JOANNA BOWEN GILLESPIE

WOMEN

SPEAK

OF GOD, CONGREGATIONS, AND CHANGE

D1193725

TRINITY PRESS INTERNATIONAL
Valley Forge, Pennsylvania

Verse 5 of hymn 304, "I Come with Joy," cited on p. 178, is copyright © 1971 by Hope Publishing Co., Carol Stream, IL 60199, and is reprinted with permission. This hymn has been revised by Brian Wren, 1994.

Verse 1 of hymn 305, "Come, Risen Lord, and Deign to Be Our Guest," cited on p. 178, is taken from *Enlarged Songs of Praise* by G. W. Briggs (1875-1959), copyright © 1931 Oxford University Press; used by permission.

Trinity Press International, P.O. Box 851, Valley Forge, PA 19482–0851

Library of Congress Cataloging-in-Publication Data

Gillespie, Joanna Bowen.
    Women speak : of God, congregations, and change / Joanna Bowen Gillespie.
      p. cm.
    Includes bibliographical references and index.
    ISBN 1-56338-104-4 (pbk.)
    1. Women in the Episcopal Church—Public opinion.   2. Women in Christianity—United States—Public opinion.   3. Episcopal Church—Public opinion.   4. Christian women—Religious life—Public opinion.   5. Episcopalians—United States—Attitudes.   6. Christian women—United States—Attitudes.   I. Title.
BX5968.5.G55   1995
283'.73'082—dc20   94-23531
                                           CIP

Printed in the United States of America

95 96 97 98 99   10 9 8 7 6 5 4 3 2 1

CONTENTS

FOREWORD

*J*OANNA GILLESPIE's *Women Speak* offers a unique view of contemporary American religion. This book describes the active, rich religiosity of ordinary women in a mainline American denomination. It has captured the intimate religious experience of ordinary believers as previous studies have failed to do. That there is a wealth of religious experience — from deep piety, to a sense of useful service or warm fellowship, to an active sense of connection to God — among women who are ordinary churchgoers is the most striking finding of this remarkable book.

Sociology is awash in studies of American mainline religion, attempting to diagnose its problems, predict its future, and measure its support. But the taken-for-granted assumption of these works seems to be that theological or spiritual inspiration has very little to do with the success or failure of these religious institutions. We also have many studies of cults and sects, of fundamentalists and communards, but almost nothing on the religious experience of ordinary churchgoers. *Women Speak* is the only book I know that captures how and when church members find satisfaction in prayer, feel close to God, respond to the melody of a hymn, or sense the divine in the act of polishing the brass and silver for the altar.

It is not that this book holds a purely positive, conflict-free view of American women's religious experience. Indeed, these pages tell stories of conflict and loss, as well as discovery and fulfillment. What gives these narratives analytic power is the book's focus on generational change, the intersection between a changing Episcopal Church and the dramatic transformations in women's lives during the last fifty years.

The book brilliantly juxtaposes the very different experience of

Episcopal women of different generations, who confront change from very different vantage points. The simplified wording of the Lord's Prayer alienates some older women who feel robbed of its spiritual resonance, while some younger women feel the prayer's real meaning is opened up to them. Some older women are nostalgic for the special fellowship that a segregated women's religious sphere used to offer, while some middle-aged women remember bitterly their exclusion from central forms of religious participation. The middle-aged women often rejoice in their new religious participation, while younger women, pressed for time, sometimes long for the friendship an older women's religious community provided, even as they put spiritual self-expression first. The rich interplay of these varied generations' experiences animates the book, making vivid the complex ways personal biographies intersect with historical change.

As I read *Women Speak*, I wondered why earlier studies had failed to create a satisfying portrait of the religiosity of ordinary church members, while this study succeeds so beautifully. After all, it is not only women's spirituality we fail fully to understand. We also lack equivalent studies of men's religious experience. My conclusion is simply that earlier researchers did not ask. Ambivalent, anguished, or perhaps embarrassed about what Gillespie calls "God-talk," they failed to address spiritual and religious meanings directly. While the standard survey or interview studies invariably ask whether respondents believe in God, and sometimes even ask whether they have had a powerful religious experience, researchers do not ask what early religious experiences respondents remember, what parts of the worship service they find most satisfying, or when they feel closest to God. One senses in the ways the women in this study responded that these are important questions to these women themselves, that they found it enormously gratifying to talk about their religious experience, and that they also recognized how rarely such topics are broached in polite company.

In *Women Speak*, questions about religious meaning were asked in a perfectly straightforward way. One has no sense that those interviewed felt they had to come up with deep, passionate religious feeling to satisfy the researchers. Indeed, it is precisely the mundane, sometimes routine things in which these women find spiritual meaning that makes their testimony so convincing.

This book will be of great interest to many different audiences. For congregation members, not only Episcopalians but those of many faiths, this book can serve as a way to explore the interaction of generations in a single community. The way religion actually feels different, and has different meanings, at varying stages in the life cycle can be a revelation for those who participate together in a religious community. And a deeper understanding of how changes in worship, religious leadership, and church practices such as separate women's organizations have affected different generations can increase mutual respect and understanding.

In the second place, this book is enormously important for women. Women's religious voice and their religious needs and interests have been neglected by both scholars and religious institutions. This book highlights the varied riches of women's religious experience and suggests how seriously these religious understandings need to be taken.

Third, scholars of religion have a great deal to learn from *Women Speak*. It reports research involving not only interviews but intensive studies of four typical Episcopal congregations. It captures the process of religious change in these four congregations, from changes in liturgy and worship, to changes in leadership, to changes in identity. Its original focus on generations produces a powerful analysis of the ways changes in congregational life differentially affect members with varying generational experience.

Finally, Joanna Gillespie's *Women Speak: Of God, Congregations, and Change* will be a revelation to all of us who participate in religious congregations and find spiritual meaning there. I found my understanding of my own Jewishness deepened by the voices of the women who speak here and by Gillespie's deep, discerning analysis of what they say.

ANN SWIDLER

Chapter 1

"NO ONE EVER ASKED ME BEFORE"

"*N*O ONE EVER ASKED ME BEFORE," mused a woman in her 80s. She had just surprised herself by putting into words a profound experience of God's presence, one she had never "said" aloud till that moment. This book weaves together many such thoughts by "ordinary" women in four contemporary Episcopal congregations — rarely articulated words about God, their lives, and the congregations to which they belong. To a woman they expressed a feeling of amazement at realizing this was the first time they — regular, sometimes lifelong churchgoers — had been asked about (or encouraged to put into words) *their* reflections on religion and religious change. The deceptively simple language in which they cast these "never said it before" responses drew into the realm of religious meaning work, families, memories, reasoning, doubts, questions about life and death, and even responses to 'scenery' such as church buildings. To my knowledge, a record of this kind of "God-talk" among women in a mainline Protestant denomination is unique — *terra incognita* in contemporary feminist and religious research.[1]

Women's words about their church identity are crucial today because both women and church have undergone enormous change since the anomalous churchgoing boom that characterized the post–World War II decades in America. Today, whether or not they acknowledge it, women are immersed in a stream of change that began with the women's movement in the 1960s. This ongoing change of consciousness has vitally affected their self-definitions, their understandings of work and career, and their attitudes to all institutions, including church.

1

One of the arenas in which women's changing consciousness has been most fertile — at the same time generating mountains of resistance — is religion.[2] Protestant and Roman Catholic Christianity is being dramatically reshaped through a significant body of feminist theology, writings that open up once-standard terms of faith, ethics, and polity to the incorporation of historic female experience. Because the resulting concepts no longer fit into or can be contained within existing explanatory structures of "church" and "American Protestant religion" conventionally viewed, it is clear that a paradigm shift is underway. New or reclaimed structures and language, new imaginative formulations are bubbling into consciousness and print.[3] But to date the least studied, least known element in the process of religious change is that involving the female segment of mainline church members in the United States.

As I immersed myself in the rich harvest of these words, they began to coalesce into a wondrously complex, multifaceted whole. It was as if I were turning over in my hands a prism that reflected bits of light from its multiple facets. These "ordinary" women form a collective archetype in the late twentieth-century "culture of disbelief"; the glints of light are refractions created by their diversity of age, personality, racial and social class identity, education, occupation, and circumstance. Beyond gender, their one commonality was the fact that they were all participants in an organized faith community, a local congregation. In the 1930s, British mystic Evelyn Underhill asserted that "the main reason" people joined a church was to find God. "God is the interesting thing about religion," she wrote, and what people are looking for in their leaders and their churches is "spiritual realism" — a genuine connection with holiness, mystery, and prayer.[4] That quest, process and goal, is embedded in these words that also map the terrain.

These reflections of "real" people in four actual parish churches open out and confound the usual journalistic formula emphasizing loss in American mainline churches: loss of numbers (members and money), loss of influence and significance (to one-issue fundamentalist, radical, or charismatic sects). A quartet of voices introduce our prism, capturing the push and pull between long-standing habits of being on the one hand, and the assimilation of change on the other. A young New England woman dismissed as irrelevant the sociable, quilt-making stereotype of female church affiliation: "I'm not into basket weaving or that kind of show-and-tell; if I'm going to spend my precious time, I want real God-talk," she said.

An older woman from the Great Plains hunched her shoulders as if against a chill and all but whispered (about the Sunday-worship innovation known as the Exchange of the Peace), "When they're moving around, out of their pews, shaking hands with each other right in the middle of the service. . . . " Shaking her head, she said, "I just don't do it. I just stand there." A middle-aged woman in the Northwest cited her existential loneliness in the midst of her congregation: "There are lots of wonderful people here in this church, with deep faith. But we never talk out loud about that kind of thing, so we just don't know it. It's not there for us to use, or to draw on." And a young Southern woman used the image of family to describe her congregation: "This is the kind of church that lives the Gospel, not just talks about it. Besides, I need a family that isn't family, one I choose instead of the one I just happened to be born into." They highlight four dimensions of the soul quest drawing women to a religious organizational belonging: the search for a direct experience of God, surviving change in lifelong religious habit, the longing for a community that allows deep sharing of ultimate truths, and congregation as theological family.

An additional reflection adds a denominational note. "I like *participating* when I go to church; I don't want to just sit there like a bump on a log." Half-chanting rubrics about posture from a childhood catechism, Anne, an energetic Great Plains 30-year-old, said, "Standing to sing. Kneeling to pray. Sitting to hear the Word." She added in self-amusement, "And shaking hands when you give the Peace. . . . I just *love* the fellowship. It makes you get into the flow. And that extends to coffee hour, too. That's real important to me." Anne's vigorous verbs challenge the mental image of stolid worshipers in proper mainline pews. How do ordinary laywomen worshipers experience God and "church" on an average Sunday? How do they find a particular religious body with which to affiliate? Does their congregation allow or encourage profound exchange among its members about things of deepest import? And what spinoff effects of congregational identity do they discern in the rest of daily life?

Women's experience is the tie that binds together and illuminates here the topic of change and the religious arena called "church." To date, that focus for God-talk has not been treated seriously by either historians or theologians. As middle-class America's traditional institutions seem to be losing their potency, it carries a special urgency.[5] Also, middle-class women in general are feeling

pressure because of the many changes that have occurred, especially in the workplace. Susan Faludi's *Backlash* is one of the latest
to document resentment directed toward women in "new" places,
and broad societal anger aroused by the changing ground rules for
interpersonal relations — such as Sen. Bob Packwood 1950s' assumptions about male prerogatives. What aspects of extra-church
change accompany women into their congregations? And who
are the "typical" congregants found in the pews? A once-thriving
church has often been dismissed with the phrase, "Nobody's there
anymore, except for a few old women." This raises another related
issue: does the very form "congregation," constantly changing in
terms of demographics and external factors, still have a place in
late twentieth-century women's spiritual universe?

More pointedly, what attracts and sustains women in this religious structure that has always been patriarchal, with minimal or
totally invisible female participation in leadership or policymaking
(until the 1970s)? What do today's women find in an institution that historically equated female passivity and subservience to
(male) religious authority with "holiness"? At the time women's
"good works" were supplying, almost solely, the funds and volunteers for outreach programs, official male voices in congregations
idealized such productive dutifulness as the evidence of spiritual virtue — and derogated mysticism or contemplative prayer
as superstition. How do women reconcile the American ideal
of individual self-development, newly significant for them in the
late twentieth century, with belonging to a "traditional" mainline
church? And what kind of emotional freight do they associate with
"tradition"?[6]

Most intriguing, what has been the impact, on women in the
pews, of new female leadership in the sanctuary? How do laywomen respond to having one of their own gender, a female priest
or minister, carry out the sacramental functions of their community — a woman presiding over the Holy Table? One young woman
felt a sense of "safety" at seeing a woman celebrate the Eucharist.
That new reality spoke to the "real conflicts" in her "gut" about
"all the male words and symbols, like bleeding Son, and a male
body on the cross." Another, from a different angle of vision,
confided that she was thrilled at having priests who are female:
"You have to remember I was nurtured on bells and chants and
'Mother Mary, pray for us'!" She still occasionally misses "the
ornate...crazy Catholic architecture, and little red lights and the

million statues.... Also, there's no *body* hanging up there on that plain wood cross."

Men's views of religion have dominated all aspects of the writings and the institutions of religion since the early church banished house churches at the end of the first century. Men's thoughts and structures have been the norm against which all church members have been measured and have evaluated themselves. A study of women's thoughts exclusively is essential to begin redressing such an incomplete view of the institution. Obviously in the long run human beings must work together to revitalize their religion, in this as in other ages. But here the primary voices are those that have been inaudible in previous religious dialogue.

Framing the Inquiry: Looking for Congregations

National media attention followed the stormy opening of ordained leadership to females in the early 1970s and reported plenty of newsmaking contentiousness about it within denominations — Episcopal, Baptist, Presbyterian. Few if any stories tracked the responses to that change among the laity. However, a Lilly Endowment grant titled "Women in Mainline Protestantism: A Case Study of the Twentieth Century Episcopal Church (1988–90)" enabled a group of us — twelve female church historians, sociologists, and theologians — to begin exploring that lacuna. The empirical centerpiece of the project consisted of interviews with some sixty women church members from age 28 to 93, in four congregations located in the four corners of the nation — women who might well be found in any neighborhood church on any Main Street U.S.A. This narrative is an expanded version of some of those conversations, using the analytic framework described in my chapter in the book that grew out of that study, *Episcopal Women: Gender, Spirituality, and Commitment in a Mainline Church* (1992).[7]

Each of four congregations in widely distant parts of the country — Grace New England, Redeemer Plains, Nativity Northwest, and Advent South — yielded a wealth of information, including: (1) responses from a questionnaire mailed to all women members of a congregation; (2) responses to a similar questionnaire mailed to parishioners in official leadership or "opinion-shaping" positions, male and female; (3) six background interviews with that same opinion-shaping leadership in the congregation — the clergy

plus five lay members, male and female — for their perspective on
the congregation and its history; and (4) structured interviews with
fifteen women, five in each of three generations. These last were
selected randomly from the pool of women indicating on their returned questionnaires a willingness to be interviewed; those names
were then pulled from a hat until we had five women in each "generation," younger, middle-aged, and older women in each parish,
with whom we were able to have extended conversation.[8]

The written questionnaires mailed to all women on a congregation's membership roll were our first public move into their
territory and their first exposure to our agenda. In each place
there were women who applauded some or much of the change
in their church, who were eager to talk with us and readily put
their names into the pool from which the allotted fifteen interviews
per congregation could be drawn. Others were uncomfortable with
religious change and used the written survey to register their negativity anonymously. A few took one look at the questionnaire and
rejected it. At a coffee hour, one woman said frankly, "Your questionnaire was so obviously slanted in favor of feminism I couldn't
take it seriously. . . . I just tossed it in the wastebasket." But such
direct dismissal was surprisingly rare. It is possible, of course,
that the norm of civility prevailing in Anglo-Protestant mainline
churches helped muffle the expression of disagreement with our
project.

These mostly white and mostly well-educated women (three-
quarters of those we interviewed were college graduates and a
sizable number had master's or doctoral degrees) were still comfortable claiming church as part of their identity, and were willing
to respond to a survey sent to them with the endorsement of the
congregation's official leadership. Situating our inquiry in a local
congregational setting meant that we had to see and understand
the women who were there, who had chosen to "stick with" their
church through thick and thin. Or they might be newly returned to
active church life after years of disengagement and thus filled with
the enthusiasm of the recommitted.

By definition, the women we could reach were not those who
had become so disillusioned with organized religion as to completely withdraw. Focus on the women "there" in the pews also
meant concentrating on the regular layperson in a clerical, hierarchical church, instead of on the ordained leaders, male or female.
Women clergy, since the 1970s, have made and are making an in-

calculable impact on the congregations in which they work. But what research exists on the topic of women and religion has focused on that most visible and photographic icon of religious change.[9] We set out to listen to those "no one ever asked before" — an observation made by almost every woman in the study.[10]

Two of the four churches were located in very large cities, one in the far Northwest and one in the Deep South; a third was in the downtown area of a medium-sized, formerly industrial New England city, and the fourth in a railroad-hub city in the Great Plains. None was familiar to our team. Both churches and women respondents are here given fictitious names as a way of honoring their anonymity. In terms of size, we selected congregations that had a weekly Sunday attendance of more than 100 but under 500, people of all ages. We looked for a "usual" Sunday morning Episcopal pattern, two services ("early" holy Eucharist at 8 A.M. and a larger "family" Eucharist at 10 A.M.), and some involvement in programs beyond the physical boundaries of their parish, for example, a soup-kitchen or nursing-home ministry.

We sought out congregations that were typical in the denomination rather than idiosyncratic, medium-sized rather than very large or very small, and "mainstream" in liturgy, not distinctly charismatic or experimental. Our aim was to collect material for a composite portrait of the women in a particular congregation that would be recognizable to other religiously observant women. Because in the Episcopal Church, as in many mainline Protestant churches, congregations with a predominantly ethnic-minority membership are still the exception rather than the rule, and require an analysis that is essentially bicultural, and in response to our own racial heritage, we felt most competent working with congregations that were predominantly white and Anglo in background. Fortunately, in each of the congregations there were women members from African-American, Hispanic-American, or Asian-American heritage who allowed us glimpses into "mainline religion" from a cultural perspective other than Northern European and "English." They were there because, for a variety of background and personal reasons, they had chosen the overall ethos of Anglican worship. One young African-American woman said, "I can visit my uncle's Baptist congregation for gospel singing and shouting if I want to, so I have the best of both worlds. But I was raised in the reverence of Episcopal churches and that's still my deepest identity." We also sought congregations where the clergy leaders were comfortably established rather than just arrived, so that women's responses to change in liturgy or gender roles could be relatively independent of the major internal change involved in adjusting to a new rector.

As it happened, the congregations we visited each reported a similar recent history. Each was enjoying the kind of renaissance that accompanies what seems to be a cyclical resurgence of young families wanting a church identity. The new members bring with them the energy of "rediscovery" after a church-vacuum in their twenties, a pattern of youthful church disaffection familiar to, even taken for granted by these women. Each of the four congregations had already had or was presently experiencing female clergy leadership. A number of the laywomen were leaders in congregational worship and served on "important" committees that had earlier excluded women, for example, the finance or personnel committees. The congregational calendars in each were beginning to reflect an awareness of the need to adjust parish meeting schedules to women's employment.

The rectors of these churches were not promoting change for women out of *noblesse oblige*, as a matter of principle or compensation for centuries of exclusion — or because more equal participation of laywomen in worship leadership was "good for them." Rather, these competent, confident male clergy supported change for women because it was a source of vitality, even of survival, for the congregations in their charge. And unwittingly or providentially these congregations had selected male leaders who enabled such change. They were men in midcareer, genuinely loved and respected, who had been situated in a particular congregation for five years (approximately). Most important, they were men who were not threatened by the idea of sharing leadership with women. Two of the rectors had associate or assistant pastors who were ordained women; the other two churches had at a previous time experienced a woman priest. By the late 1980s, laywomen were visible in all four congregations as ushers, lay readers, serving on vestry and all other administrative committees, and in outreach commissions.

We introduced each conversation with a list of the five themes on which we wanted their reflections. First we asked each woman for the earliest remembrance she could summon of "something transcendent," something she had called God or "knew" as God, whether or not it was so named at that point. Second, we inquired about any awareness of God or religion in the landmark events of her life: the decision to "leave home," or choice of career; decisions about marriage, parenting, divorce; the death of a parent. Had those turning points intersected with any religious insight or awareness? In what ways had she thought about God in them, or asked for divine guidance?

Third, we asked about the woman's symbolic universe — in what forms she found it expressed. We wanted images and visceral memories, color, sound, birds or animals, stained glass, hymns, trees, clouds, Sunday school (or nursery rhyme) characters — anything that was rooted in spiritual association or insight for her. Each person's "holy ground" was a crucial revelation of the ways she related to abstraction — "church," God, Jesus, the Holy Spirit — and fellow human beings. Under the fourth theme, we wanted her experience in her congregation. We wanted a narrative of how she got there, how it and she might have changed, issues of leadership or participation. As the fifth, concluding theme, we inquired what each would name as the most precious dimension of her religious life thus far. In her experience of faith, or in the church (or both combined if that was her experience), what spiritual insight or learning would she most want to see preserved and transmitted to succeeding generations?

The conversations covered the entire gamut of human experience, a cornucopia of stories. Some women in each congregation seem to have had picture-book childhoods, others experiencing the depths of rejection and alienation — even for a time the despair of homelessness. Some are in long-time marriages, some recovering from divorce, alcoholism, or other types of addiction. Some struggle to cope with disabling illness, soul-searing loss, remarkable healing. While each woman's story merits its own full-length narrative, the succeeding chapters, one per parish, weave into that congregation's synthesis only some, not all, of the voices, and only segments of the various interviews.

Since our inquiries took place in churches of the same denomination (although in widely separated geographic locations), the distinctiveness of each congregation's character or ethos is in some ways surprising. Although women in each pew in each location use the same worship manuals, the Book of Common Prayer (1979) and Hymnal (1982), they rarely commented about their shared national church identity. Visiting one congregation at a time, worshipping at its services, reading bulletin boards, and exploring the community context, we became aware of a consistent theme or imagery in each congregation's self-identification, an overarching "congregational idiom."[11] An uncanny unity of image and the language in which it was expressed characterized the accumulated reports from each congregation — the written questionnaires, the transcribed tapes of conversations with women and various opinion-shapers. A given congregation's way of talking about and seeing itself seemingly produces an unacknowledged but real consensus among its members. For good or ill, the women in each of the congregations identify with the *persona* of "their own" parish far more than with the denominational identity and ethos. They have chosen to be "there," and in a kind of feedback mechanism they both absorb and reflect the imagery or "personality" of their parish.

I have attempted to preserve the distinctive sound and mindset of a woman's voice and words, with a few clues about her age and background. Names and biographical events have been scrambled somewhat, geographic descriptions made impressionistic instead of concrete. The mosaic of a single congregation uses only fractions of any one individual's thoughts, and only hints of the whole life. In paring the quotations to a focused point I have sacrificed leisurely description and the false starts and stops that tend to characterize thoughtful self-exploration. Reducing these verbal gifts of self to mere words on paper constitutes a necessary but regrettable injustice. I wanted as many facets of religious reflection and exploration as possible here, in print, to "catch the light" in all their variety and depth.

Also, I do not claim a definitive reading of each church's "congregational culture." The viewpoint here is partial, by intent. This volume concentrates (for once) on only women members' experience and perception of it.[12] The records of the conversations make a type of hybrid oral history or extended autobiographical reflection.[13] The thoughts themselves are inevitably shaped by the religious goals of the inquiry and the actual physical location within which we sat as we talked together — usually a parish library or classroom. In addition, each person's spectrum of religious experience has its own uniqueness. A third qualification is the way I have discharged my responsibility as participant observer, "reporter," fellow seeker. My choices for this written narrative were made on the basis of realities in their words that struck deeply responsive chords in me (and others who have read various versions of this synthesis). No one else can be held accountable for them. I have not tried to verify or substantiate my interpretations with any of the women whose words appear here. A fellow churchwoman and scholar, I am their compositor, shaping and fitting fragments of their individual thoughts into a whole that ends up a mosaic or a prism.[14] I have interpreted each woman's words and the patterns of their collected voices as faithfully as I could. Other researchers with other interests might well have emphasized different themes or reached differing conclusions.

Our conversations can best be described as a type of negotiation, a dialectic of experience and interpretation evolving unconsciously. Their design, originally conceived as "interview," quickly turned into dialogue. Questions and responses flowed in both directions. The women were as interested in us and our project as we in them. A bridge-generation woman from the Northwest unconsciously elicited affirmation about her perceptions: "Don't you see this same thing where you are, back in the East? I know it's not just here, in this church. It's happening in the schools, in business, and in other organizations as well." Although we touched on the same themes with each woman, the reflections took distinctive directions; each heard and picked up on differing facets of one or another of the themes, in her own way. One woman wrote me a few months later, "I laugh every time I think of our interview. It was a wonderfully animated and *fun* conversation. I don't think we kept to your agenda at all! When my mind moves, it goes like a rocket and is ten minutes ahead of my mouth (and two days ahead of my pen), in a rolling free-association that would intrigue a Freudian and delight a Jungian....I just don't usually share these free-for-all thoughts so wildly and rapidly 'in public,' so to speak."

Generations in Four Congregations

"Generation," a way of thinking about time, is the interpretive template applied to these conversations. The concept of generation was first given social-scientific application early in the twentieth century as one means of interpreting the rise of European fascism.[15] It provides a perspective on "the times" and helps account for what people in varying age groups think of as "knowledge." It can explain the contrast in emphasis on what is "important" to one group that is ignored by a later one. People who have grown up in the same time frame and location are predisposed to view the same things as "fact." Generational perspective explains what might be called "fashions" or eras in language and word usage, each age group employing its own images to make sense of daily life. The reference points of varying age groups also illustrates the reality of "generations of ideas."

Major events that reach into every corner of a culture, such as a war or an all-encompassing economic depression, are likely to be experienced in unconsciously collective ways. Although the impact of words in public print and on newscasts powerfully implants images and symbols that then become a common currency, generational absorption goes beneath media influence. Without particularly intending to, people in a given age group assimilate similar ways of viewing, feeling, and referring to such major events. The words and concepts thus widely shared take on the function of symbols or code words that can reinvoke and recapitulate that experience. The shortage of nylons during World War II and the visceral remembrance of anti–Vietnam War protests are symbolic language for those who "know" them and recall the same associations around such phrases.

Each generation, then, has a memory bank of images and code words that instantly summon specific implications to its "members." These generational symbols emerge when groups try to explain their perception to other groups — a generational mindset offering evidence of "membership" in one's own era. In this perspective, code words serve as generational demarcation, helping to pinpoint a shift between generations. Generational codes also offer a wide-angle vision that incorporates the world outside the church, interrelating historical and sociological details. While perceptions of change, "the church," congregational membership, worship, and ritual are themselves intangible, generational markers make visible the process by which those perceptions and attitudes are modified, discarded, or replaced (however glacial in speed). Generation thus constitutes a kind of vertical boring down through successive layers of symbol and language.[16]

Two vivid, widely shared generational notes among these women appeared around the adoption of "new" words in the Episcopal worship language during the 1970s and the change in women's expectations about "dressing up" for church. While an older-generation woman misses "the old familiar words" of the Lord's Prayer — "Our Father, who art in Heaven" learned as a child — a younger generation woman is already so accustomed to the contemporary language, "Our father in Heaven," that the earlier version seems archaic. Many older women object particularly to the substitution "Save us from the time of trial" for the old phraseology, "Lead us not into temptation," though both are followed by the same words, "deliver us from evil." "I'm open to many...even to *most* of the changes," declared an active older woman for many in her generation, "but *not* the Lord's Prayer. That's where I draw the line." In contrast, a young Southerner celebrated the new wording of the Lord's Prayer: "At least now you can look at how to fit God into life in 1990, instead of in the Dark Ages!"

A middle-aged woman from Redeemer Plains recalled the strikingly abrupt relaxation of "requirements" about dress for church-going. She could "remember...practically the very minute when wearing hats to church changed from being a requirement — you felt undressed without one! — to something that just wasn't done anymore." Summarizing her generation's remembrance, it was "too formal, too fussy, embarrassing and old-fashioned, somehow. Suddenly you were *overdressed* in a hat!" Coming to church in "blue jeans" was a further generational demarcation, an idea that horrified some of the older women but had come to seem the ultimate statement of feeling "at home" and "accepted" among some of the younger women.

The idea of generation has received astonishingly little application in local congregations, where there is often a wide range of ages in a relatively small organization. People are often reluctant to acknowledge "generational consciousness" and its powerful effects — until a corporate conflict illuminates its usefulness. One of the younger generation, describing the "inflexibility" of the older women in her congregation, reported that they refused to even *try* the jobs of lay reading or ushering newly opened to women. "They just can't even seem to imagine themselves doing those jobs," she lamented, "any more than I...." She stopped, then bravely finished her thought: "any more than I used to be able, in high school, to imagine that girls could *ever* be acolytes.... You know, candle-bearers in the procession. Only boys could do that in the church I grew up in. It never even occurred to me to *ask* if I could — it was just totally unthinkable. I guess that's how they [the older women] feel, actually."

The American myth of individualism is absorbed by women as

well as men, an unquestioned assumption that each person alone is
responsible for her or his own thoughts, own soul, own spirituality.
The ability to acknowledge the influence of others is not a "habit of
the heart" we have been taught to value. In fact, the polar opposite
is true: ideas must be made to sound like "one's own." The goal is
to "sound" independent of others' words and ideas, and thus independent of one's generational time-frame. The idea of emotions,
reasoning processes, and ideals being invisibly transmitted to us,
through relations with fellow human beings, is something we are
not supposed to admit. It is derogated in intellectual work, as if
one's thoughts somehow emerged from nowhere. Even in religion,
women's need for relatedness and self-disclosure to other human
beings has been devalued — perceived as a character weakness they
should try to "outgrow."[17]

Still, despite our pervasive attempts to achieve individualism
and supposed "independence," any group of people who share a
certain slice of history will also share overlapping generalizations
and images, clues to "generation."[18] Actual chronology — years of
age — is significant only when linked to a state of mind. The point
at which "generation" becomes useful is when it helps us locate an
internal response to some event or happening in a real, historical
time. Understanding one's response as part of a wider pattern —
a realization that makes each individual feel less vulnerable — as-
sures us that we were indeed participants in a current of ideas and
experience from a given era and setting.[19]

Each woman here defined the course of her life with the
same landmark cultural events — the ideals, hopes, and anxieties
that formed the common generational landscape of her cohort in
twentieth-century America. For the older generation of women
in the four parishes (age 60 and above), the overarching external experience has been the Great Depression, while each also
unconsciously assumed the personal expectation of stable, lifelong marriages. Women between the ages of 40 and 59, here
called the bridge generation, have two defining pivots; those at
the upper end of the generation had their marriages and horizons
shaped by World War II, while the civil rights movement and the
contemporary women's movement defined those nearer 40. The
women 40 and under date themselves in relation to participating
in or resisting the many upheavals generated by and around the
Vietnam War.

The vast shift that led white middle-class women to leave home for paid work, directly related to the women's movement, was interpreted by each bridge-generation woman as her "own" decision — a telling illustration of cultural individualism in the mental world of these educated women. That change in attitude in fact constituted a generational mindset and "social movement," though it consisted of "countless separate decisions of individual women," each within her own family and educational circumstances. No outside force imposed on any of them this changed view of employment outside the home.[20] (This observation relates only to women in the middle class, of course; women in less secure financial circumstances have never had a choice.) For many of these Episcopal women, the idea that they could *want* paid jobs was a mind change that turned on its head the assumption on which they had been raised — to be proud of *not having to* help support the family financially. The "choice" of being comfortable in deciding to have a career or job evolved, for the 1970s' cohort of middle-class white Protestant women *as individuals*, out of their changed perceptions of opportunity in the external climate of new possibilities. Financial need had some, but not the definitive, influence on that decision, which each woman thought she was making "on her own."

The overall effect of this shift created new dynamics in their congregations and assumptions once taken for granted now become history.[21] "All the women in this congregation now work outside the home," they generalize, when in actuality they are thinking of that proportion of women who formerly had the leisure and economic security to fill their time with volunteer jobs. Taking one's own era and situation as the standard illustrates "generational fallacy." We unthinkingly assume that commonsense ideas prevailing in our youth have always prevailed, and will continue throughout our lifetime. Inevitably, then, each generation finds itself confronted by what they come to see as outmoded meanings and assumptions. Generation provides us with insights that helped put "change" in the spotlight in the four congregations.

Dynamics of the Inquiry

This inquiry into religious change among women, a topic usually protected under the rubric of respecting personal privacy, may have been given legitimacy in the eyes of the women we spoke with by being conducted under a funded research project. In contemporary American society we are accustomed to the idea that "knowledge" and "information" enter public discourse through surveys, polls, and recorded interviews, especially when later that idea or information appears in print. We take for granted the assumption that an inquiry supported by a foundation grant must *ipso facto* be worthwhile.

Whatever the strength of that speculation, these "informants" seemed very willing to respond, to become friends and fellow-seekers in a process as involving for them as for us. In the narrative the reader will occasionally see my interaction with the speakers when the conversation becomes especially mutual. None of the standard research labels — "interviewee," "informant," "subject" — seem either appropriate or adequately descriptive so I use them as little as possible and with apology. Perhaps the great revelation of the process came to those of us who were the inquirers. We were the ones who received the full experiential learning: that collecting religious thought and experience is the ultimate human-to-human disclosure. Discussion of doctrines or church polity could hardly have created the same dynamic sense of personal revelation and discovery for them and for us. In this "traditional" denomination, where individuals connect with a church by assenting to and participating in its rituals and symbols (rather than by having to identify a moment of conversion or deep spiritual insight), women found "trying to put it into words" for us acceptable, even stimulating.

This prism of women's thoughts, then, creates a complex whole. It refracts the light of broad institutional change as experienced at the local congregational level, intermixed with all the personal psychological and spiritual stages women "naturally" experience over a lifetime. Perpetual change, although invisible, is the reality in which all people and churches live, move, and have their being.

After the completion of the interview phase of the project, I wrote thank-yous to each of the women who had so generously spent time putting into words their intimate religious insights and experiences. I often got responses in return, thanking me for expressing gratitude to them, probably also for having brought this interest and attention to a public focus in their congregations. My notes to them had acknowledged the imbalance of the process: it was their words that became the grist for our research mill and would be further transformed by me into "our" prism. I had ventured to hope that our conversations, incredibly productive and beneficial to us, might also have held some rewards for them. "Thank you so much for your letter," one young woman wrote me back. "My empathy for fruit trees — harvested and then ignored — absolutely vanished." After a few more thoughts, she concluded, "I've actually been wanting to thank *you*, for stirring the waters of my personal Episcopal experience."[22] In the chapters that follow I attempt to honor the bond thus created.

Chapter 2

GRACE NEW ENGLAND AND "WORK"

*T*HE FIFTEEN WOMEN with whom we talked at Grace cast much of their religious self-explanation in terms of work. The idea of active "doing" threaded reflections about secular, personal life as well as congregational identity. "I just don't know what a person does if you don't have some place to go when you wake up each morning," one in the older generation said. On the other hand, the meanings of "doing something" varied for the generations. "Women today don't seem to respect home and mothering as work; I guess I have to figure out whether or not I do," one of the younger generation said. The standard by which "doing" was measured also has shifted. "I really feel better about myself," explained a bridge-generation woman, "when I'm doing what's right for me, not what people have always referred to as 'women's work.'" Their use of work as reference point and metaphor came to sound like a substitute language for other, more conventional terms of spiritual self-definition — piety, devotion, faithfulness. In all four of the research congregations, we noted that typically "religious words" had only a minor place in the vocabulary of these interviews about religion. (The one exception was the term "love," which the women in all four parishes often used as a synonym for religion and spirituality.) But "work" was the most frequently used verb and noun here.

The fifteen women interviewed at Grace ranged in age from a woman over 90, who was polite but disengaged from the congregation except for the weekly Sunday service, to a busy young mother in her thirties, employed part-time "to help with the mortgage payments" and with no time for herself. Several used the label "feminist" about themselves, others avoided it. The women placed themselves along a narrow spectrum from acknowledging the benefits of the women's movement to courteous avoidance of it. Some viewed open avowal of feminism as somehow disloyal to the males in their church. But all the topics we covered — employment, leisure time, congregational membership, and commitment to larger social issues — sooner or later related back to a quality of effort or work. Activism was the key emotional value in all these conversations about women, religion, and change.[1]

Perhaps a residue of the traditional New England heritage, a strand of Protestant work ethic still flourishing in the cool green geography, helped turn "work" into a staple conversational theme. A young waitress in a local restaurant could be questioned by customers about her employment. She reported being made to feel defensive about the disposition of her own time — her "excuse" for working. How could she be "away from her kids"? Their query, expressing a conservative point of view in an avowedly "Christian restaurant,"[2] symbolizes a nearly obsessive focus on work as a measure of identity, and an angle of church membership identity.

Paid employment has indeed become the norm for the middle (or bridge) generation of women at Grace. Each person's story centered around that issue, inserting the element of conflict over the valuing of paid versus volunteer work for churchwomen — literally a line of demarcation for that generation. But the older women also needed to use the label "work" to validate their membership and contribution in the congregation. Even the 90-year-old woman still spoke of her daytime hours in terms of working in the office of her retirement-community residence (as a volunteer). Within this sample of white middle-class women in a New England church, "work" came to seem an irreducible component of identity, religious and secular.

An interesting explanation about the apparent dominance of work at the congregational idiom at Grace may be attributed to us, the outsiders coming in to inquire. Our initial foray into a congregation took place at Grace New England, where we tested the workability of our questions. Something of our own research need, the desire to obtain "substantive" materials in an area that can be very abstract, "religion," may have cued these first conversations toward concrete information — encouraging the use of terms invoking effort, work, time spent. Culturally we assume time is "worth more" when it is described as filled, busy, productive. An inquiry about the function of religion and congregations can easily elicit the language of effort to give it importance. Or, as it appears from our experience of four different parishes, a congregational ethos admiring effort and work in religion (as in many other areas of life) is indeed the essence of the congregation at Grace, the characteristic that draws and sustains it.

The men with whom I spoke in the background interviews, as well as the women themselves, also used the word "work" in an admiring way. "Action" and "activity" were the terms of approval for fellow congregation members. Passivity was definitely negative. With the exception of a few women who described themselves as spiritually empowered by regular participation in the informal Tuesday evening Eucharist (described below), spiritual concerns were not much put into words — in marked contrast with the women in Advent South. Or perhaps they were viewed as too private to share. One bridge-generation woman was comfortable using the word "conversion" to describe her reawakened faith — the exception. The few who invoked charismatic vocabulary — praying, speaking in tongues, healing — still also invoked the imprimatur of work, referring to those expressions as their personal "work" or ministry.

The divine wellspring of this activism remained an open question during our visits. We saw hints of it and heard some talk around the edges of it, but only in the conversation of a few. There is, of course, precedence for an emphasis on activism. Historically, Protestants have not considered time or energy spent on meditation or introspection as "work"; time invested in actions that relieve suffering and poverty is somehow more legitimate than just praying. Further, in clerically hierarchical churches such as the Roman Catholic, the Episcopal, or the Lutheran, women's cultivation of their own inner lives has rarely been given priority. Also, among many Protestant women there is a dread of sounding glib about something as personal as one's soul. For a variety of reasons, possibly including the agonized conscience of Yankee spiritual geography ("nothing is ever enough"), activism was the accepted identity at Grace. Also related to this inhibited spiritual vocabulary were the modest claims the women made for their own spiritual insight and authority. At least in conversation with us, this hardworking, committed group of women gave "work" rhetorical precedence over everything else.

Of course in biblical times, women's way of talking about their religious calling was also through work. The women around Jesus created their participation through what they did, for example, the woman who washed Jesus' feet (Matt. 26:6–13), the hospitality of Martha (Luke 11:38–42). In the culture of late twentieth-century American Christianity, work that brings a financial return is a sure way for women to be taken seriously. On that account, Grace New England's unique women's organization, the Gift Workshop (described below), not only garnered special admiration from all the women with whom we spoke (and the men as well), but in its own way epitomized their view of "work." The older women at Grace who manage and staff the Gift Workshop fill their days producing handcrafted items to sell, the way old-fashioned, full-time volunteers did. But these workers also operate a self-sustaining business and service-providing organization, catering meals and maintaining a parish gift shop along with making and selling their products. They reap multiple rewards: appreciation for the financial return on their efforts, the providing of something "worthwhile" around which to organize their personal lives, and creating actual volunteer "jobs." Their works give substance to the theme of "work" at Grace New England and also illustrate specific generational issues.

The Physical Context

The physical plant, the church and attached parish hall, is situated some forty or fifty feet back from the unusually wide main street in this midsize New England city. It sits between a modern "glass-box" bank building and an older block of storefronts. The reddish-brown sandstone walls and stained glass windows (now protected by Plexiglas) are darkened by age and automobile exhaust. The lawn and shrubbery have been recently spruced up in keeping with the stores nearby. The "downtown" area of the city, a few blocks from the river, is recovering from the economic downturn of the 1970s. Nothing in the immediate vicinity of Grace looks seedy anymore, although the sidewalks have their share of streetpeople who belie the business district facelift. One of the congregational leaders noted the human cost of these improvements: "It's pushed out all low-income housing. And of course young families now can't afford to live in the city at all, let alone near the church." This demographic change is particularly troubling to those who remember a more neighborly feeling in the imme-

diate area. On Sunday mornings, the only human traffic in the
downtown area is churchgoers.

Grace is an imposing Victorian Gothic presence on Main Street.
Its primary late nineteenth-century donor intended a physical and
symbolic statement about the Church at the Heart and Center of
the city, a legacy that is still part of the congregation's consciousness. One of the young women commended it to us in defense
of the gloomy exterior: "This church *ought* to be in the middle
of things! We shouldn't run away to the suburbs and leave the
downtown problems." However, the realities of its late twentieth-
century center-city location mean that its weekday face onto Main
Street is opaque. Only the tall, closed, and locked fire engine–
red doors relieve the intimidating exterior. There is no hint of the
church's brilliant scarlet, sea-green, and gold interiors, the original late Victorian decor to which the sanctuary and nave were
restored in the late 1970s. Only on Sunday mornings when the
red doors stand open is the contrast between inner color and outer
somberness visible.

Just inside the Main Street doors, five rows of back pews have
been permanently removed. This creates space for social gatherings
of parishioners during the coffee hour, a function formerly prohib-
ited by the physical limitations of a linear parish house attached to
the church. The parish offices are a similar solution to this structural puzzle; a computer perched in the secretary's office and the
"machine room" where the bookkeeper works seem to have been
shoehorned in. A nursery classroom and clergy offices occupy the
rest of the first floor. The basement level is a warren of Sunday
school rooms lighted by high, narrow horizontal windows near
the ceiling. A vast Victorian staircase leads to the second floor's
huge kitchen and dining room that have become virtually unus-
able for large parish gatherings; the climb is too steep for many in
the congregation. An apartment for the sexton and family occupies
a third floor. Since Sunday morning coffee hour has become "the
fifth sacrament" (postworship sociability around coffee and cookies given ever larger significance in contemporary church life), the
lack of ground-floor space was a major logistical problem. Their
adjusting sacred space to make room for sociability was a creative
response. Space for automobiles was another problem that could
not be foreseen a century earlier. Fortunately, on Sunday mornings
the congregation can use a nearby municipal parking lot.

Church competition in this downtown area is high: within three blocks are a Congregational, a Methodist, a Baptist, and a (huge) Roman Catholic church. A synagogue has anchored the other end of the Main Street business district for well over half a century. But Grace has something none of the others in this study can boast or bemoan: a history of more than 250 years. One of the oldest Church of England parishes in the New England area, this is its third building. "Too much history" may strangle the present congregation, some say. Maintaining a huge, inflexible set of buildings in a neighborhood that changes around it is a financial burden that seems disproportionate to some in this congregation.

On the passageway leading from the front of Grace into the parish house are two bulletin boards. One is for "outreach" notices (posters and announcements are placed there by parishioners, not by committee or clergy) such as "Women Can Get AIDS, Too"; the picture of a maimed child with the legend "Stop the Contras"; and a Health Care Center program on Female Alcoholism. The other features "in-house" information about the congregation and denomination: adult Christian education programs, a daycare clearinghouse bulletin, a women-helping-women group.

Although the communicant list numbers well over 800, an average Sunday attendance of approximately 200 (counting those at both the 8 A.M. and 10:30 A.M. services) populates the nave a trifle thinly. The congregation at a typical Sunday service, not a festival like Easter or Christmas, is likely to consist of twice as many women as men. The growing Sunday school serves about 120 children in the primary grades. It meets separately until the worship service is three-quarters concluded, at which time the children join their parents for communion. The competent choirs, adult and youth, each have about fifteen members, and are directed by a professional organist/choirmaster. They sing with energy. As in many predominantly white congregations, Grace has a sprinkling of worshipers who are people of color. All but about 2 percent of the membership is white, although the family names on the membership roll now reveal many more names from other-than-English background than would have been found a century earlier. Old Yankee families are now "the minority." But Grace, we learned, is still a "family" parish, with 60 percent of its members married or living in family groups. The singles are mostly widows, and divorced or never-married men and women.

The city, originally a New England mill town, also hosts a small, progressive, coeducational liberal arts college. "We're not really a

college town, even if the university is the largest single employer
in it," an economics professor in the congregation explained. "It's
probably best characterized as industrial heartland; it was formerly
a big blue-collar town. Now of course it's lost any small-town fla-
vor." A retired scientist put that change in human terms: "People
are afraid of strangers now. You no longer have the feeling you
know everyone you meet." Given this setting, the people who come
to Grace for "their" church are a loyal and determined lot.

To fit into Grace New England, to feel a part of this congregation, "you have to be a real do-er, you just have to get active." One
young woman reflected, "You have to be self-initiating, *you* have
to take the lead in talking with other people. You aren't expected to
hang back; you can't just show up for services and leave. If you did,
no one would take the initiative or go out of their way to talk with
you." As proof of this, one said she made it her secret undertaking
to draw new members into fellowship during the coffee hour. None
of those with whom we spoke invoked the "Social Gospel" label —
the early twentieth-century emphasis on social needs in poor urban
areas — but Grace clearly cherishes a late twentieth-century version
of it. Their favorite self-label is "outreach," which is part of the
overarching rationale of "work" against which women members
measure themselves.

Asked about the fuel of this activism, the respondents' standard reply was "the Eucharist," a code way of naming worship
their core element. Additionally, most of the women cited participating in one or another of the subcongregations as a source of
nurture. These informal friendship or work groups — relationships
built around shared tasks or affinity of interests — constituted the
congregational glue. Once alerted to their existence, we could begin to see the evidence. Unspoken bonds, smiles, meaningful hand
squeezes passed between many of the women. Several mentioned
fellow-congregants with whom they felt "close enough" to bare
the most painful concerns. One young woman specifically said
that women "belonging to the same congregation" enhanced the
possibilities and "permission" to seek that type of closeness. At
Grace, this female subculture provided its own subterranean emotional and spiritual supports, making concrete the organizational
and theological dimensions of membership. The men with whom
I spoke did not mention infrastructural support or the awareness
that women members enjoyed such support.

Grace attracts few college faculty and fewer students, even if it is known for its liberal stance on social issues. Members are largely middle-income; Grace Church has "no lawyers or doctors, but lots of nurses" was one pithy summary. By no means the high-prestige church in the city, its membership is about half college-educated; fewer than 40 percent have family incomes over $50,000. Nevertheless, "we are really a 'program church' now," one of the congregational leaders said.[3] With energetic clergy leadership, "we're more oriented toward causes and crusades than being primarily a 'family church.'"

Grace does not attract young career-émigrés as does the First Congregational Church around the corner. "[Grace] is definitely not the yuppie church in town," observed a youth-group leader. Nor does it appeal to individuals not "in the mainstream," such as those who are homosexual, according to a male parish leader. Someone wanting more "anonymity" in a church, he surmised, would commute to a larger city parish in the metropolitan area about twenty minutes away. "Also, we're not worshipful or reverent enough for real Anglo-Catholics — although the mood of our worship has moved from being very informal and 'low church' to using a lot more ceremony and candles."

Others who wouldn't be comfortable in this congregation, said a vestryman, are the politically conservative. "They wouldn't appreciate our general stance of being critical toward government and certain public policies, or the underlying sympathy with issues like socialism and pacifism." A young mother, raised Lutheran, recalled that Grace "once had the reputation of being very stuffy, a true Episcopal church, you know, very WASP. . . . I always heard, before I joined, that if you didn't have pearls and furs to wear on Sunday, you shouldn't really go there." But in the 1980s any such identity with a "landlord" status has vanished. Only the exterior architectural shell continues to suggest that self-image.

Right after World War II, several satellite groups spun away from Grace to establish mission-parishes at the edges of the city. Those new congregations dwindled and closed in the 1970s, having lasted only a generation, but while some families happily rejoined the "mother church," others never returned. It had come to seem a "downtown cathedral" that made them uncomfortable. Then followed a shattering decline of membership and finances during the 1960s and '70s. At Grace, clergy leaders had "burned out" or went "off on their own tangent." Occasionally that tangent was a "cause," such as reaching out to migrant workers in the area.

But such programs failed, perhaps because of social-class naiveté. Today the older generation, surviving the memory of the "bad old days," rejoices in a resurrected congregation. Everyone mentions the "return of young families." The sense of having endured "the worst that could happen to a congregation" helps many older parishioners accept changes they might otherwise resist. And although many still characterize Grace as "graying" — the depressing self-identity they internalized during the decline — the age balance has shifted. The congregation is "blooming" with the cyclical reinvolvement of families with young children.

Grace's most valued, conscious self-description is "outreach," a concrete expression of their activist ethos. The example nearly everyone mentioned — "You've heard about our Shut-In Eucharist, haven't you?" — is a twice-yearly service organized for shut-ins. Nursing- or retirement-home residents who are mobile are transported to the church by ambulances and vans that can accommodate wheelchairs. The logistics of assembling such a congregation — where to park thirty or more ambulances, how to line up the wheelchairs so they will all fit in the sanctuary — were reported to us in detail and often. It is as if rehearsing these mechanics conveys their religious meaning. The guests are participants in a "healing Eucharist," at the end of which the clergy and lay assistants move among the wheelchairs and pews, touching each individual with a hands-on blessing and prayer for healing.

This is followed with a lunch contributed by the congregation. The lunch is served on tables placed around the edge of the nave and in the "coffee hour" space near the street door. Each guest receives a handcrafted memento from the older women's Gift Workshop, one year a decorated felt butterfly (symbol of Jesus' resurrection), another year a felt "rainbow" pin (symbol of God's promise after the Flood). Sandwiches, salads, and cookies or desserts are donated by those who cannot be present because of other obligations during the day. The visible rewards of this ritual occasion go to the givers because many of the guests are unable to speak or acknowledge their experience in an audible way. Aside from any psychic and spiritual benefits to the guests, however, the congregation feels profoundly blessed in the giving. Because the occasion has such a high value in the congregation's self-image, it can also attract negativity. One older member undoubtedly had this event in mind when she wrote about what seemed to her an overemphasis on "outreach": "There ought to be more 'in-reach' to the members than reaching to outsiders."

A problem identified by both clergy and laity was "time," time for gatherings other than worship. "Getting adults to come out to meetings" on weekday evenings has become next to impossible, many said; increasingly, church activities must be limited to "one specific weekly time-slot — Sunday morning," one of the clergy reported. Even if a few members still live within walking distance, women's understanding of their "extra" time in this era has all but abolished midweek gatherings. As with physical structure adaptations, there are now time adaptations. Sundays and "church time" are used for all varieties of "religious business." For example, the vestry that formerly met Monday evenings uses the hour or two immediately after the main Sunday service once a month. But parents of high school children find soccer games yet another competitor for the "hour" (or morning) reserved for Grace. Sports are encroaching on even the once-inviolate New England Sunday morning block of time.

Still, a variety of organizations somehow continue to meet in spite of the general lament about time. These include a small (perhaps a dozen or so) Prayer and Praise "subcongregation" that holds an inclusive-language liturgy every Tuesday night, complete with guitars, folk music, and a Eucharist; an ongoing Bible study group of about twenty people, led by one of the clergy; the Altar Guild; and the remarkable women's Gift Workshop that has a steady workforce of between eight and twelve postretirement-age women.

This informal work group has no "officers" other than a treasurer and chairperson chosen by consensus. Anyone who shows up is welcome to pitch in with the tasks in progress, or just sit and visit. The first floor of a parish-owned house adjacent to the church property has been turned into a kind of "clubhouse" and activity center, organized and administered entirely by the Gift Workshop. A huge supply closet holds the three-foot rolls of bright felt from which they fashion stuffed animals, children's wallhangings, and Christmas decorations. The former dining room is brightly lit and inviting, cups of tea perched among the bags of sequins and white stuffing cotton on the four long tables that make a huge square work surface. Any visitor is urged to join this relaxed assembly-line where some eight women are cutting and gluing. Some years their handwork products net substantial amounts (the highest to that

point had been $30,000), which the women themselves designate
to charities, inside and outside the parish.

Equally important, participants in the Gift Workshop perform a
ministry (though that would not be their word) of service to each
other. "We look out for each other. Sometimes we have our own
Bible study, or one of us reads something aloud while the others
are sewing or cutting," one of the regulars explained. "And when
someone needs to go to the hospital, we drive them. We care for
our own." Their cash contributions, which have made such improvements as the wheelchair ramp at one of the church doors and
new carpeting in the chapel, help account for the unusual degree of
respect with which Grace New England speaks of its older women.
This is a gratifying exception to the societal view of that generation. Even though the kind of handmade items and foods they
produce remain in the category of "traditional churchmen's work"
and are in a sense "out of sync" with the younger generations, the
workshop earns high marks in and beyond Grace. No one here
would write off these older women as no longer productive. They
wield too much financial clout.

One whose initiative had been key to founding the Gift Workshop summarized the equation of work and spirituality that describe this subcongregation at Grace: "When I first saw this room,
and learned that it could be made into our workroom, I felt God's
hand between my shoulder blades — just literally pushing me forward as I walked into it." She had brought a mental picture of a
place that could be "workshop" and "clubroom," a place where
her sociable faith and skills at crafts could be united in concrete
actions. "And I said to God, 'I think this is it.' After that everything just fell into place." Such "work" was her gift, her particular
calling: "It's what *I* have to give, what I know how to do."

A small adolescent youth group is again flourishing, after some
years of nonexistence. There is a couples' club, leftover from the
marriage boom immediately after World War II; its membership
is now aging and widowed. It has become, according to one report, "nothing more than a burial society. They complain about
no new blood joining them, but it's remained a closed group and
has effectively kept newcomers away." This group represents a negative generational phenomenon in marked contrast with the Gift
Workshop. It, too, is a generation-specific "organization" with an
even older average age. However, the Gift Workshop's openness
to any and all interested "strangers," plus the desire to mount

commercially successful activities, have created an entirely different self-definition and therefore response from the congregation. In fact the workshop women (and the congregation) use a thoroughly modern label to describe themselves: "We are a support group," they report with satisfaction.

"Sunday Church" at Grace

A friendly bustle greets the first-time visitor who steps into a church service at Grace. At first the formality of the huge sanctuary space contrasts uneasily with the overall demeanor of "comfortable informality," but the easy rapport in the congregation and its energetic worship quickly won us over. One visit in May, the final meeting of the Sunday school until September, included a lateral celebration of a spring floral tribute to mothers. Each child received a tiny potted marigold to take home, celebrating both occasions. Happy confusion abounded; there was no embarrassment or feeling of invisible boundaries being trespassed. During the Eucharist, the Exchange of Peace (shaking hands while saying "The Lord be with you," or "Peace be with you," or just "Peace") was prolonged and generous. People were at ease in the worship space, and welcoming to strangers. The vested figures on the raised platform of the sanctuary were both male and female; the congregational singing was vigorous. The choir members were engaged participants, not aloof performers.

The clergy team is much appreciated at Grace: the rector and associate rector, both men, and an ordained woman who also directs and supervises Christian education. Members credit them with bringing the congregation out of its "bad period," with the smooth acceptance of an ordained woman as part of the staff, and with enlightened leadership in social ministries and outreach. The rector is a man in his mid-50s, a competent administrator, a good preacher, energetic and forceful. "The only time I ever received a standing ovation from my vestry was during the fuel emergency several winters ago, when I walked in and announced I had just offered the sanctuary, in addition to the parish house, as sleeping places for the homeless," he recalled. He is married to a career health-professional; their children are grown and gone. He welcomes the noise and confusion that accompanies the children when they come from Sunday school into the main eucharistic service, defending it against those who find it distracting. "Let's not be afraid of the uproar created by the children," he reassures complainers; "at least it proves we're not dead."

The copastor, shortly to retire, has led the ongoing Bible study classes over the years and done much of the pastoral work. The ordained woman on the staff, in her mid-40s, came into the leadership as Christian education coordinator for several parishes, including Grace, but will become his full-time replacement. She is appreciated for the way she has revitalized the Sunday school ("something most men pastors aren't very interested in, or any good at if they are interested," one woman said) and as a spiritual counselor. She is also admired by the women of Grace because her move toward ordination allowed them to change their attitudes along with her, rather than alienating them. "I think we are all indebted to Joan, by the way she moved in this process. We all loved her before she got ordained, so we just continue to love and respect her now that she's a priest," a bridge-generation woman explained. "Her ordination, which took place here at Grace, was a real celebration for all of us."

Within the context of buildings, worship, and activities at Grace New England, the women who gave us their reflections and experiences had some distinctive and many similar thoughts.

The Older Generation

Gertrude, a retired nurse, now spends most of her days at the Gift Workshop; Marguerite is still employed in a doctor's office but is a lay leader in the worship life of the church; Evelyn works at Grace in both paid and volunteer jobs — as a part-time office employee and as a lay leader. Priscilla, the oldest of the four, is a retired church musician. While only Marguerite spoke openly about her inner life, "work" was their primary language of obligation and loyalty to this congregation — their badge of self-worth.

Among the dozen or so older daily workers at the Gift Workshop, Gertrude, in her late 70s, was clear about the importance of that daily work in her life. Her assessment of change included some disappointment in the younger generation. Gertrude's entire lifetime of work, professional and voluntary, was, in her mind, "church work." "What I have done for all those different organizations is church work, as well as volunteer work," she said.

"I think of it as bringing something of the church to the outside." This encompassed her understanding of lay ministry, the
relationship between the church and the world, and altruism versus self-fulfillment. Younger women in her church characterized
that depth of religious identity as "ministry," but none of the
older-generation women in any of the four congregations were
comfortable applying that label to their work. For them, "ministry" was a word for what ordained men did. Since recent ill
health has curtailed her work, Gertrude lamented, "I used to be
out every day doing community work." Asked if she could now enjoy some recreation or leisure activity, her response was a brusque
"Never have . . . waste of time."

The annual parish fundraiser, a bazaar, now starts from a financial base: every woman in the congregation is canvassed for either
a money contribution or something to sell. Gertrude commented,
"Of course there's a lot of giving that goes into that, from the different organizations and all the folks who work on it," but "if it
weren't for the Gift Workshop, it would be kind of sad around
here, as far as money-raising work is concerned." All the "regular workers" are older women: "I think the average age is in the
70s." She is proud of the "products" resulting from this fellowship. "Everything contributed is turned into money, one way or
another!" When asked if Grace New England still uses church suppers to raise money, she answered yes; a few of the men now "pitch
in" with the cooking. But the younger members don't, she worried. "It really bothers me — where are they now? Our group gave
a card party to raise money for camp scholarships for the kids."
She spoke as if the older generation had arranged it entirely for
the young, not for any of their own satisfaction in doing it. "There
were seven tables, but more than half of them were filled by the
older women. The people in this parish just don't seem to get behind a lot of the things they [we] do. You see all these young people
[in church] and you wonder, where the heck *are* they?"

Gertrude also thinks it's time some of the retired men became
involved in fundraising activities and "did" more. "I firmly believe
the men should be getting together more and doing something as a
men's group. I think the women are more active because it's always
been that way. Men should cooperate more in projects that women
sponsor." She paused. "Of course, I don't know how you're going
to get them to do it." There should be a shared sense of responsibility. "I would hope the young women would have more feeling

of cooperating. . . . The Gift Workshop works very hard on things, and we really don't get regular support from any of the younger ones." It hurts to be unappreciated. "Of course, it's a changing population. . . . It's not their thing to just sit and sew. But there are other things they could do." And she recognizes differing economic realities. "Of course, a lot of them are working, I know, but. . . . " Church loyalty nowadays, even just in terms of attendance, is pretty feeble. "This is probably because people are so much more independent, going so many different ways these days."

Although she expressed a longing for deeper companionship, Gertrude herself does not attend the women's monthly Bible study. "It wastes so much time that I just don't commit myself to that." Then she returned to the symbol of her dismay: "It's women, again [that attend the Bible Study], most of them the same ones that always do the work." She has absorbed the view that something involving "only women" is intrinsically less worthwhile, even as she treasures companionship of the Gift Workshop that she has found life-giving. "We're the only ones around during the day to do things." In light of her diminishing energies, her standards for being a contributing member bring a sense of despair — she envisions no other measure of self-fulfillment.

In contrast, Marguerite, a young (in her early 60s) member of the older generation with bright white hair, participates in the new work for women — a different universe from the Gift Workshop. Her personal calling among the new roles open to laywomen is the ministry of healing; in addition, she arranges the schedules for all lay assistants at healing services. She welcomes this administrative task because of the fulfillment she finds in healing itself. "The whole healing process is just nothing but love," she reflected. "When you lay hands on another person and pray, it's just a total pouring forth. I'm drained by it for a whole day or so after. And at the same time I'm walking off the ground. I'm just so filled with joy at being that kind of channel." She was particularly moved by her recent participation in the Shut-in Eucharist for wheelchair-bound guests. "That is just so wonderful." She sat silently for a moment. "You never know how they're going to react," she continued. "Most of them will say, 'Oh thank you' [after the blessing]. But one lady, as I started to go on by, grabbed at me and said, 'Come back, come back.' 'What's the matter, dear?' I asked, and she reached out her arms to me. 'I want to hug you.' "

Her favorite biblical images for meditation are "the healing ones," especially "the one where a man on a pallet is lowered by his friends through an opening in the roof so Jesus can heal him. Or the woman who touched only the hem of Jesus' robe and her bleeding stopped." Tears welled in her eyes as she named the images at the core of her spiritual identity. Both she and I, women of the older generation, were raised to consider tears self-indulgent rather than associated with spirituality, so Marguerite was forced to wonder if they sprang from a holy source. "Crying around other people used to bother the living daylights out of me," she went on. "It really *embarrassed* me. Now, at least, when I find myself crying with someone, I'm assuring them, 'It's all right, it's okay, I'm not upset. I'm just moved.'" But she dreads the thought of manipulating people through her weepiness. "I really try *not* to use tears in that way. But I am a crier; I can cry...." She paused, then exclaimed, "I have cried at the drop of — even when they just sing the Lord's Prayer (you know, the familiar one by Malotte) at a wedding!" We laughed in mutual recognition. "Anything beautiful can just completely undo me." She was one of the many who made an intuitive connection between tears and moments of spiritual insight, in spite of its being "so un-Episcopalian!"

Marguerite's paid job is that of medical assistant, but she has come to see her employment and her church life as a seamless whole, all of it a channel for God's love. "When somebody who doesn't know me, except at the office, and who doesn't belong to this church, and doesn't know what church I belong to, or even if I go to church...when she comes up to me and says, quietly, 'Marguerite, please pray for me,' and then walks out the door, you think maybe.... Well, maybe my faith *does* somehow show!" She "hadn't been particularly nice" to this woman, or given her signals that were different in any way from her interactions with others in the waiting room. The first time this happened, "it kind of floored me. I came right to the Prayer and Praise group that evening," her particular group-anchor in the congregation, "and shared it. But you know how it is: once you find a spiritual center, you can go any place and be drawn to somebody who has the same feelings. All of a sudden they can tell, they can identify that they are sharing something with you." At this stage in her life, personal spiritual growth is Marguerite's primary and consuming interest; at the same time she is also dealing with her husband's retirement, her mother's terminal illness, grown sons who have yet to get married, and a list of nursing home residents whom she visits regularly. A secondary

satisfaction in her congregational "work" is the close working relationship with the clergy it provides, as well as a visible place in the
leadership. She sees it as a means of serving that is also enormously
fulfilling.

Some older women recall longing throughout their church lives
for more central connection with the congregation's worship, and
they are gratified that the church is "beginning to wake up." Evelyn, however, a no-nonsense woman in her late 60s with steel-gray
hair, credits the business world rather than women's newfound
spiritual authority for this long-awaited institutional change. "I've
always wanted more scope for women in this parish. The previous rector just tried to buy me off, to keep me quiet — because
I had a lot of opinions. He sort of bought me off by making me
the first lay reader. But of course," she added with heavy irony, "I
couldn't be — *women* couldn't be — a chalice bearer!" Women assistants able to "pass the Cup" and actually handle sacred objects
symbolize religious equality to Evelyn.

When she finally became Grace New England's pioneer female chalice bearer, she experienced disapproval. "One woman
wouldn't receive communion when women were serving." But that
kind of resistance is a thing of the past, with the exception of a
few who just want "to keep the church pre–World War II." She
now enjoys a sense of partnership with other leaders. "In this parish, women have a quite...a fairly strong voice. Today's women
have gotten much more aggressive, due to being out in the business
world." And it was women's increased confidence from job experiences that forced men to listen to them. "The church, formerly,
was always run by the men, and we couldn't say much about it."
And even if she had felt comfortable speaking out, it would have
been unavailing. "All of a sudden they find we do have something
to say about the way things run, in other places...so we're offering our opinions here. It's just brightened up this place." She
added, "Women have always been much more forward-looking
than men, in most cases; women here are now coming out of the
closet. They're doing a great deal of good for this church!"

Evelyn has been married forty years to a religiously observant
Jew who supports her involvement at Grace, and that of her children, while faithfully attending his synagogue. Recently, already
aged 70, she was forced to retire from an office-accounting firm. It
was a traumatic dislocation: "Nothing, absolutely nothing to do, is
just sort of mind-boggling." The rector then offered her the part-

time job of treasurer for the congregation. "Having this to get me
out of the house . . . has really been very good for me, because I'm
not one who likes to sit around and do nothing. Never could."
When asked whether the original needlepoint canvasses she designs
and works are not a compensatory kind of "work," she dismissed
them as a mere "hobby." What she is really proud of is mastering
the computer. *That* is real work: "I know now that I, at my age,
can do a spreadsheet!" She added a self-effacement typical of her
generation. "It turns out I'm not as inefficient as I thought I might
be." Work at the church has helped her deal with her husband's retirement; he deserved it, he'd earned it, "he's worked ever since he
was 15." But "it was quite different having him around the house
all the time."

Until her children reached junior-high age, Evelyn had "stayed
at home," meaning unemployed in the wage market. For women
of her generation this left the days to be spent in volunteering,
"work at the church. I had a good example for this, in that my own
mother did a great deal of it. And while my grandmothers didn't
work [at paid jobs], there was an awful lot of volunteer work done
by them. Of course their main task in their day was . . . they kept
their households together! But that didn't keep them in the house."
Thanks to her present arrangement of two days paid work each
week and assisting in the worship, "I've sort of backed away from
being involved in too many other volunteer activities." She resists
the label "vestry rat" (one who spends "all my time down here at
the church"), but she is deeply gratified at being in the center of the
workings of the church and staff. "It really is a big part of my life.
Church to me is the center of things." Personally, "actions, which
I hope speak louder than words" are the expression of her faith.
"I just try to do what I think is right. . . . I try to greet the newcomers." She is her own "greeting committee": "When I see a new
young family in church, I try to find out who they are and a little
bit about them . . . to draw them into some fellowship, that way."

Presently, Evelyn feels too happily occupied to join her age
group at the Gift Workshop. She had once imagined that would
be her work, after retirement, because she enjoyed crafts. She is
charitable about their complaints of being overburdened. "Sometimes they feel as though they're being asked to do too much,
and sometimes I think they might be, for their age. But in this
day when so many women are working, those of us who are not
just have to carry a little heavier load." In her estimate, a very

high proportion of the women in this congregation, "a good 75 to 80 percent, I'd say," are now employed outside the home. "A number of activities that used to be 'women's activities' are just no longer done," she sighed. "But we're pulling together pretty well now, men and women. Of course women have always been more forward-looking...but we and the parish are getting out of ourselves now and more into outreach. And that's good." Both Marguerite and Evelyn derive self-confidence and spiritual strength from work in the central acts of congregational life—worship and healing.

A fourth older woman revealed the deep sense of disruption of the ways she had related to the congregation as a church musician. In her 80s, Priscilla's "work" contribution was now limited to the Altar Guild. Slight but sharply firm of tread, she opposes most of the liturgical changes Evelyn and Marguerite enjoy. Widowed and living independently, she recently "gave up" being in the choir but still sings at services in the nursing homes. A lifelong Episcopalian and member at Grace, she is aggrieved by changes that impinge on her personal worship and on "her" field, music. "Sometimes I have difficulty handling changes in the order of worship, and the wording of the prayers. Not just here at Grace but all other churches." The problem is vanished predictability. "You used to be able to go to any Episcopal church anywhere, and know that when you prayed, you kneel; when you listened for instruction, like the psalms or sermon, you sit; and you stood to praise. But now, heavens! You don't do any of those things alike. You go to one church and they do one thing, to another church where they do something else, and you're uncomfortable, because you don't feel at home." More in bewilderment than anger, she added, "I don't know why they ever changed that."

The new wording of the Lord's Prayer is the ultimate offense. "Of course, the Lord's Prayer is something I really am adamant about, because I will not say that contemporary one. I don't care what anybody around me is saying, I just say the one I was brought up with, and I see no reason for changing. I really don't know what was wrong with it." She warmed to her thesis: "I can't see it, so much change...in the Prayer Book, and all. The '28 Prayer Book that we were fond of...." She paused. "Well, I've learned to accept the new one *somewhat*," she emphasized. Then, returning to the theme of displacement, "But I'll never accept it completely, because it changes so many of the things." She turned esthetic objections into concrete and literal (as well as metaphoric) loss. "I've never found my way around in the new Prayer Book yet! I spend half the time finding my place, and then, just when I get there, everyone else is all through and they're on to the next thing."

She knows that age has probably heightened her resistance to change, especially in the church musician's tool, the hymnal. She had had to retire from both paid office job and volunteer singing in churches, on top of the death of her husband after his long illness; plus she had to "give up" the family house. Her distaste for the "new" hymnal is further compounded by a generational identification with colleagues who have been forced out of paid church jobs as choir director or organist. "I don't think 'they' did a good job on the hymnal, the printing, and . . . they changed some of the wording in the hymns. The additions and deletions, the hymns they put in, and others they took out. . . . " Obviously "they" (the hymnal commission) are a hostile regime. Otherwise how could "so many excellent musicians have been fired"? The villain *per se* is the church's infatuation with change for its own sake.

Also the laity are "taking on too much responsibility," tasks that belonged to clergy in Priscilla's experience. She blames it on an aggressive laity demanding more say in things, at Grace and other churches, rather than seeing it as a reinvigoration of the "priesthood of all believers." And the clergy are not fulfilling the role she expected, a sure sign of institutional decline. She isn't thrilled with an ordained woman as clergy leader, but she isn't as "opposed as my husband would have been. He just plain wouldn't be here." She does approve of laywomen on vestries and parish committees — they "do it every bit as well as men." Her opinions are valid, she believes, because of her many years as a professional participant in church music. "Sitting up there in the choir for so long, being part of the service itself . . . something should have brushed off on me, don't you know. And knowing all the different rectors, in the different places where I sang. I have an overview of the Church." Her years of Sunday morning proximity to the clergy and helping to lead the service authorize her standards. "I recognize all that background that clergy have to have, and their dedication to this job, and. . . . " Here logic bowed to a cry from the heart. "They're *supposed* to be Father of the flock. Just like being a father in the family." Her Altar Guild work seems distinctly less important than being in the choir, certainly less visible. "Everything's entirely different now."

She feels little emotional connection with the present rector at
Grace. "He's really good in terms of causes. But, you know — kind
of over-human." She evidently means the lack of awe-inspiring
quality in his style of management, his down-to-earth manner. "If
I weren't built the way I am, I probably wouldn't even be in the
church." Then she added, "But I do respect him, and we know
each other real well." A specific objection is people calling him
"Mister" rather than the honorific "Father" — and the fact that
he encourages it. She sees lack of respect for the clergy as generational. "I can't call anybody 'Mister' who has spent his life's
work getting ready for the ministry. It's the kind of profession you
have to work at, you know. And...today people don't acknowledge that, when they speak to him in that flat way." To Priscilla,
lack of deference to churchly authority simply compounds the loss
of "excellence" in an institution that has always represented 'the
best' to her.

Her grievances include congregational behavior. For instance,
standing to receive communion seems unworshipful to her. "They
don't give you time...you can't even kneel anymore!" Less reverence toward ceremonial in general is offensive. The aura she had
cherished is gone. "Now, when you sing some of the beautiful
anthems...and take part in the processional and all that, people in
the pews may not even acknowledge the cross." As a choir member
processing down the aisle, singing the opening hymn, she had been
gratified by the congregation's unified bowing of heads. "Half the
time now, the processional cross goes right up the aisle and nobody
even notices or bows their head."

Despite her catalogue of losses, however, Priscilla remains ebul-
lient. Each day as she opens her eyes, she recites the wondering
acclamation, "This is the day which the Lord hath made; we will
rejoice and be glad in it." Of course, Priscilla never "needed" to
spend time with the women in the Gift Workshop. Her own work,
and the opinions and standards it has formed for her, remain the
core of her religious identity.

•

The written responses on the questionnaires noted some of the
virtues this generation could now claim. A few named explicit spiritual gratifications: "I feel I am growing and changing as I strive
toward a closer walk with God." A woman in her 80s wrote, "I
have come to know God within me only after my middle years,
though He was there all the time. But I wasn't always sure of it."

Another wrote that she had been raised in the belief that God was Good, but only now felt able to "rest" in "the feeling, the knowledge, that He is omnipotent, omniscient, omnipresent." Another penned an image from childhood to describe the depth of her closeness to God: "I've always felt that He is my shepherd, that He loves me, and that I can tuck my hand in His if the going gets rough. What more could one hope to understand as the years go by?"

The Bridge Generation

The women in this generation have a complex, even conflicted, view of what it means to contribute to their congregation. They feel it involves "work," effort, something beyond mere attendance, but the new item on their horizon is paid work, which tends to diminish the value of the old-style "women's church work" exemplified by the Gift Workshop. They are sharply aware of the contrast between the ideal of selfless volunteering they were brought up to expect of themselves, and the self-fulfillment they now feel free to pursue in church as in other areas of life. They choose tasks that involve them in the direct "religious work" of the congregation, as lay leaders in worship, even though or precisely because it separates them from the once-expected pattern. They, the world, and their church have definitely changed.

Two of them, June and Joy, consider music and choir membership their "work." Like Priscilla in the older generation, the choir offers them both personal and spiritual fulfillment, and makes them feel they are contributing. "To me, singing is worship," explained June, presently a corporate secretary. A genuinely sunny person who was not a complainer before women had as much scope in church or world, she has no complaints now. Her daughter is "married to a minister," which gives her an "insider" perspective on institutional change and the dynamics between congregation and leaders. Having an Episcopal priest son-in-law undoubtedly cued her to name "sermons" as an important element in her personal worship, but she was one of the few women in our talks who did. "We hear fine sermons at Grace; all three of our clergy are just excellent preachers!"

June was full of admiration for her clergy, especially the ordained woman, Joan, and the way she has contributed to Grace New England's "natural" acceptance of women clerics. Her only reservation about change produced "just a little sympathy for the men" at Grace, like her husband. Men "might be feeling as if nothing in the congregation is left for them distinctively. Maybe we should let men keep the ushering!" But she laughed at her own suggestion. In an era when complaint garners more attention than equanimity, June epitomizes openness and stability in the midst of change.

For Joy, a professional academic, singing in the choir also carries special meaning. "What I like about the choir is actually participating in the service in that way. Singing *is* the worship. That's the kind of prayer that works for me." She loves the liturgy, the music and the prayers. "I don't mind the sermons, but they don't seem to me to be the most important part of it." Like other bridge-generation women, Joy experiences worship less in terms of words or listening to an exterior voice than through internal, esthetic experience.

Two major personal traumas were keys to spiritual growth as Joy neared 50. One was parental: an adolescent child's depression and drug problems, now somewhat abated. The other was professional: fighting for her own academic job as director of a special program. She had been appointed to this newly created position in a nearby college without the crucial professional base of tenure. When the program was incorporated in the college curriculum, she found she had to compete in a national search. "I'd been used to fighting for my kids, and for other people and causes. But I finally realized I really had to just set out and fight for *myself*, for my own right to this job I'd created.... That was a really important step for me. It has changed me, in a positive way." Like many comfortable middle-class, highly educated women, Joy had never known how to fight, "how to be ... angry, how to express anger. Trying to fight with my husband used to be a major thing. It terrified me so, I thought our whole life would come apart, because I'd never seen it. My mother never let us fight as kids. She'd grown up in a turbulent household and she wanted hers to be peaceful," meaning that emotion had to be denied or tamped down. Joy found she had achieved a new level of autonomy. "So I feel like ... I've finally grown up." For a number of women in this study, anger was a way station on the path to selfhood, most often when they were dealing with occupational fulfillment. Asked whether any "jobs" within the congregation were still seen as "belonging" to one gender or the other, Joy responded, "Well, change in that regard is very slow, of course.

As a feminist, I naturally support the Gift Workshop women. But I had to make the point to them that I wouldn't again say 'yes' to something as small, as harmless, as their request to make tuna sandwiches for some occasion." That kind of traditional women's work contribution "simply didn't sit well with me." For other women, however? "I know it is something they love to do; the care and design they lavish on meals for this parish is incredible. But what about the fact that it's a traditional, and therefore perhaps demeaning, role they're playing? I don't know." She paused. "It *is* a benefit to the parish, and to the people involved. If that's what they want to be doing, I suppose that should outweigh any stereotypes in my mind about the exploitation of women. Some things have to evolve gradually, I think. Too-abrupt change simply loses people." Are there some arenas in which women's contributions to the life of the congregation are more welcome than others? "Myself, I never had the sense that I would be stopped from doing anything that I wanted to do, in this church. Well, yes . . . I might be stopped for other reasons . . . but you wouldn't want to print that!"

The social world of the choir and her part in its worship function let Joy see it as a foundational cell within the corporateness. It is her own subchurch within the congregation. Many bridge-generation women in the four congregations named smaller groups or specialized "communities" as the source of their spiritual nurture. "Choir members don't bother socializing outside the choir, but within it, we know each other pretty well. It takes that kind of structure to bring you together with people you wouldn't be with otherwise — not unless you had this kind of purpose." She acknowledges the benefits of a community "not otherwise part of your world," and of "just plain *habit*" of observance: "The worship on Sunday is very important to me. Just the routine itself — coming here every Sunday."

Joy's religious idealism is captured in such symbols as "the lonely poor person, the outcast who becomes religiously significant" and a leader for justice, the way she sees Jesus, Gandhi, Martin Luther King Jr. She shared the vision at Grace of what it took to build a congregation's internal cohesion. "When people work together for a cause, along a common path, community is accomplished, especially when it's something difficult or challenging. That does an even better job than being in the choir, or something that could be purely social, because you are all committed to accomplishing the same goal together."

Jane, now employed as an office manager, believes she is the
kind of person who basically resists change. But she expressed
no regret over the change that discarded previous definitions of
women's churchwork. "I'm not into fairs and that kind of thing,"
she said flatly. Just turning 50, Jane has suddenly confronted the
illness and death of a parent, a daughter's serious trouble with the
legal system, and her own health problems, including the onset of
diabetes. "I suppose hitting middle age is harder than it would have
been if things had gone along without any change. I don't deal well
with change. I'm very conservative in that respect." The birth of
her son's out-of-wedlock child was another shock, though she and
her husband were now deeply grateful for a grandchild. In all these
traumas, Jane found her nurture in the on-going Bible study group:
"How I distanced myself from all those problems was with the
Bible Study. This is a really close group. I can deal with everything
better there, with those people, because I'm in a spiritual context."

Jane's office job, "with a fairly rough group of people," is a
daily challenge to her religious self-definition: she has to resist the
"lower" language and demeaning gossip. "It's very easy to fall
back into a more worldly attitude." Her new church work in mid-
life has been a marital enrichment program for couples; she and her
husband served as its national officers. Jane enjoyed and learned
a great deal from administering the national "office" for that organization from their home. "My actual physical work, now, with
this church, is about five hours per week. That includes Sunday
worship, Tuesday Bible study, ringing the bells in the church tower
every week, and my personal reading of a spiritual nature." Jane
also serves as lay reader, crucifer, and chalice bearer. The varied activities through which she expresses religious commitment created
some friction in their contrast with her secular job.

Jane thinks she has more trouble than most maintaining a psychic balance between accepting and resisting change. "Once I get
into something new, I have no problem with it. I have some modern attitudes, but I like the old forms of worship. I'm probably a
mixed bag." She fears that she doesn't relate well either to the elderly or the very young: "Sometimes when the kids in the church
are making a fuss...it bothers me terribly....It all depends on
what my needs are at the time....Sometimes it doesn't." And she
"finally got up the courage to drop out of the ECW," the traditional churchwomen's organization, because only the most elderly
women still continue in it. "From what I perceive here at Grace,

no one looks to see what gender you are, but rather how well you can do any particular job, and if you like to do it." And she applauds the congregational emphasis on outreach: "People here are involved in feeding the homeless...in the abuse houses, halfway houses, shelters...civil rights...." But causes and enlisting volunteers are still promoted as one's personal choice, not a demand for congregational conformity. "Nobody stands up on Sunday morning and says, 'Because *I* believe we should be doing this, that's what we *all* have to be doing.'"

Since she is one of the few who have experienced diocesan and national levels of leadership, Jane enjoys a picture of the international Anglican communion and the abstraction she called "the church of the people of God." "Being part of that organization expanded our understanding of our church." But she surprised herself by liking one of the most drastic changes: "I'm actually a little proud of our church having a new bishop that is a woman!" Her basic self-definition stresses practical, step-by-step religiosity. "I think I am somewhat more realistically inclined than someone who considers herself more 'spiritual.' I think my spirituality is rooted quite strongly; it's not pie-in-the sky. It's on a day-to-day basis, not the overly dramatic 'I need you *now*, God' type of thing. And it's not a charismatic feeling. I don't consider myself charismatic, but I do consider myself spirit-filled." In fact charismatic Christians "come across as a little pushy." In spite of all she has assimilated, Jane still approaches the new with caution.

Mary, another bridge-generation woman, is entirely opposite — embracing change in every aspect of her 60 years. She has finally been able to "kick the habit of smoking," and the house is free of children. And she is proudest of having completed college. Initially she had been frightened "because I was always the only middle-aged person in a class of students the age of my own children." But it was "the best thing I ever did." And it had only been possible through "a lot of support from female friends." After that she had a job in the public schools, but it became important that she manage the office for her husband's business, a decision that wasn't easy. "Working together...it's as if we're different people in the office, and then back in our house." Now that they are alone again, they are in the process of rediscovering each other.

Mary went on, "Our relationship has grown stronger because the kids are gone and we now have time just for ourselves. We're learning how to enjoy each other." She laughed when her husband actually said one day, "I have to remember that you're part of my life again." He had suddenly realized "it wasn't all right for him to just go off and do his own thing in the evenings anymore. That male independence in marriage comes from the way we were brought up," she interpreted generationally; "that's the standard of twenty and thirty years ago talking." Until she re-entered college and her entire worldview opened up, she had accepted the wife's role as "staying at home with the children" while the man was free to go out with friends or to meetings anytime. "When the kids leave, all of a sudden you say, 'Hey, you're not the person I married!' "

Although Mary loves the congregation and always has, she is critical of its somewhat compulsive activism. Grace is not enough of "an open, sharing community." It is characterized by "tasks and announcements. We aren't willing to show our own needs," she observed, probably "because it might open us up to our vulnerability." Five years ago, when her "daughter went off to college, more people went out of their way to speak to her at that Sunday morning farewell service — showed more awareness of her — than during the entire time she was growing up here." An older daughter, born deaf, had also grown up in that congregation and received much more attention. "If this congregation really could talk more openly, and share, and really say 'I need some support,' people here would realize what 'church' really was, what praying together . . . being part of it . . . is all about." In her view, Grace New England lacks the glue that could draw people into deeper spiritual involvement: "How can we do all this work without more openness with each other?" She herself is at an age where she wants fewer activities. "I think we need more emphasis on supporting what people are actually already doing, the kinds of quiet good work being accomplished right here and now." However, what she means by accomplishment is not sewing and cooking. She hungers for conversation, a meeting of souls rather than hands.

Describing what nurtures her soul, Mary "loves the liturgy most of all. It's not only a time to come and be involved in the service, and see friends that I don't see the rest of the week — but time alone, with God. It's both friendship *and* religion." Mary is another middle-aged woman at Grace New England who loves Joan, the woman priest, for helping her through the momentous change of women's ordination. Joan kept the process of preparing for ordination from being "merely" political, Mary said admiringly. "She wasn't one of those women's libbers seeming to say 'No one can stop me!' Joan went about it just very quietly and didn't make any great pronouncements." Then, fearing she had painted an overly passive portrait, Mary added, "I don't mean she was meek or anything, it was just very natural. She was a person who clearly had something that should be shared. She wasn't doing it for women's rights or anything else," a stance that would have tarnished the change in Mary's eyes.

Mary believes that this woman priest's deep spirituality and capacity to prevent open factionalism were the agents of blessing that transformed Grace New England. Locating her approval historically, Mary recalled the earlier hostility to women and change she felt. When she chaired the stewardship commission some years back, she was roundly scolded by an older-generation woman for "daring" to "stand up in the pulpit" and appeal for increased pledges in the Every Member Canvass. "Only *men* were supposed to do that!" But that kind of gender rigidity no longer has much power. She gives highest praise to the institutional changes that have made it possible for Joan to be a priest and for her own lay leadership. The beauty of it all, she muses, is that change was led *by a woman* openly sharing her calling with everyone and carrying them with her, emotionally and theologically. Overall, Mary loves Grace despite its inhibited spirituality. "I think there aren't too many Episcopal churches that have reached the level of acceptance about change this one has."

The youngest woman in the bridge generation, Harriet, announces herself on the cusp of change, personal and spiritual. She literally rejoices in her recent experience of "salvation," a word she uses unself-consciously (one of a very few women who do in this report); she has been rescued from deep psychic and physical despair. A business crisis accompanied several years of escalating marital tension. As a result, she was hospitalized with a bleeding ulcer. "That night I got down on my hands and knees, and just said, 'Lord, *You*'ve got to take control of my life. I can't do it.' And soon after, I really was healed." Now divorced, she is exploring ways to translate this life-changing spiritual benediction into words and actions helpful to others. "In spite of my brokenness, I'm beginning to find I can reach out religiously to others," she acknowledged. "Actually, it was people in this church who helped me to see . . . to realize that it was important to separate myself from my husband's severe emotional problems."

Three people helped: an office friend unrelated to this congregation, with whom she shares a prayer group during lunch hour; an African-American woman in the congregation at Grace; and the woman priest at Grace who became her spiritual director and friend. She also had the help of a professional therapist. These gave her the strength to confront what she saw as marital failure ("I'm a Christian, and Christians just don't get divorced"), along with the belief she couldn't possibly abandon a really sick man ("He needs me, I just have to bear it"). She had even let herself accept responsibility for her spouse's suicidal impulses. Finally, the therapist's psychological absolution freed her: "He's the one who's psychotic. Whatever you are, you are not causing your husband's psychosis." In her new inner life, she recently received the "gift of tongues," a level of spiritual expression in her praying that "I've never had before, nor ever thought I would. It's wonderful."

Harriet realizes she could be called a workaholic. "I'm very much a Martha, I'm such a do-er. It's been hard for me not to put down the Mary part of me. But now, I'm seeing it more as . . . I'm more able to wait for God, on a very deep spiritual level, to tell me what to do." Her attitude toward "work" has been transformed: "When the activity comes because you want to share the good news of Christ, it's very different." Like others in the bridge generation at Grace, Harriet has no interest in the "women's work" tasks of hospitality or handwork. She is forthright about her need for self-focus, in that sense being more like the younger generation than her generational assignment. "Anything that I do on my own time has got to be related to my own personal growth. I don't have time for crafts." She still "helps out" in Sunday school because her seven-year-old son attends and she wants to learn all she can from her friend Joan, the priest, an expert on Christian education. Of course she values the older women's Gift Workshop but "I don't think I could ever do that. I've no interest in making show-and-tell things." Still she appreciates its immense benefit to women of that generation. "They're performing a ministry with women that is really unbelievable in this day and age."

Seeing her congregation through a more spiritually focused lens, Harriet longs for Grace to become "more spirit-filled: we still need to open up a lot more." She also longs for more profound willingness to "minister to, and be with, the real down-and-outers. It's . . . we're all so white-middle-class here. My friend in the congregation who is black, says — only half in jest — 'I'm going to bring you down to the Salvation Army some afternoon, so you can see just how white you really are.' " Concluding, Harriet dreamed aloud. "Sometimes...It would be fun...if this old building weren't here, if we could start from the ground up.... What would it be like to build a new community? Because, really — there's no 'history' living here anymore; I mean there aren't a lot of wealthy people here, which used to be our history." What would Grace be like in a new incarnation? "If we could start over, we could build a new, more Gospel-based kind of congregation."

Gloria is engaging and open about her own spiritual agenda, and the distance she feels from the congregation at Grace. A young grandmother, barely 50, Gloria is only peripherally related to Grace because the spiritual companionship she needs seemingly can't be found there, she said somewhat sadly. Although "raised Episcopalian," Gloria attends only the midweek Prayer and Praise evening Eucharist; friendship with several of the women in that subcongregation is the sole link sustaining her denominational roots. She and her husband had transferred to the First Church of Christ, a move congenial for a man who had grown up "in one of those clear-glass-windowed, plain, white-steepled churches in Connecticut." Did she miss the experience of the church of her childhood? "Yes, speaking of windows: I miss the stained glass windows, and the dignity, the order, of the liturgy." But during the several years they worshipped at Grace, the congregation of her birthright seemed not to touch on her needs. "I was just never asked for anything here," she mused. "I always felt people here didn't really know who I was."

Ten years ago Gloria worked "practically full time as a nursing-home volunteer," loved it, and began to think about studying for a degree in gerontology. Then she had to face her mother's final illness and decided to bring her into their home where she cared for her until her death. After that, Gloria toyed with the idea of a job: "I almost felt guilty that I didn't have the desire to climb the corporate ladder — or something like all the women I knew." Then she and her husband discovered they were needed as legal guardians of a four-year-old granddaughter. Their drug-addicted, institutionalized daughter could no longer care for her child, Felicity, who came to live with them. Asked how on earth she had survived the horrors of suing her own daughter for custody, she said instantly, "Oh, my faith, definitely. Without it I would surely have gone under." Extensive psychological counseling helped, but the need for daily, hourly sustenance through unthinkable pain of "failure with my daughter" led beyond therapy into spirituality.

What suited their new family configuration best turned out to be a basic liturgical link with "her" church but membership and community in "his." Gloria was one of the women in the four parishes who spelled out a disciplined daily routine of Bible study and meditation. She had a long list of favorite devotional authors and books, which types of prayer were most helpful in which circumstances, and hymns she sang while driving her car.

In her new congregation Gloria enjoys leadership in the adult education forum and a close friendship with the female pastor. She and her husband appreciate the varied "family" groupings they have met, companionship with single parents and other atypical child-rearing arrangements. "If I were hungering for friendliness and wanting a congregation that fed me more than just on Sunday morning," she explained, "I would have to say First Church is the right one." Although she regretted leaving her birthright church, the decision "had just turned out to be a blessing" on many levels. Nevertheless, the words of the Prayer Book were embedded in her soul: she would "never lose that." Some of her memorized daily prayers come from the old (1928) Prayer Book, because "the old Thee and Thou grammar" is so comforting. Over the years, liturgy is the only thing that sustains the Episcopal corner in her soul. "It certainly has not been the warmth or friendliness of this bunch of people," she reflected. In the new responsibilities of second parenthood, a "new" denominational community is also right.

Each of the bridge-generation women at Grace spoke of the sense of release from traditional church confines for women, following the women's movement changes. They enjoy their new possibilities, though they still feel obliged to justify or explain their choices. They eagerly embrace lay leadership roles as work closer to the "real business of religion," once they were free to think in other terms than quilts and coffee hours. Perhaps because of the excitement of exploring new territory, they are not yet able to re-evaluate work in the kitchen as one aspect of spiritual experience.

In their written responses, "religious satisfactions" are personal and spiritual rather than institutional: "Developing a more meaningful prayer life"; "Having a personal relationship with God"; "Being more appreciative of other people's similar spiritual awareness"; and the hope that people are "accepting God's power in their lives, more caring toward each other." Balancing that, their "religious frustrations" are indeed focused on the institution: disillusionment with "politics" in the congregation, and "frustration with the bureaucracy." Several were discouraged that too small a proportion of the congregation has changed; only a segment of it is willing to "participate in study groups or retreats," and new challenges in social outreach. Only a small portion are willing "to move away from a 'safe' spot. As a church we're too content."

The Younger Generation

For the women under 40 at Grace New England, definitions about what is or is not "work" embraced motherhood itself. For Angie, completing an unfinished college degree; Bettina, working part-time but primarily occupied with caring for two preschool children; and Cathy, "retired" from teaching with a first baby, the issue of "personal time" versus "work" was acute. The exception here is Alison, a young African-American woman with two preschool sons who has always taken a paid job for granted. Her white contemporaries, however, see it as an existential problem they have to rationalize and spiritualize.

An avowed feminist, Angie opened the conversation with her ethical conviction about caring for her own kids, "not leaving them to someone else to raise." Her own childhood had not been typically American, she feels, because her immigrant father assumed that girls didn't need higher education. After ten years of "dead-end jobs," she married, had two children, and was just completing her junior year in college. "Not to brag," she smiled disarmingly, "but it's been one set of successes after another." However, that change complicates her work as a mother and raises problems with her priorities. "Last weekend for example, I went to a seminar all day. Which was almost like playing, I had so much fun. . . . It was on how biography is a way to study history. Then Sunday, there was church in the morning, and my son's birthday in the afternoon. You can see how much I tried to jam into two days."

Angie feels trapped in a dilemma, "a feeling that I must *go out* and have a career." She wants to believe that "being at home with two children" is itself a valid career at this stage of life. But "a lot of women just don't see that as worthy of a life investment. So I'm having to grapple with whether I do or not." In the intellectual

world she now inhabits, a location that gives her the extreme satisfaction of developing her mental powers, her parental standards
of responsibility are considered bad news. "I find that women are
the most scathing critics of a decision to stay at home." More dis-
maying to her feminist identity, women she knows and admires
are vociferous about the "male, professional-career" model as "the
only valid pro-woman stance."

"It's very hard," mused Angie. "I met a woman at the seminar
last weekend who asked me, 'Are you employed outside the home?'
It's an awkward question, but very powerful — which is why it
had to be asked so carefully, so deliberately." She pondered its implications. "When people ask me 'Do you work?' my jaw kind of
drops. I'm taking three and a half credits at college, I have two kids
in grade school, I do church and all the PTA things plus the laun-
dry — though my husband and I share housework pretty equally —
and still I'm asked do I work? What more do they want?" It is a
matter of principle for her to avoid "being disloyal to women who
are working," because she defends their right to make that choice.
She longs, however, for reciprocity. "I would appreciate...being
respected for my decision, even though it doesn't bring in a lot of
cash. It seems as if that's the only thing people want to know about
your decision, how much money you make."

Angie is an idealist about Grace — what it is and could be,
especially its social involvement. She noted its Christian commitment to outreach, "that it does reach out, that it opens itself
and is available...geared toward the community. No matter how
much trouble it is, we take responsibility for it." Current international conflicts are a topic on which she wants her church's
moral perspective. "In this age of nuclear war, and South Africa,
and Nicaragua, *church* has to be one of the places where people
learn about these issues...where people are helped to know how
to think and feel about them. They're certainly not going to get
anything like that from the TV news! Most people probably won't
pick up a book about Nicaragua, but if they hear a sermon about it
they might say, 'Gee that's interesting, I think I'll do a little research
on that.' That kind of influencing is exactly what the church has a
responsibility to do." She endorses the use of church facilities by
"outsider" or secular groups. "I see all that as part of our mission.
It's real important to our identity as the church on Main Street. We
can't just move to the suburbs and be closed off from the world.
I'd leave this church before I stood for that!" She thinks the major-

ity of the congregation is pretty modern: "I think 'modern' means being able to accept changes like women priests and... women's [larger] place in the church." She used a generational rationale: "The old have had things their way for ages, now it's our turn."

Angie has a very clear appreciation of organizational dynamics. "I think conflict is good for this congregation... disagreeing over how to spend our money, which projects to work on. As long as people fight about those things, they're interested. The minute they say to the vestry, 'Go ahead, do what you want,' we're in real trouble." The majority of her own time and interest centers in religion and the church. "But," because of the college schedule, at this point, "when I talk about volunteering, I mean only attending church, period!" (She also sings in the choir.) Before starting college, she had volunteered in more conventional ways: initiating a women's outreach group that gathered Christmas presents for needy children, and ensuring that casseroles got delivered to the sick members. "Now that committee is composed of both men and women." Here she is, she laughed, a feminist who belongs to no women-only groups! And presently her faith has to be nurtured through her mental and spiritual activities, not specific tasks. "I guess *living* the life of commitment is the way we try to do it, my family and I... making it really an integral part of our daily lives. I don't know if that's what Jesus had in mind when He said 'go and tell,' but that's what I'm trying to do right now."

Bettina, a young mother of children aged 2 and 4, was "not comfortable with a lot of modern stuff" about women because it offers so many "confused priorities." She is disturbed by the antagonism she receives at her evening "waitress job" in a Christian restaurant, "real women-against-women stuff." She explained, "I can't afford to go back to the university for my master's degree in education because I work at night. If I don't work at night, I don't have the money to meet the payments on the house. It's really this big 'Catch-22.' I have a degree, I just can't teach because I haven't completed the state teacher certification courses." Then she added, defensively, "I don't even know that I *want* to go back to work during the day. I want to be home when my children need me."

For Bettina and her former Roman Catholic husband, Grace New England is alive and "really going places." She loves the worship, the singing, the sermons, and the rector who is a real leader. His wife is a good bridge-generation friend. Of course Bettina has already discovered the truism describing most organizations: there are "the few people that do everything, the core of the parish, and then there are the peripheral members who come occasionally. And last there are people who get lost in the shuffle. But overall there is a definite people-center to this church." What she thinks this congregation could do better is "try to touch people so that they *will* come more often, and...realize what a good thing...what a Christian service community can really be." This was her most direct reference to spiritual challenge. Her view of commitment, however, like most of those in her age group across our four parishes, is individualist: "If you want to put your soul into it, that's up to you. The ministers can't reach inside you and say 'you've got to do this.' *You*'ve got to unlock yourself."

Bettina is concerned about the image of the church, newly significant to her, in the secular world. "A friend of mine — she's involved in the religious education classes — she and I were just saying how few families in the [housing] developments where we live go to church. It's like you are a minority if you go to church." Adolescence in general seems to her to be a period pretty well lost to religion. "Those years, you just kind of hang out. I don't think anyone really wants to go to church from age 15 to 21. Then, when you're more normal, in your early 20s, you start to care. You suddenly snap your fingers and say 'Wake up! There is an afterlife!' "

But her present overarching concern is childrearing in an "alien" context — an un-Christian, materialist world. First, "in order to have time with my children, I sacrifice everything else." This limits her involvement in jobs that could make her more a part of the congregation, like tending a booth at the bazaar, "which always takes place when I'm working at the restaurant." Then, as a parent, "you want the best for your kids, and you want to have a nice house and — say, a new Ford Taurus! Me with my '74 Maverick! But in order to have the lifestyle where your kids can *do* things besides just go to school, you have to bring in between $30,000 and $40,000." She tries to summon empathy for women who couldn't sacrifice "fifteen years of a career" to stay at home with little children, but the choice of full-time employment strikes her as totally wrongheaded. "It's such a waste! The child goes to daycare, leaves the house from 5:30 in the morning until 5:30 at night, eats, and goes to sleep....I always ask: why have children? Of course, that's not really a popular opinion." How to realize one's potential is a constant existential puzzle. "All the friends I know work around that, all the time — juggling schedules, holding down a menial job, finding time to be with your husband."

Bettina's ambivalence has recently been heightened by cross-examination from families "eating out" many evenings, as she waited on their tables. "Those are the ones who ask, 'What do you do during the day?' But when I answer, 'I stay home with the kids,' it makes them defensive, because they don't. There's . . . like . . . this great big *blaming* me, or *blaming* themselves, because that's not what *they're* doing." She sighed. "So then they ask, 'Well, who's home with your kids now?' I say, 'I'm home by 9 P.M., and my husband has given them supper and put them to bed." The part-time job that is somehow "beneath" her, necessary as it is, undermines her self-confidence. "A lot of the ones who are working feel bad," she believes, "because they're not at home, but . . . they need to go out and do it." She groaned. "It's a no-win situation. Heaven forbid there's a woman who stays home, and doesn't go out to work at all. 'You don't work at all?' Women beat each other up over this philosophy." And she doesn't expect relief in the near future. "Only when your kids are in school does it let up. At least, what I'm hoping is . . . that the worst is from birth to five years." Bettina summarized her quandary with a gendered assessment of present-day femininity: "Women just plain feel guilty! They go to work and feel guilty, they feel guilty if they're not working."

Active participation at Grace is open to anyone of either sex who will volunteer, Bettina concluded, and "people will love whatever you do, whatever you decide to give. But you have to want to *do* things, to really work at it. . . . It's up to the individual how much of yourself you want to put into the church. Or rather, into Christian service. Right now, my time is such that I just plain can't. It's all controlled by having to pick up my son at nursery school and my daughter from a friend's house."

Alison, a scientist by profession, recently moved to this locale. Her husband, between jobs, is currently doing the childcare for their preschool sons. She grew up in an historic African-American Episcopal Church in Baltimore. "I always envied my brother when we were kids: I wanted to be an acolyte like he was, that's what I wanted. The candle lighting, and the robes, leading the procession, being part of the service. . . . It seemed to me that if I'd been up front, it would have been great. I wouldn't have had to sit and fidget through the service." Presently she finds her religious emotions absorbed by and expressed in terms of family. "Since my

mother's death, I've taken on the elder-sister role, trying to keep
the family together. It's funny how almost immediately, I thought
'now it's *my* house where the holidays will have to be held.' And
I also started worrying about my dad. Even though he's perfectly
capable of taking care of himself!" She is aware that assuming responsibility for everyone's emotions is her way of trying to step
into her mother's family role as kinkeeper. It also is a way of fend-
ing off grief. With a second baby, it has been hard to "find a time
to grieve, a time when I could let myself fall apart. Finally, now,
that's coming. . . . I'm dealing with it, through prayer."

When asked whether images like All Saints' Day and "the fellowship of the saints" had become a more profound symbol after
the early deaths of both her mother and her brother from diabetes,
she laughed. "Having them up there in heaven in a way almost
restricts my prayer life instead of opening it up." Expanding the
image, she said, "Praying is like a family conference, now . . . with
confession! I can almost feel myself holding back, censuring what I
say, now, because they're up there, they'll hear it, they know." She
then added somberly, "Also I'm thinking what I should have said
to her before she died, but didn't. I see that my mother keeps on
living, through me. I can constantly see myself doing things, making choices, that have their basis and values in her example . . . for
instance, the goal of graduate school." She and her husband are
both graduates of Ivy League universities and worked overseas in
the Peace Corps, where they met. "I can see that I have *already* set
my sights on the boys getting *at least* a master's degree, just the
way she did about us! And my oldest son isn't quite four!"

As evidence of a deepening spirituality in her daily life, Alison
finds herself "doing things at work that I never did before, like
wearing a cross. It's as if I've finally figured out it's okay to go
public with it." She also enjoys a lunch-time prayer group near
her office that she attends with a new friend from the congregation. Motherhood has made her, like her mother, "more willing to
fight about things I don't think are right. And yet I don't like the
fighting image at all." She mused over this sudden disregard for
pacifism. "Well, there are some things I just have to fight for. For
Christianity, for my faith, I would fight!"

What would she choose for her special contribution as a member of the congregation? She is still considering various possibilities. "Maybe intercessory prayer. That's new for me. I think it
would fit under two headings: it's an aspect of friendship, and I

can also call it 'work.' Or maybe I'd like to join the choir, or be
in the Bible study group." She thought a minute. "My time is just
so limited now, whatever I do will have to be really important for
my soul." Of the younger generation at Grace, Alison is the most
comfortable with religious terms and the only one who mentioned
anything to do with "soul." "I used to love to spend time, alone, in
churches...to just absorb the quiet and the sacredness within the
walls. But marriage changed all that. And now, with kids, actually
what I need more than anything is just plain Alison-time." So far
she believes that egalitarianism at Grace New England, men and
women sharing the same jobs within the congregation, is still more
surface than substance. Is it only the female of the species that
thinks "work" is an essential component of religion, she wondered
wryly? Is it only women who believe that making an active contribution is a badge of belonging? Even now, at this "improved"
moment in time, "the fathers who take turns helping in the nursery
still let their wives 'volunteer' them," she observed.

Cathy, a new mother of an infant daughter, taught school for a
decade. She is happily "retired," as she put it, in her mid-30s. Having endured several miscarriages and a long wait for this baby, she
is basking in motherhood. She loves finding a place in the congregation, new to her, where her husband has been a lifelong member.
Baking, cooking, and all the "traditional" women's-work tasks are
her recreation; Cathy already has a freezer full of cookies for the
next bazaar. Church is both "the social and spiritual center for
their family," she stated. She is grateful for the preparation sessions
they attended before the baby's baptism. She also loves the congregation's warm participation in their new-parent joy. She is not the
least reluctant to "stay at home." Volunteer churchwork and family are the only work she cares about, for now, at least until her
child reaches school age. Because of the pleasure she derives from
doing crafts and handiwork, Cathy is the one younger-generation
woman who has a special relationship with the older-generation
women and the Gift Workshop; she even joins them occasionally
with her baby daughter nearby in a basket, a gesture of female
solidarity across the generations.

Several of the young women wrote searching notes on the survey. "Where is God in AIDS? I had a friend who died of it last
year." "My understanding of God has muddied considerably since
my youth," wrote another, "but my need for Him has dramatically
increased." Another wrote frankly, "I'm still unclear who God is,

but I begin to be readier to believe He's there for me." Another chose a jaunty metaphor: "Jesus is a peer, a helping hand on my shoulder."

•

Women in this congregation reflect what might be seen as a quintessential strand of Protestant cultural influence, one putting work and effort at the heart of all that matters. While women in the other congregations also used work as a measure of religious identity, none used it as often, or evidenced a similar level of fascination with and analysis of work or action as part of a spiritual and congregational identity. Some of the women at Grace expressed a concern over too much emphasis on "doing," on activism as a substitute for private inner nurture, on busy-ness as an incomplete measure of faith and self-worth. Still, in each of the generations at least one woman — Marguerite, Mary, and Alison — spoke more about issues of the life of the spirit and less about work as a value.

The emphasis that Grace has seemingly placed on "works" or tasks is painfully apparent in its older-generation women. The opposite side of that standard of self-worth is the fear that in spite of all their efforts, the changes happening in the congregation justify their anxiety about their church's longevity. Participating in a congregational identity that overemphasizes work implicitly devalues worship, the bedrock of religious community. Many of this older generation discount their own inner lives, clinging to the label of activism as the only guarantee of spiritual community. "Going to church" isn't enough, but merely the surface of a religious identity. "Being in church," by itself, has been stigmatized as passive. They have absorbed a kind of schizophrenic evaluation. All women at Grace who responded to the questionnaire ranked "regular worship on Sunday mornings" as both their "primary church activity" *and* their "source of spiritual nurture." But among the older women only something that is "more than" praying and Sunday worship can assure them their church "is all right," and that they are all right in it. Which makes Gertrude, one of the older women, puzzle about the young who do not share that measure of importance: "Where the heck are they?"[4]

In view of the actual quantity of service and services Grace New England puts out, Gertrude's disappointment, expressed in code terms of fear for the future of the congregation, has to be a generational mindset. Overvaluing "work" of a certain kind makes the older women undervalue the considerable outreach that is actually provided. If actions above and beyond membership and attendance are the primary, intrinsic Good, their life stage itself — increasing frailty — becomes a judgment. If the one expression that really counts, in terms of commitment to one's religion and congregation, is the ability to make extra, active contribution, and if that "work" is valuable only when it is a concrete physical task, their value to the congregation is called into question.[5] This generation has never had the comfort of believing that their prayers or presence were blessings in and of themselves; they must worry, at bottom, that they will one day be cast out if this congregation's primary religious evaluation no longer applies to them.[6]

It is instructive at this point to place the emphasis on "works" (as a primary aspect of a member's value) in the context of gender. To re-ask Alison's question, how many male congregants at Grace measure their spiritual commitment or fulfillment in terms of activism? Do they similarly equate "doing" with organizational importance and "influence" with significance? Or was the idealization of activism women's specific way of staking out and claiming a place for themselves in the congregation? Even after several decades of the women's movement, some women have not internalized the same "green light" for self-development and self-cultivation, in church and world, that men take for granted. Women historically have had to "carve out" space for themselves in hierarchical institutions, a function that tends to create intensity of commitment.[7] Whether or not men think of congregational activism as *their* responsibility in the same way the women do, women here still view male congregational leadership as "the norm." Any advances in that arena are somehow still surprises or bonuses, not yet taken-for-granted enough to escape comment. The bridge generation's delight in lay-leadership work is its clear testimony.

Many Protestant women, including those at Grace, have indeed carved out new and different space in their religious organizations since the 1970s. To some degree they all express an understanding that volunteer, unpaid contribution to the church is a central meaning of "congregation." Generational contrast is found in where that meaning lies on the spectrum of reasons for membership. Does membership at Grace exist to promote and channel these women's self-giving, as it seems for the older and some bridge-generation women, or is it primarily a means of self-fulfillment — perhaps one among others — as it seems among the younger women?

Influences from the larger culture, rather than the congregation, constitute the struggles the younger women are confronting over paid versus volunteer work. Faced with the complex, multiple demands they must juggle as parents, workers, members of Grace, and spiritual seekers, they see themselves caught in a societal conflict that overvalues paid work and undervalues child nurture. The experience has both a gender and a generational twist: in this new age for women, a career in the world, the kind of work that men traditionally did, has become the only "work" that "counts." Bettina and Angie are torn between childrearing as vocation and the cultural goal of autonomous, self-determined womanhood as defined by a career. They happen to be in the career-oriented segment of New England society because of their education and aspirations. Unfortunately, their privileged social-class location acts to expand, but also contract, spiritual self-development. Working out *their* self-worth in terms of "work" is the effort, valued or not by their religious organization, on which they expend much emotional and spiritual energy. Alison stated it for them and all younger-generation women: each needs time for her own soul most of all.

Among the bridge-generation women, the age group increasingly moving into leadership, changed definitions of work and church have opened horizons that were literally unimaginable a few decades earlier. Along with that comes the ability and the responsibility to question the authority of both clergy and tradition. Increased confidence in their own perceptions, thanks to experience in paid employment, has strengthened them. Another is the more collegial administrative climate adopted in some of the large corporations near Grace, where many of them are employed. The rector suggests that this organizational change alone has made an impact on the congregation's internal dynamics. Within the congregation, links among the congregants themselves — small "primary group" friendships or quasi-family support groups — have taken on more importance than the hierarchical member-to-rector, follower-to-leader links that formerly prevailed. "People in the congregation seem to be disagreeing more with each other and less with me" was his summary. At the same time, contemporary clerical management of churches has indeed promoted a less hierarchical process of administration and decisionmaking.

Our women informants "credit" most of the changes within the congregation, including "pulling Grace along concerning women," to the rector. In their view his ability to reactivate Grace's social-gospel identity is the important factor. "He's the one who got this church out of the stupor it was in for years and years," one woman pronounced. They attribute to him and the other clergy more credit than their own change, an indication that "things being pretty modern" at Grace have not altered as radically as they like to think. In a congregation where the contemporary Social Gospel identity is idealized, a masculine, this-worldly emphasis dominates the congregational worldview. Perhaps some of the women are tempted to interpret the new organizational power now open to them as spiritual power.

The women with whom we spoke are indeed among those at Grace who believe that any job they want to hold in the congregation is open. Even the most powerful taboo — women leading worship and celebrating the sacraments — is gone. Harriet, the youngest of the bridge generation, illustrated this with a grass-roots, women-in-the-pew measure: "At announcement time, now, a woman can get up, wherever she's sitting in the congregation, and make an announcement about something as specifically feminist as the battered women's shelter — and there's nary a raised eyebrow." At the upper end of the bridge generation is Mary's benediction on the present state at Grace. "We've incorporated so much change in the past decade, let's stay modern. Let's not be stuffy, let's not fall backward."

Although the fragments of these women's lives cited here illuminate the dominance of the theme of "work" among the many religious characteristics of this congregation, they also suggest multiple riches below the organizational surface. They illustrate the ways in which three generations of women at Grace New England themselves identify with what makes the congregation tick and how they have carved out space in it for themselves. In various ways "work" gives a highly rational shape to religious identity at Grace, and many seem to believe it functions (with greater or lesser satisfaction) as their form of religious nourishment.

Concerns about one's "institution" are ultimately about survival, one's own and the congregation's. The anxiety of the older women at Grace is particularly poignant, since the kind of self-less work that was their generation's role for churchwomen helped keep the parish alive. But the other side of that kind of work meant that efforts directed toward their own needs — spiritual, developmental, even recreational — were deemed less worthy, even discouraged. Today they are finally encouraged to state their own needs in the congregation. Still, they are situated on stony New England soil that yields only to Hard Work, if at all. They and their fellow congregants grew up in a church that mistrusted spiritual "softness." Women who claimed the right to focus on their own inner lives were once viewed as a threat to the congregation that depended on their carrying the congregational burdens. As Max Weber noted in his great historical overview of religious institutional evolution, "mystical saints" were a contradiction in terms for Protestants.[8] The self-absorption necessary to discover a personal spiritual path could easily have led women to focus more on their own inner growth than on meeting everyone else's needs. In this locale, it may be that a cultural residue of that congregational ethos still sustains a gendered version of work as selflessness among women at Grace.

Chapter 3

REDEEMER PLAINS AND "CHURCH"

*A*t Redeemer Plains, in the deep Midwest, each woman's story seemed to be about finding her own right relationship with the congregation. The topic of "church" — as an ideal, and as Redeemer itself — dominated our conversations. At first we had to wonder if this unanimous appreciation of Redeemer was an attempt to present us with a perfect parish, a church without blemish or strife. Later, the significance of the individual's *choice* behind the explanations in these narratives became apparent. "I just plain went church shopping," one young woman announced. "I was looking for a place where I could feel a spiritual connection, right within the context of the place." A bridge-generation woman exclaimed, "Give me a church that has good Bible study or something — just don't expect me to sew." An older-generation woman for whom it meant task involvement — membership in the Altar Guild — took a didactic stance. "Every Episcopal woman should work 'on the Altar,'" she pronounced. "That's how you learn your church!" Each demonstrated her own generation's perspective on what had made Redeemer the "right" church for her.

A swirl of meanings about 'the church' seemed more fascinating to the members at Redeemer, were closer to the surface, than to the other congregations we visited. Against a backdrop of negative experiences in other churches, they spoke of the church building itself, this particular congregation, and its sense of spiritual magnetism. The women were eager to put these thoughts into words because many of them had consciously chosen this particular religious home, we learned. The act of sharing their stories aloud and enjoying our responses was strengthening to them. Many had made

61

their choice at some cost in family relationships, which added to the intensity of their reflections. In a locale where the land itself signals continuity as far as the eye can see, a woman's selecting a religious belonging into which she wasn't born is a major act of differentiation. Additionally, people in the Midwest take religion seriously; Redeemer's context is a community in which church membership is an expected part of everyone's "identity kit."[1]

The need to exercise and defend one's choice of church membership undoubtedly heightened the awareness of change itself. It was not hard for the women to name the stages of inner adjustment through which they had moved, from one self-image to the next to a present "self." While a few were "born into" Redeemer families, the local spiritual geography keeps the idea of change in religious identity — with accompanying, sometimes painful psychic and familial adjustments — very present in their consciousness. Each knew friends or relatives still struggling to "free themselves" religiously from some of the more fundamentalist or legalistic churches that abound in their setting.

Like women in all patriarchal religious structures, the women at Redeemer have had to "carve out" space for themselves. But the image of carving out space can also be a metaphor for the entire congregation. In its regional context Redeemer is a refuge for religious choosers. People in an earlier century who joined this denomination corporately carved out church "space" that was socially and theologically independent vis-à-vis its neighbor churches. Episcopalians have always been a minority church in the vast midsection of the continent. A goal of "carving out" and emphasis on "choice" formed the subtext of our conversations about change and the church, differentiating Redeemer Plains from others in its locale and from the other three churches we visited.

A congregation like Redeemer, containing a high proportion of those with the liberating experience of having selected instead of merely inheriting a religious self-definition, develops a distinctive corporate ethos — a lived ideal of peaceful co-existence with fellow refugees.[2] Women started from varying beginning points but the end of the search was Redeemer. They identified a subconscious "safety" in its liturgy. They were thankful for a form of worship giving them an internal freedom and dignity — a religious system where "people don't have to conform" to "every jot and tittle" of dogma, "just the central things," that is, Christianity and Protestantism. But more it spoke to them innerly, viscerally. Their sense of relief — of having arrived at this oasis in what seemed a religious desert — was palpable. Of course, several articulated the potential danger in such uniform self-gratification. Pilgrims such as themselves might so rejoice in their "privilege" that they begin to worship the sheltering walls themselves. But the apparent joy each seemed to find within Redeemer's own internal pluralism evoked a loyalty that was indeed distinctive.

A small city anywhere, not just in the Great Plains, can be stifling; many of the women mentioned the need for "breathing space" and a place to examine new ideas, to think new thoughts. Redeemer is a place where "it's all right" to grapple with matters of faith and ethics instead of "swallowing whole" a given set of beliefs and expectations.[3] People especially value Redeemer for offering this type of "independent sector." Perhaps that is one reason they identified themselves more readily with the name of the church, Redeemer Plains, than with the denomination. The "right to think for yourself religiously," one of the main benefits of the American form of denominationalism, was clearly a key emotional element in their choosing to affiliate with Redeemer.[4] The women expressed their satisfaction in statements such as "I'm here because Redeemer is a place where you are *expected* to think for yourself" and "I joined this church because it encourages you to use your own mind, not swallow something whole." The model of individual responsibility and commitment associated with Redeemer is a welcome contrast with congregations demanding conformity.

This congregational idiom — the right to think for one's self — paradoxically created its own kind of uniformity. The special ethos of Redeemer, its "personality" to which they all responded and then adopted, honors choice and made them see themselves as progressive — pro-change. In the mood of openness permeating our conversations and informal gatherings, there was a general eagerness about "the new." Those we spoke with have a greater awareness of secular (media-diffused) change than of specific canon-law changes in the national polity of their church but they see themselves on the side of change *per se*, especially the young. Their fearlessness illustrates the truism that larger cultural currents of "change" are really the accumulation of countless individual decisions — assimilation at the personal, invisible level of choice. Women at Redeemer took from the women's movement the aspects of "the new" that they could appropriate and constructed (most subconsciously, a few consciously) their own version of change — using the tools they had at hand.

The clearest example of a generic approval of "the new" emerged when we talked about women clergy. At the time of our visits, Redeemer had little direct experience of women priests. They anticipated having a woman-seminarian "staff intern" in the near future but had experienced women priests at other churches or diocesan functions. Yet they brought an expansive personal response to the *idea* of "priests who are women" — a welcoming openness that expressed Redeemer's own sense of being an independent sphere. That contrasted with a negative view of the label "feminist": very few referred easily to themselves as feminists. At the same time, only a few (in the older generation) resisted the denominational changes of liturgical language and women lay readers. Women's employment outside the home is clearly no longer an issue, though it had been. Perhaps being insulated from the reality of ordained female leadership, to this point, meant they were free to project only positive responses. Redeemer's independence vis-à-vis its neighbor churches, and the relative cultural sophistication of these women — who displayed a cosmopolitan frame of reference in sharp contrast to the more restricted mental worlds of many of their neighbors — was evident in their lack of defensiveness as they talked about change and this church.

The Setting

Redeemer Plains is housed in a neat, modified A-frame building with an attached one-story parish hall, set in acres of lawn at the edge of a small midwestern city. The entire "campus" conveys a plainness that is dramatized, on stepping into the church, by a stunning two-foot-wide band of contemporary stained glass windows at clerestory level (just underneath the meeting of roof and wall, but above eye level as one sits in the sanctuary). The windows are a glowing iconography, symbols of Nature and the sacred such as a bird in flight, wheat, fire, a potter's wheel, a cross, and the Chi Rho (the ship of the Church) under sail.

The sand-pink stucco exterior does not prepare one for the impact of these visual sermons.[5] The interior tone is sand-beige and light-colored natural wood, heightening the deep purples, greens, yellows, and blues of the windows. The overall effect is immensity contained in an enclosure — the moderate-sized sanctuary. The choir loft and pipe organ are in a gallery at the rear of the nave. Outside, on the horizon behind rows of houses and grain elevators, is mile after mile of undulating grassy plain. Anxiety about another Dust Bowl crops up in conversations among those old enough to recall the earlier one. The relative emptiness of the landscape reinforces the sense of "haven" in church buildings that seem to nestle in a great bowl of plains-land.

Redeemer has 270 communicants and an average Sunday morning attendance, at the 8:00 and 10:00 services, of 135. At the early service perhaps as many as thirty people sit, widely scattered, in the nave; at the main service, the pews seem well filled with people of all ages. The male rector is supplemented and complemented by many laymen and -women who quietly assume the many tasks and roles required to maintain the congregation. This small band of Episcopalians in a rural sea of dogmatists radiates a striking sense of unity. Redeemer knows itself as "the parish of choice" in this railroad-junction city of 15,000 and some fifty-two churches. Nearly half the present members of Redeemer are fairly recent refugees from Missouri-Synod Lutheran, Roman Catholic, or splinter Protestant churches. The older members are also descendants of an earlier wave of "choosers," making this identifying ethos both historical and contemporary. Although Redeemer is primarily (60 percent) a congregation of families, single professionals in nearby colleges, industries, or medical facilities find its reputation for "religious independence" appealing. People interested in "making their own decisions" view Redeemer as *their* kind of congregation, a contrast with the usual Episcopal image of political and social conservatism.

Episcopal parishes were first established in the Great Plains in the 1830s — the result of competitive missionary campaigns between the High Church or Anglo-Catholic wing of the denomination, and the Low Church or Evangelical majority. Thanks to the missionaries who were first to work among them, early white Episcopalians in the Plains were likely to be high church, a religious identity that made them even more unique among Protestants in that locale. But Episcopal minority status was also tempered by its location on "an opening frontier." Historically, those congregations were forced to be more flexible out of necessity. Since women converts outnumbered men, Episcopal churches in rural areas in the late nineteenth and early twentieth centuries allowed women considerably greater parish and diocesan participation than prevailed in urban, male-dominated parishes back East. However, during the twentieth century, male hierarchy in Great Plains Episcopal churches became as established and unquestioned as elsewhere.

Redeemer's new buildings and setting belie its history of more than a century. The congregants of the 1960s, now the surviving older generation, made the enlightened decision to build anew on what was then the outskirts of the city, in response to the post–World War II need for education rooms and parking. Four of the nineteenth-century stained glass windows from the original downtown building, now demolished, are lovingly mounted on the walls of a room in the parish house that has been converted into a chapel. They provide the only visible link with the congregation's earlier structure.

Of the women who returned our questionnaire, 60 percent have some college education but only one-quarter are in families with an income of $50,000 or more. Wages are generally lower than on either coast, as are living costs: 56 percent of the women reported personal income between $10,000 and $20,000, the lowest of the four parishes. Even so, Redeemer has a higher percentage of law and business professionals than the other three congregations in our study, and a higher percentage engaged in civic leadership — the elite of that city. Two of the women we interviewed have run for public office. The rare African American or Latino resident drawn to Anglican form and ritual is welcomed. The congregation's sense of its uniqueness results in racial openness that is rare in a setting where white middle-class propriety assumes separation according to skin color. But unless the ethnic-minority worshiper is also well educated and at home with "English culture," he or she does not usually choose to join: "Our worship is just too formal," several people reported. At present one black and one Latino, both professional women, are members.

A special sense of gatheredness and dedication pervaded our exchanges at Redeemer. The rector was one of several members who noted, "People here are more likely to call themselves 'a member of Redeemer' than 'Episcopalian.'" In this context, that is code for claiming the distinctiveness of the parish but soft-pedaling any culturally aristocratic connotations. Trying to explain why she loved Redeemer, one young woman cited some of her neighbors who were in the habit of lacing casual biblical quotations into the conversation. "Whenever we're talking about religion," she reported, "I don't know if it's my background or what...but I just don't feel real comfortable saying 'Do you recall when Jesus said so and so?'" Episcopalians here are biblically literate, perhaps more than their contemporaries in other parts of the country except the South. But she implied something more than social-class reserve toward verbal "proof-texting." Scriptural reference in everyday conversation is not part of the lay spiritual lexicon at Redeemer — it is considered an affectation and therefore inappropriate.

Although the surrounding geography is agricultural, none in this congregation live any longer on farms, or make their livelihood in agriculture. The older generation recalled farming as a "hard life"; they were offspring of the ambitious farm youth who "got away" from its drudgery and isolation. Today they relate to their agricultural context the way a suburbanite relates to the city: They recognize that it is essential and symbolizes their commercial bedrock, but it is no longer "their" world. Men in the congregation have jobs in oil, or are lawyers, businessmen, and merchants; a number of men and women work in the helping professions, nursing and teaching. Congregational members also exhibit unconscious refinement of dress in relation to their setting — the men in business suits on Sunday, the women wearing classic, cosmopolitan tailoring. In terms of appearance, Redeemer's congregation could blend invisibly with any somewhat formal urban church.

Their rector of five years, a soft-spoken man in his late 40s, is credited by everyone for the present atmosphere of harmony and unanimity at Redeemer. His calm, low-key manner has coaxed order into parish administration and relaxed residual suspicions from its recent history. A series of leaders who came and went too quickly — troubled rectors whose personal problems damaged Redeemer psychically and financially — was blamed for the previous disharmony. Pastoral care is done not just by the ordained leader; rather, it is a wholistic, mutual ministering to each other that is encouraged and nurtured by this priest. One of the older-generation women said fervently, "I just hope I die before this one [rector] has to leave!" Many told us, "He's the best thing that ever happened to this parish."

Bridge-generation women cite his assistance in their spiritual interests: his support of expanding women's leadership roles in the worship life at Redeemer, promoting a more enlightened connection with such world problems as racism, homelessness, and

the feminization of poverty, and active programming for local issues. Thanks to his musical background, his favorite recreation
is singing in the community chorale — plus "going fishing on a
sleepy afternoon." His wife is a teacher and fellow musician. Their
daughter is away at college.

Worship and Community at Redeemer

The Sunday morning is as cosmopolitan as the congregation's style
of dress. During our visits, the well-trained choir sang an eclec-
tic variety of music, from Bach to "modern anthems." The hymn
singing was strong, the mood formal and reserved. The dominant
tone was one of reverent dignity. There was also an observable demeanor in the congregation that could be understood as crucial
to "getting along in a small town." During the worship services
themselves, the worshipers maintained a mask of external privacy.
People who later became outgoing and friendly during the coffee
hour assumed an inward-turning, solemn facial expression as they
sat in the pew. It was as if an invisible wall surrounded each person
or family grouping. The few unguarded countenances I saw during
services were those directed at children, who were also decorously
behaved.

The self-censorship unconsciously cloaking each person's public
self-presentation during worship has its influence on the param-
eters of open discussion. A young businesswoman, formerly one
of the leaders of youth activities, said, "This small city has everything you would find in any larger place, including racism and
homosexuality." But conversation about such issues is mostly kept
under wraps, "masked" by the unruffled exterior. "Controversial
topics" are dealt with largely by avoidance. "No one here talks
about homosexuality," she said, though there is plenty of awareness and much private conversation about it. A positive by-product
of this careful surface harmony is that even "a divorced mother
with a teen-age daughter" could be immediately "welcomed into
the congregation" — something that differed from her experience
in other small churches in the Plains. Her single-woman status had
sometimes elicited coolness, even suspicion initially.

One of the women leaders in the congregation registered the
rare negative under the surface at Redeemer. She had recently
been forced to recognize what seemed to her some antiwoman-

leadership sentiment. "If you had asked me a year ago whether there were any barriers against women leaders in this congregation, I would have said no. But the recent election to the vestry really shook me up, because a highly qualified woman was defeated by a younger male — for no apparent reason other than that he was a man." It seemed to her "just plain sexism." The friend she had supported was a woman who had held responsible positions in the city and as a professional out in the world. "*He's* never done anything in the congregation, except usher," she added. It was a radicalizing experience for her. She now questioned whether there was another principle operating, previously unnoticed. What did it take to qualify a woman for election to the vestry, in the mind of this congregation? "It almost seems as if the only way to elect a woman is to put up someone whose experience is in business or finance. That can't be right, either; is the only skill required for vestry leadership 'male,' in another guise?"

An older congregational leader, one who has given years of faithful service in many positions — director of acolytes, vestry member, head of the Every Member Canvass — articulated what seemed to be the mindset of the older generation toward change. In the plain speech of the Plains, he presented a disarming mixture of courtly good manners, deep religious devotion, loyalty to Redeemer, and half-humorous, ostensibly grudging, acceptance of modernity. He claimed that his psyche had an "almost innate resistance" to many currents of change, including those around women in the congregation's leadership. Even more, he opposed what seemed to him the current politicization of homosexuality, not just in the national media but also in the national church.

While expressing regret that he still found the mere topic of homosexuality anathema, he also found that he had made accommodations to other, once-unthinkable kinds of change almost without realizing it. "I was against every single one of [the changes]," he said. "I was opposed to girls becoming acolytes. Then I was against women on the vestry. Next I was against having women as lay readers or chalice bearers. And I was certainly opposed to women as ordained deacons and priests. I was opposed to *all* of them. *Every single one.*" With magnificent timing, he added a rueful afterthought: "And I've been proved wrong, in every case." We both laughed. This patriarch would not characterize his acceptance as "real, internal change" because it came after the fact. He had resisted until the ground on which he stood was no longer

there. His resistance seemed to derive less from secular political conservatism than from a generational code and mindset —
archetypal gender rigidity, if presented as charming civility. Because
he takes his own Christianity seriously, he accepts responsibility
for his resistance to change, at the same time acknowledging that
change itself is a constant.

People at Redeemer are aware of social problems in the larger
society: racism, crime, drugs, Third World warfare. On this dimension Redeemer is one of the most liberal churches in the area,
members reported. A single issue of the parish monthly newsletter, for example, contained information about where to drop
off clothes and food for Thanksgiving baskets, a letter thanking
volunteers and contributors at the settlement house in the nearest city, a letter announcing hurricane relief in the Caribbean from
the Presiding Bishop's Fund for World Relief, and an exhortation
from the Audubon Society ("Think globally — act locally"). A
large basket just inside the door received canned goods and clothing donations each Sunday morning, as people came through the
entryway. In that sense, Redeemer Plains members are "outsiders,"
or cosmopolitans in their own territory. Despite its geographic and
political location, Redeemer is anything but provincial. The congregation is no more remote from urban ills than a church in any
suburb anywhere.

The unity within the congregation seems to require few subgroups (or organizations) beyond one for the adolescents, a youth
group, and the service provided by the Altar Guild. Young people
are involved in a variety of issues, including peace activities. Inter-
church youth-group competition is a morale builder in a city where
church identity is one of the major arenas of sociability. Developing some kind of city-wide "youth hangout" is a serious topic
both for Redeemer and its Presbyterian neighbors. A senior warden
noted empathetically that, in a small town, the thirst for excitement
drives adolescents to court danger — like slipping out at night, after parents were asleep, for high-speed joy-rides in the family car.
Drugs are available many places in the community. At least at Redeemer there is an openness about such information; the problem
can be publicly named and discussed.

What about traditional organizations, such as the Episcopal
Church Women, once the primary means through which women
related to their church? "We no longer have any separate women's
organizations," a woman in her late 80s announced with pride.

She didn't think about the all-female Altar Guild in that meaning, since that work is perceived as a devotional service, almost a form of personal worship, rather than the traditional "women's work" implied in her announcement. A majority of the women at Redeemer expressed pleasure that they had "gotten rid of" or "voted out" the ECW some years in the past. In their view this was a progressive step. Redeemer women do not put on bazaars or handicrafts fundraising events — another distinction in a city where women of other denominations are renowned for, and raise, huge amounts of charity funds with "homemade" products. A number of Redeemer women confessed that their need to be different from those women is a significant factor in their disengagement from "traditional women's church work." They want to serve their congregation, and Redeemer encourages it, in "higher," more directly religious ways: assisting as lay assistants at worship, along with a more egalitarian sharing of the maintenance tasks.

For instance, to cover the congregational functions once managed by the ECW alone, there is a hospitality committee made up of couples and singles that is responsible for organizing all social and fellowship events, for example, weekly coffee hours, the annual parish overnight camp-a-way, and so on. Any recreational or community-building subgroups, such as two (mixed male/female) volleyball teams, are ad-hoc groups that may spring up for a time and then dissolve — an example of the kinds of companionship available in an already cohesive identity. What Redeemer seems determined to avoid is separate constituencies or competing subcommunities. The dominant need for unity proscribes any organization that acts as "its own little church." And there is no sense of congregational passivity, of people sitting back and "letting others do it." Just the opposite: the congregation at Redeemer seems to function almost like "a Committee of the Whole."

Parish cohesion and a feeling of hard-won "social space" in an uncomprehending external environment are central to Redeemer's self-identity. By virtue of its unique status in its context, people in this parish can view themselves in an almost "privileged" relationship to the outside world. This freedom allows them to envision responses to many problems that are as yet theoretical in their location. It helps explain the enthusiasm with which these women explore the meanings of "church" and their church.

The Older Generation

Women in their 70s and 80s have made brave and creative adaptations to the changes in the congregation, finding ways to continue their girlhood pattern of "remaining in the background" even in the 1980s and '90s. Their generation had been encouraged to think of itself as the "Marthas" of the church — the stereotype of bustling female practicality that puts dinner on the table — instead of idealizing the dreamy and pious "Marys" who prefer sitting at the feet of Jesus. When they were cut off from Martha-dom by the dissolution of the ECW in the 1970s, some found a way to continue all-female church work in the Altar Guild. One energetic woman near 80 has undertaken the task of organizing midweek hospitality after a funeral service. They feel great affection for the rector who brought hope when the congregation was deeply troubled. Their gratitude translates into respect for his leadership and the changes he has brought, plus a sense of mutual responsibility for the congregation. Another, over 80, confided, "Whenever I'm needed in the office, I love to help out; I'd do anything for our rector."

Audrey, a farmer's daughter and helpmeet wife, expressed her religion in terms of her Altar Guild work; Isabelle is a long-widowed former Presbyterian-turned-mystic, who has cast off the many "practical" jobs in which she was involved earlier, and now feasts only her soul and mind; two retired public school teachers, Prue and Carolyn, talked about how they experienced "church" and religiosity through women's work, and how they felt about its changes. Even those who had "worked [for pay], part time" in a husband's store or an office do not think of themselves as having any public role other than through women's church organizations and women's clubs. In their small-town, middle-class, churchgoing world, their creativity has always been channeled into group money-raising projects for the church. That framework developed their administrative skills and in turn gave a larger importance to their fundraising.

These women have not viewed such activities as having any social significance, nor do they see them as a key component of community-building. They may have heard clergy credit them with expanding God's kingdom on earth. They know, in reflection, that they poured their faith into bazaars or guild meetings — concrete tasks and products that become somehow acts of worship.

Few holy words ever emerged from that type of activism. Women of that generation were expected to derive spiritual nurture from what they did in public liturgy at regular services, or through the reserved formal "devotions" (routinized prayer and scripture readings) at their women's meetings. Developing their own interior lives was a private matter, not a topic for sermons or study meetings. Warm memories gave layers of significance to the companionship they had found in an organization like the ECW. Some of them grieve over its demise. They continue to adapt, however.

Audrey, a brisk, angular 80-year-old, expanded visibly when she talked about *her* "traditional women's work" — the Altar Guild. Even in the days when the ECW still existed, her major contribution to the congregation was through Altar work. She has always been more comfortable expressing herself through work with her hands than in words. Polishing the brass altar rail and the silver communion vessels, making things "just shiny and pretty," was her most profound spiritual satisfaction. "I would come out here to the church and shine brass all by myself, in the quiet and still. I just loved to polish. And it was the only place in my life, working on that altar, the only time that I really felt.... " The enormity of what she was saying stopped her words. Her voice broke, her eyes filled with tears. "That was when...I knew He was there." For her, polishing was an act of love, the gleaming communion rail in a silent church her "holy ground." My own eyes misting in empathy, I thanked her for telling me. "Never said it before," she responded. Then, astounded, she added, "No one ever asked me before."

In Audrey's generation, Altar Guild work provided scope for leadership and the companionship of other women. She enjoyed shaping recruits into a well-disciplined, faithful service corps. "I was 'on the Altar' for twenty-five years, and directress of the Altar Guild for twenty." The expression "on the altar" was a code for her generation. It locates this kind of work at the spiritual center of the congregation, the altar, while the workers remain invisible — part of the background. "I loved it," she reminisced. "You were your own boss, you and your girls. No one bothering you." She also felt (without claiming it) altar workers were a "team" behind the ordained leader. Being the recipient of the priest's plans for the service, marking the readings for him in the Service Book, putting out the right altar hangings — these were the ultimate "insider" jobs for laywomen of the older generation. "Every Episcopal

woman should work on the Altar," Audrey enthused. "That's how
you learn your church."

The Altar Guild was also her "ministry," a word she and others
in her generation would never apply to their own work. "The girls
I trained, and worked with, they just never said no," again a code
for praising women's generosity and self-giving implicitly, rather
than saying it directly. That shared love and labor was her supreme
expression of caring for this congregation. "I loved them. I loved
doing it for Him, and for our priest, and for our people." As a
young bride she had come to her husband's church and yearned
for a special way to express her new commitment. "I always felt:
this Altar work is one thing I could really *do* for my new religion
that I loved." Her hallowed path into the sacred led through "servant" tasks: preparing the table for the Holy Meal, ensuring that
all the accouterments for each step of the ceremonial were in place.
"Today I see people who don't know their church, who can't even
follow their Prayer Book...." She viewed them as deprived rather
than obtuse: "You see, if I hadn't been 'on the altar,' I wouldn't
know, either." No other churchwork open to laywomen in her
generation could have so adequately nourished her spirit and her
practical nature.

"I think we're quite modern at Redeemer," announced Prue,
65, recently retired from teaching in the high school. "Women
here participate in everything but the men's choir! And men are
in everything but the Altar Guild." For her, the disappearance of
gender-bound tasks is a measure of Redeemer's progressiveness.
"We don't have a women's group as such, anymore, and I think it's
good." She meant the ECW, not considering the Altar Guild in the
same category. "But I must admit, I was *thrilled* when I saw that
first woman lay reader up there in the chancel! I think it's great,
although I wouldn't have liked the idea of a woman rector a few
years ago."

In general Prue feels that all the changes in the church, not
just those around gender, are for the better. "We're a lot more
caring for needs outside the church now, you know. I mean the
missionary-type caring." She distinguishes the new ethos of community involvement from the old: "Not that women sit around
and make bandages, and that kind of thing, anymore. But...what
with working through Lazarus House — you know, the settlement
house in the city — and lots of us doing volunteer work there,
we are much more outgoing...we are friendlier." She seemed to

be describing an expanded mental world. "It used to be...when you walked into the Episcopal church, you didn't talk; you didn't even look around. Visitors really did feel we weren't friendly and warm." We laughed together at the 1950s Episcopal stereotype: "God's frozen people." Prue compared that unwelcoming image with another generational symbol that had vanished. "That's kind of gone out, along with wearing hats."

Warm remembrances of the ECW revealed Prue's ambivalence, however. "We used to be very active; every year we had a project theme, like table settings for different holidays. We'd set them up in each classroom, and in the parish hall. Or tours of the houses, all decorated for Christmas. We even sometimes had tents put up out in the parking lot, and we'd do crafts and sell things we had made.... We met regularly to accomplish those little projects." In the midst of her positive memories, the dismissive adjective "little" revealed the standard church derogation of women's cooperative fundraising projects. "And the guilds met regularly, once a month. But then — when we dissolved those? Since then, it's really been zilch. Completely! If any of the women are doing any money-making projects...or are meeting, other than aerobics during people's lunch hour, I don't know of it." Having resurrected the memory of satisfactions, Prue began to speculate: "You know ...I've wondered if it isn't time, maybe, to...meet, not just about money making, but...just to get everybody together." She confessed she had already gone as far as to "put [that suggestion] in the rector's 'Suggestions Column.'" Then she came back to the reality of the present. "But women today are so busy, they don't look for meetings to go to. When I was in the Altar Guild we used to do extra things, like put on congregational breakfasts on festival occasions like Easter. But that's too hard for young mothers and working gals today."

Another teacher in this generation, Carolyn had been forced back into teaching after a divorce. Now in her late 70s and retired, she said, "I was shocked when I discovered that the guilds...that women's groups had dissolved." On second thought, she added, "Of course, I now see that I played a part in that. I wasn't helping them any. I had to go to work so I had a good excuse not to be involved any longer, it seemed — I couldn't go to afternoon meetings anymore. Besides, I felt I didn't have to do that sort of work anymore." Part of her welcomed the freedom from being obligated to traditional women's tasks. "The ECW is missed, of course. Because we had a good time doing those money-making things. I can't really say we had any great religious experiences in those guilds, but the fellowship...it let you get really well acquainted with someone you just nodded to in church. We old ones often talk about those days...those bazaars involved everyone in town, you know, and we worked — I felt like — we were all putting our talents to work for a reason."

On the other hand, Carolyn is at a stage of life where she is "not wanting to be tied down." "I refused lay-reading because of my...health and wanting just to be free on the weekends." At the same time, her view of what it meant to be part of a congregation requires working with and for it. "I feel like a great big zero, because I don't do anything." However, she defended her current inactivity. "But I have done it. I know people detest your saying, 'I've done my share.' But I'm just not going to come out and teach Sunday school anymore. I'm past that." Listing what she does presently, "I visit in the hospital; sometimes I work at the city settlement house. And I help with the rummage sale, if they have anything like that. Oh, and I do Meals on Wheels. But I'm not doing that other kind of volunteering anymore." The activities she rejected had once been the lifeblood of the parish women's own world. Her present activities "fit" her present life better but they don't fill the void created by a vanished "women's community" in the congregation, or her generation's understanding of "church work."

Isabelle, formerly active in Church Women United (an ecumenical women's organization), a participant in civil rights crusades, and a lifelong Presbyterian, has belonged to Redeemer only a few years. Now well past 80, she recently discovered a strong streak of mysticism beneath her childhood Calvinism, and is delightedly educating herself in its devotional literature. She quoted spiritual guides such as Thomas Merton and Henri Nouwen, and is supported in her exploration by a female spiritual director in the congregation, with whom she exchanges books and meditational tapes. Although unable to kneel for prayer because of her arthritis, Isabelle is filled with zest by her new immersion in Anglican piety. And she would rather read a new book on contemporary feminist theology than "go to meetings." After decades of activism, Isabelle is simply spending time in the presence of God, feeding her inner self. Everyone ought to take "a few minutes each day, where they can be absolutely quiet, and ask themselves 'Why am I upset about this or that?' — and then, of course, just to praise God and thank Him." What is "new" and exciting for her, at this stage in her life, is the spiritual realm. "I have a special word that helps me every day. Actually, that's it: The Word. 'In the beginning was the Word and the Word was God.' It clears my mind. I know where I am."

Isabelle enjoys poking fun at the traditional ways women like her have been expected to "do" church. "Potlucks drive me crazy," she exclaimed. "Presbyterians can't meet without eating. They're forever having the women, and even the men — everybody together — 'bring a dish'!" Bored with what now seems a disproportionate emphasis "on food, and on women in kitchens," Isabelle waxed eloquent about her awakening to worship. She is the typical evangelist, wanting to share her discoveries. She has no patience with resistance to change in her newly chosen congregation. "Women in this parish who've been here the longest" are the worst; they are "slowest about asking to do the new things for women," she said. "I think we should banish the phrase, 'This is the way we've always done it!'" Doing anything with one's hands other than turning the pages of a book is definitely a lower order of activity — literally beneath her. Having placed her faith in action all her life, Isabelle now feasts on meditation, Anglican devotional writers, and worship.

In a generation shaped by "traditional" ways of relating to a church, older women have no way to express their commitment other than to continue some kind of "serving," even without the organizational framework that was "theirs." Three of them still identify with the old-style "maintenance mentality" that made women so fruitful in the era when they joined Redeemer. They continue in a mindset that expects to fall to and "do whatever needs to be done," remain in the background and expect no recognition or thanks. What spiritual community they knew (and could talk about indirectly) was captured in organizational "frames" — ECW, the Missionary Society. During the 1950s and '60s, direct spiritual connection between women's work and any sense of spiritual mission became attenuated, gradually undermining the purpose initially motivating those gendered organizations. The person open to a deliberate spiritual quest, Isabelle, is working at it solo. She has rejected the women's work that absorbed her younger life in favor of a view that mental activity, meditation, and contemplation are spiritually superior.

On the positive side, age has allowed the women to have a

more conscious appreciation of congregation as "family" and their source of community. They really know, on a rational level, that they no longer have to make things or produce bazaars in order to justify their place in the congregation; they only continue thinking in those images because they know no other way of being. They find satisfaction in dropping in to the parish house on a morning and cleaning the stove, or wrapping presents for the settlement-house children. Choice is more distant for them; their feeling of responsibility for this beloved parish and its maintenance is the channel through which they can best express their spirituality and "church."

The Bridge Generation

These women's lives embody the daily experience of change. Janice, married, a former nurse, is now engaged full-time in a healing and counseling ministry and is training for the role of spiritual director; Dorothy, a lay reader and chalice bearer, is a college professor with several grown children and a happy second marriage; Elizabeth, a musician, is married and teaches French in the high school; Estelle, married, is a local businesswoman and active in city government. Each is conscious of having breached barriers that once barred women from participating as leaders in the worship. As Dorothy said, "I actually remember looking at the altar and thinking, 'They need a woman up there.' So! I volunteered to be the first lay reader, and now I'm a chalice bearer. I remember saying to myself at one point: They need women up there in the chancel, just like they do on the city council. And by the time I'm 40, I hope to be doing both."

These women want tasks in the congregation that are explicitly connected with worship and policymaking. And not merely waiting for it to happen, they view themselves as agents who bring about these changes. They have relegated a women-only church organiza-tion to a banished image. An organization like the ECW no longer has a halo in their understanding of congregational membership. As with Estelle of the older generation, high-minded (nonkitchen) work is more in harmony with their professional weekday selves.

The senior member of this generation, Janice, a clear-eyed, dark-blonde woman in her late 50s, was herself a bridge between the former church organization, the ECW, in which she had been an active leader, and the new view of religious self-fulfillment for women. Her present identity is found only through spiritual studies and counseling, which has led her to devalue what she had previously done. In her enthusiasm for the new spiritual leadership open to her, she has dismissed her former work (president of the ECW) as a form of "role playing." Although it was the older generation's own form of "church," organizational religion never dug deeply enough for her.

A self-taught theologian, she is remarkably conversant with both current and traditional theology, knowledgeable about many types of worship. In the past and in a more rigid congregation, some of her "unconventional" spiritual explorations might have gotten her ostracized, or labeled eccentric. However, the congregation and the rector value her and welcome the insights she has brought home from retreats — for example, at a Roman Catholic monastery or a New Age seminar. She works with local prayer groups and has a personal ministry of healing. Janice is now totally absorbed in a religious citizenship far different than she could have imagined even a decade earlier, but to which she feels somehow she was destined from birth. The many strands of experience and instruction to which she has been exposed — growing up in the Far East with evangelical missionary parents, and training for a nursing career in the United States — come together in her present calling.

A full-fledged mystic, she is equipping herself for the relatively new role (in most Episcopal congregations) of spiritual director. She has channeled her leadership skills into "doing a lot of counseling, dream analysis, teaching classes in dreams, and creative visualization" and a healing ministry in which she often works with medical professionals. "I'm also a massage therapist now." Far from these particular activities being "new" to her, she believes that "the forms are what is new," since all this was latent in her earlier spiritual self. "All through my work as a nurse, I think I was given a kind of sixth sense about how to heal; I prayed all the time for God to use me." She credits the healing touch of her hands to Asian gurus' influence throughout her childhood. With her hands opened expressively, she explained, "You just tune yourself to the universe.... It has nothing to do with me or my ego. It goes right through me. I'm only the channel." Also studying creationist and Native-American "cosmic understandings," Janice thinks of herself as "kind of a bridge between the medical world, the religious world, and the New Age perspective."

"Presently I'm working with a lot of people who are very angry at the God image. I'm discovering that there are a lot of abused young women out there...abused not just physically, but even more powerfully by the fears created in them through the abuse of priestly authority, and the Roman Catholic Church." Absorption in her work serves to isolate Janice to some degree. "I'm not a real conversationalist....I'm okay in one-to-one conversations, but...." A jaunty phrase described her single-mindedness: "I have an agenda and I go for it." Any loss of the community of women she once found in the ECW organization has been totally supplanted. When asked about it, she said, "Traditional women's work? You mean handwork, basketry or weaving, needlepoint, stuff like that? That I have never been involved in! We used to have a Guild, a subgroup of the ECW, that did that." As president her job was administrative. There were "teas, very elegant teas, very Anglican things — and little programs and films, and a lot of God-talk that didn't take a lot of intelligence or depth. Oh yes, we used to put on bazaars and auctions. Once, I remember, I even wrote to the queen of England, asking for a donation for our auction!" Her favorite part of the job had been intellectual: finding speakers that would "challenge them." At the same time, women's organizations were increasingly influenced by the trend toward reliance on experts instead of volunteers and enthusiasm: "We only invited women as speakers who were really trained, out there doing something," she recalled. The movement toward increasing specialization, even in church, helped undermine the value of a cadre of women generalists.

Janice described gradual disenchantment with churchwomen's organizations. "This little town has so many clubs. The ECW was just a repeat: it became a very clubby thing, only one conducted under church auspices." Women's direct link with humans in faraway places, through collecting and sending supplies to missionaries (and distributing funds for other charities), was no longer a clear animating vision. Layers of organization at the national level intervened between the women and what had been their concrete spiritual connection. Along with bureaucratic administration of the mission activities that had once been "theirs," the clubwoman ethos contributed to the ebbing of the ECW.

Redeemer women, in Janice's assessment, "are now way ahead of that game. Oh, there might be a nucleus that's still stuck in that image." She discounts the once-routine physical or material contributions made by women, and the secure place in the background it provided them. "But mostly we're just neat, neat people, not at all into the artificial." She dismisses as "artificial" what had once been bedrock for Redeemer. When she observed that women's "organizational life" at Redeemer is "not as good as it used to be," what did she mean? "Only that there is a lack of interest in it," she said, meaning the former ECW. "Women today aren't really drawn to that kind of thing any longer." Then, qualifying her dismissal, she added, "The only people that could be really interested in the ECW anymore would be the older women who would like a social group." Because Janice is amply fulfilled in her new directions, she has little empathy with feelings of loss among the older generation. Becoming a skilled and knowledgeable interpreter of spiritual experience and literature absorbs her fully. Fortunately, the rector utilizes her gifts as spiritual counselor instead of being threatened by them. She is a mentor for women in the spiritual community at Redeemer and beyond.

Dorothy, aged 46, a smartly dressed, very attractive professor at the state university, articulated carefully the profound spiritual nourishment found in her activities at Redeemer. Her change to Episcopalian several decades ago was not the turning point in her life. That had been "a total conversion to feminism when I was a young adult," which strengthened her enough to do the unthinkable and get a divorce. That in turn precipitated all other changes including church membership. As a girl, she had chafed at the "superiority" of males, while her brother carried the weight of family expectations and had grown up defeated — he was the one who should go to college and graduate school, not Dorothy. After leaving her first marriage, taking her two young children, she entered graduate school and found it a "heady" world — the first place where her intellect was valued. In the process, however, "I had to make myself so strong" that "I shut out everything else, even God," for a long time. "I couldn't, I didn't dare, need or rely on anyone or anything." Several decades later, established in her field at the university and in a contented second marriage, her spiritual self is finally being allowed to re-emerge. She once again feasts spiritually on the sustenance of "the form and the ritual" at Redeemer. She tried to describe her deep love for it. "I don't feel particularly close to the people in this church, other than while we're sharing the same worship — actually in the church at the same time. But I love this church, and this building."

Her real discovery as she reconnected with "church" was the unimagined depths of psychic and spiritual fulfillment open to her when she began assisting at the Eucharist, serving the wine. "There's a rare beauty in serving the chalice to people," she reflected. She finds herself moved by the kneeling posture of the worshipers, by the beauty of hands cupped and raised to receive the bread. A numinous sense often seems to surround her as she moves along the communion rail. "That act simply dispels my nervousness, my self-concern. I guess I would compare it with a 'runner's high' — where you can get rid of yourself and simply go with the Spirit, be borne on the Spirit." When she first returned to active church attendance, however, Dorothy found the Exchange of the Peace, an innovation introduced during her absent years, "hard to take." Turning to others and shaking hands impinged on "my own private communing and praying"; it broke the mood into which she withdrew when she sank to her knees in the pew. After entering the sacramental aspect of worship more deeply, she now finds "the Peace" profoundly moving — a "genuine moment of touching. I sometimes wish I could just hold a person's hand a bit longer...say something more meaningful. Like 'How are you, really?' or something that means 'I really care, I'm *with* you.'"

A highly paid researcher in her scholarly field, Dorothy is moderately empathetic with those still bound by gender limitations. "There are still women here who see their 'place' as only in the Altar Guild, not as a lay reader; as only in the kitchen or doing something social, not as a vestry member." She greatly anticipates the congregation's future experience of women clergy, and thrilled at hearing about the consecration of the first woman bishop in the Episcopal Church. She was one who noted the potential danger of Redeemer becoming trapped by its own "elitism...and emphasis on form." She worries that "this congregation...with its self-satisfaction...could just shut itself off from three-quarters of its surroundings." But she also acknowledges that she has a part to play in avoiding that insularity and protecting her source of nurture.

A younger (44) bridge-generation professional, Elizabeth is a teacher who pours much extra creativity into needlework, painting, and music. In her mind, as in Dorothy's, there is no need for a traditional woman's organization as generator of service activities. Each woman can find her own areas of ministry, and no one needs another organization as a means of relating to the congregation.

She gives Redeemer high marks for its "modernity." "This congregation is quite remarkably even in terms of the balance between men and women as leaders. There just aren't a lot of activities right now for women, specifically, to be involved in." She corrected herself, "Oh, possibly Sunday school; you could say there are more women than men doing that, typically." Then, illustrating the egalitarianism, "on parish-community workdays, for example, the women aren't just in the kitchen, men aren't only outside working on the grounds; it's pretty even, really. The same thing is true of fundraisers. The work is pretty evenly shared." Speaking from within her own life of professional interests, she said, "I think most women here would say, if you asked them, 'I don't have *time* to do needlepoint or work for a bazaar.'" Even the casserole for potluck dinners was too much: "It's hard to get things prepared, even just for them."

Elizabeth's deepest spiritual longing is expressed in speculating what it would be like to be "part of a sacred community or a religious order — very closely interwoven like a family, but even better than a family. . . . I imagine, somewhere, I dream about living in a group that has a joyful, intimate relationship through prayer, and song, and music." Traditional women's work assignments, often typical in such an organization, are not part of her vision. She, too, seems to hold mental Christianity — religious and esthetic "sharing" and exploration of theology — as a higher form of spirituality than kitchen work.

A businesswoman, Estelle, nearing 50, manages a local store. Energetic and intense, she announced that the part of her religion she is really "serious about" is "Bible study and theology." Raised in a strict Lutheran congregation, she had in her youth felt a strong call to the ordained ministry, but was told emphatically to forget it. She had hoped that teaching in a parochial school would be an alternate path of service and self-fulfillment, but all it did was expose her to the personal and theological devaluation experienced by all women. She found herself in painful combat with Lutheran clergy. The recollection still rankles, bringing angry and painful tears to her eyes: an arbitrary decision upheld the rule that she, a laywoman, could teach male children only up to the age of 12. In spite of her intellectual and managerial competence, she could not be accepted as a teacher for high school–age boys in that parochial school system.

The scars from that church experience, now long past, are still

raw. Even if there were a women's organization at Redeemer, Estelle would only be interested in an "evangelistic type of outreach-
group" or some other active witness, "No formal organization or
sewing-circle...or whatever. I'm not much for sewing and that
type of thing." Anger at her former church contributes to her rejection of the whole concept of "women's work." She wants to
be associated with women who are in charge, not followers: "The
women I'm involved with are more out in the working world than
in the sewing circles." She found her spirit cautiously expanding in
the atmosphere at Redeemer, her first experience in a church that
encouraged her to use her mental capabilities. She is grateful and
believes she has found her context, finally.

Finding a place — Redeemer — that is congenial and freeing
has transformed the entire framework of the female support system that was once standard in the congregation. Bridge-generation
women at Redeemer incarnate these two choices: the choice of
that particular congregation, and the option to choose a mode of
relating to it that is right for them as individuals.

Janice and Dorothy identify their choices and self-perceptions
as direct products of the women's movement; Estelle and Elizabeth
do not consciously link the two. None of them any longer assume
that their time and volunteer work "belong" to someone else —
husband, family, or church — although all of them have these relationships as part of their lives. Although they hunger for spiritual
feeding in the community of the congregation, the very thing they
don't need is an additional structure to maintain. They want direct
nurture. They have "freed" themselves religiously from traditional
women's work at Redeemer (the activity of "sewing" seemed to
be their code). They differentiate themselves from the women in
nearby denominations who are limited to handwork. Oh, those
women "do it very well, exceptionally well," Estelle exclaimed.
"It's that they aren't allowed to do anything else."

The pattern for Episcopal women that prevailed until the 1960s,
the ECW organization, has faded into a historical artifact here,
along with the Episcopalian churchwoman stereotype of gentility
and taste, and an exemplar of domestic skills. As Janice pointed
out, their expression of faith had produced "very English teas"
with linen napkins and graceful flower arrangements. But at the
same time the "gracious homemaker" image overshadowed other
forms of spiritual self-expression, women were treated to sermons
idealizing the biblical stance of Mary who sat pensively at Jesus'

feet and spoke of spiritual things. Mary was usually contrasted favorably with her sister, Martha, accused of too much fussing and busyness. Mary was the one Jesus said had "the one thing necessary" — giving her total attention to Jesus — while Martha kept to the duties that must be accomplished for life to go on. It was a curiously inverted message to women in a church that depended on their products and money-raising activities, but shunned their contemplative gifts. Nevertheless, praying was rhetorically idealized as the ultimate attainment of women's religiosity. Ironically, that is the freedom these women explore today, except that its support comes through the expansions created by the secular women's movement, not "the church."

Today women's service work moves in Mary's direction, away from the arena of Martha-dom that was their prescribed location, even while rhetorically devalued and assigned "lesser" importance. Congregational culture now exalts women who work in words rather than food, women who are professionals or managers.[6] The mindset about relating to one's church, for this generation of women, is shifting toward the same values we now reward in secular achievement — away from domestic and concrete "serving," toward the "higher" and more abstract tasks of mental activity, theologizing and praying. The idea that even the most humble act can be holy, that even something like cooking can be a sacred activity, is today being re-explored by the younger generation.

The Younger Generation

Women under 40 in this congregation view it as the place where the public and private spheres of their lives intersect. Five of the six voices here are recent converts to the Episcopal Church. Michelle, the only "born" Episcopalian, is a young office manager, married, with no children; Doreen, a nurse, is a recent immigrant from Roman Catholicism and another part of the country, newly married to a middle-aged divorced man; Jackie, a local girl, is married and has two preschool children. She holds no full-time paid job. Laurie also grew up in the city, is a school administrator and in a recent second marriage. Christine, the youngest of this group, has a toddler daughter and a part-time job as medical technician. Ann, the congregation's treasurer, enjoys an appointed job because it places her in the midst of policy discussions and decisions made by the

governing body of the parish, the vestry. These young women are a
generation who take for granted all public activities: jobs, school-
ing for themselves and their children, ski trips, art museums, local
political activism. Also they do not question whether or not they,
as females, will be able to do whatever they wish (or are able to
do) in the congregation.

Their independence from the limitations that surrounded past
churchwomen, especially in this locale, is total. The actual range
of possibilities open to them may account for the nostalgia with
which they speak of "traditional churchwomen's work" — that,
and the high profile attached to women's handmade products
(quilts, ceramics) in the Great Plains. They have not experienced
being directed to handwork only, as the older and bridge women
have. Leadership in any role, even formerly "male" ones, doesn't
have to be romanticized. They know about barriers keeping them
from any church office only by hearsay.

For them, the congregation they have chosen is blessedly free
of the strains they associate with other church choices. The multiple dimensions of their busy lives make them search for cohesion in
the "free space" they find at Redeemer. They are welcomed and encouraged. Although they see the constricting effects of "tradition"
on women in the more conservative denominations around them,
these young women are free to see themselves as impervious to —
above — that type of constraint.

Michelle, an executive just over 30, enjoys her career in an
office-management firm. She grew up in an urban Episcopal church
some distance away and remembered fondly the "Sunday school
room, the little chairs and table, the whole thing. I remember my
confirmation very well; I could even tell you about the dress I
wore." Her exuberance and good spirits mask a sadness just under
the surface, it seems. She is happy that her husband agreed to join
her in attending Redeemer, and that she is among the women at
Redeemer now able to function in the new role of lay reader. Still,
she thinks "many of the women here are probably more traditional
than modern. I don't know if this parish would readily accept a
woman priest. I would, gladly, but I'm not really sure how many
others feel the same way."

Michelle is thrilled that there is "a woman bishop in our
church" in the East. She knows that her Roman Catholic friends
envy the rich community she has found at Redeemer — the image
of a church that is open to change, all kinds of people, and chal-

lenging ideas. "Unless the Roman church does some changing, the Episcopal church will increase drastically," she declared; "[the Roman Catholics] just have too many laws, too many regulations." Michelle gives high marks to the diversity at Redeemer. "We have a very strong parish relationship...and anybody's welcome here, regardless of age, or race, or sexual preference, or gender, or income level, or anything." To express her approval in highest terms, she added, "Because that's what Christ, and Christianity, is all about." She surprised herself with her final phrase. As a "born" Episcopalian, her words are usually conventional and nonreligious. She is unused to hearing herself use "churchy" words outside the worship service itself. But her delight in having found a parish like Redeemer, located on the cutting edge of religious idealism, is infectious.

Doreen, a nurse, and her new husband for whom this was a second marriage, have both recently converted from Roman Catholicism. After trying several Protestant churches, they chose Redeemer as their new church home. She is still finding a way to relate to the congregation. She expressed a yearning for the old-fashioned guild, a handwork-and-crafts group where she could enlist her considerable skills and find a participatory sense of belonging. To her that would represent service, work for a larger purpose (and therefore "holy"), and an organizational excuse for work-validated links with other women.

Doreen is a little lonely. Her husband has grown children and his work. She has her job as an accountant in a local hospital. Although Redeemer's liturgy is enough like the Catholic one to offer her some familiarity, the culture of this city is strange to her and she misses the bonds of female companionship that enfolded her nearer her family. The choice of Redeemer is right, closest to what they had known, but they know they haven't picked up all its internal clues as yet: they don't really quite know how to be Protestant yet, she laughed.

Then she got more specific. Although Redeemer as a congregation is "friendly," the bare esthetic of the sanctuary conveys a chilling spiritual austerity to her sensibility. "I miss all my statues," she whispered. The rosary in her uniform pocket is her secret, physical companion. When I asked if she would like to join a group of Altar Guild women in the next room, who were busy making lapel crosses out of palm fronds for the Palm Sunday congregation, she responded eagerly, "Now that's just the kind of thing I'd love

to be part of!" Expressing commitment through her hands seems
the surest path to her new identity, but she isn't quite sure how to
find its heart. Doreen won't feel as though she "belongs" until she
is sharing in concrete "work" for the parish.

Jackie, 27-year-old mother of two preschool children, is not
employed outside the home, although she and her husband make
extra money by catering parties occasionally. In spite of her youth
and innocence, Jackie's faith was rock-solid in her soul. When she
was only a child, she actively canvassed all religious options in the
area: "I hit every summer vacation Bible school in town." And as
a newly married young adult, she repeated the process. Raised as a
kind of roving Protestant, mostly Methodist, she and her husband
jointly tested several congregations: "We went to the Methodist
Inquirers' Class, and the Catholic Inquirers' Class, and then the
Episcopal one," after ruling out the Baptists and the Disciples of
Christ. She is grateful to the Methodist minister "who finally suggested we try Redeemer. We hadn't thought of it ourselves. But
because of my husband's being raised Catholic, it turned out to
be just exactly what we were looking for." At the time they were
auditioning the Catholic church, Jackie was pregnant with their
first child and was horrified to learn she would have "to be remarried" by a priest in order to legitimate the coming child. "So John
and I just looked at each other and said 'That's crazy! So long,
Charlie'!" Now, she beamed, "we're very happy in the Episcopal
Church.... It turns out to be the structure that I really wanted."
Jackie likes the rector, the Prayer Book, the hymns, the liturgy.
What she's heard about past Episcopal women's church organization, the ECW, has made her nostalgic for the fellowship and
nurture "that women used to have in their guilds." Spiritual images
that bring tears to her eyes are associated with her grandparents,
with whom she'd been very close, and a few of their "legacies":
a cross-stitched quilt and the photograph "of me on [Grandpa's]
lap, when I was a six-year-old elf in the school play." She makes
her own angelic connection with them. "And I still, whenever we
pray for the people who are dead — you know, the communion of
saints — I pray about them. I don't know if that's silly or not, but
I do it, every single Sunday."

Jackie and her husband consciously cultivate friends and family relationships. They have a religiously concrete understanding of
neighborliness. She sometimes has "slipped money to the rector"
to be given to a friend who couldn't meet her fuel bills; after pray-

ing about it, and talking with the rector, she confronted a neighbor whose gossip had injured another friend. Her brother had alienated himself from the family to placate his mentally ill wife, an extremely painful experience for the entire family. "When this happened, it got me into ... made me stronger with my parents. I kind of became my mother's protector; I had to fill in where my brother wasn't."

Jackie applauds more women's leadership in the congregation, though her newfound loyalty to this church and its rector tends to make even abstract discussion of a woman priest seem "disloyal," somehow. She then qualified that comment. "I think ordained women are needed. We've always been taught, in church, from a man's point of view. I'm not a real big women's rights person, but I can see how a woman would bring a different light to the scriptures — the way she perceives them. I think you need both male and female points of view." Because she has chosen "relationships" as the focus of her Christian discipleship, "the place where I really work on expressing my faith," she especially wishes she could experience the legendary sense of community that existed when women did work projects together.

"What would be fun," Jackie mused, "would be going to other people's homes and doing your cross-stitch, or some craft, for a couple hours, while you sit and visit. And you could see ... I'd be interested to see some of the other people's homes, and how they live." This was more than mere curiosity; it was a direct expression of her relational spirituality. "I think you get to know a person a lot better when you're in their surroundings. It feels more personal." What she values most about her faith is "the way I feel in my heart ... the way I feel inside, when I go to church, or read the Bible. . . . The real important thing to me is making sure you take communion every Sunday, and that you read the Bible every day." Moving from external to internal definition, she said softly, "Just the person you are, inside, is very important. I think you need God, and you should know Him, and know all about Him. But I think you know Him better, and understand Him more, if you know yourself more, in your heart. I think just what you do ... feeds what you are, inside." Then she put her credo in denominational terms, one of the few in this study who did. "I just love the Episcopal church so much, I want everybody to. All my friends." As the interview ended, she said, "You know, I love talking about all this stuff, the church and how I feel about it; I don't get to do that very often. It's made me think: 'How do I *really* feel about it?' I don't think I'll *ever* leave the Episcopal church. I love this church, and the way women are in it."

Christine, another young mother (28) with a year-old child and a three-quarter-time job as medical technician, also mythologized the "fun women used to have" in her thoughts about her new congregation (which she joined because her husband had grown up there). Any work organization today, however, should welcome men as well as women. "My husband likes to make things, too; maybe we could have a group that included the men." Gentle, soft-spoken Christine has often had to confront death as a respiration therapist. A terrible trauma she recalled was being part of a resuscitating team that tried to save a pregnant mother and her three children after a car accident. "I was in the emergency room and we had them all lined up, each of us working on a child [doing CPR]. I had the little three-year-old girl." She paused, then spelled out what made it even more horrifying. "The father of these children had just started his new job as an ambulance driver, it was only his second day on the job, and his was the ambulance that went to pick them up...not knowing it was his own family. They'd hit a cement bridge abutment." The father had brought a priest into the emergency room to baptize the children even as she and the other technicians continued trying to revive them. "And he'd just lost his entire family!" Her own tears flowed. "For him to have thought about that, while we were still working on them.... It was so moving. We were all crying, and working...." The recollection made her gasp for breath. "Officially they hadn't been declared dead; we were still pumping their hearts and breathing for them, and...I remember, we continued for a long time so that they could...be baptized." In a world of daily tragedy, Christine's own small child is infinitely precious. "I constantly ask God to help me watch over him and try to keep him safe."

During her pregnancy, for a time there was concern over some indication that the fetus might have Down's syndrome, and Christine was confronted with the most agonizing potential decision of her life. "Because of my work experience, I'd always thought that if I knew the baby was going to be very, very severely defective, I would have an abortion." She has seen "babies suffer so much before they died that I always said I could never see a baby of mine go through that." But when the time came, "there was no way, even if they had told me positively that the infant was damaged, that I

could decide to have an abortion." She refused a definitive test because she couldn't bear to face the decision. After a safe delivery,
she found herself saying, "Thank you, thank you, God; thank you,
thank you," an on-going litany in her head.

Praying, sometimes in words, other times just in images, is as
natural and unself-conscious for Christine as breathing. Holding
the baby in her arms as they open the curtains each morning, she
finds herself saying, "Thank you, God, for a beautiful day." She
prays in the car on her way to work. "I talk to my grandmother,
or my cousin, or whoever. I believe that when someone is dead
you can still communicate with them somehow, so that's part of
my praying, too." She looks forward to the time when she will be
able to take a more active part in the congregation. "Maybe my
husband and I could be greeters, or some sort of shared job." Pondering about this new church, she wonders: "Do women always
work more in this congregation than men? Or maybe they don't,
but it seems that way."

A vibrant, dark-haired school administrator, Laurie, 38, came to
her interview directly from her daily jog, still in running shoes and
shorts. Traditional or "background" women's work has no place in
her overcommitted family and professional life, she declared. She
has married a second time, five years after a divorce, and still has
two high school–age children at home. But recently she joined the
Altar Guild, to enjoy its sense of community and female nurture:
"As a feminist, I wanted to be with a group of women."

Laurie's arrival at Redeemer was preceded by a lengthy quest.
Her childhood family was large, eleven children in all, and poor,
definitely on the fringe of middle-class life in this city. An alcoholic father, "really a hippie, that's probably why he was such a
social outcast," was responsible for "embedding some of the ideas
of 'hippiness' in me — like not always judging other people, trying to see some 'good' in everybody even if they do bad things."
Her mother's stability and employment as a nurse kept the family
together and supported it financially.

Laurie's earliest learning was how to protect herself from the
turbulence in her home. A shadow crossed her face as she recalled,
"They would be shouting, and fighting, so I would just leave home.
Just run away — literally or sometimes in my head." During one
such flight, she had her first experience of religious transcendence,
God's presence surrounding and sustaining her. She was nine, sitting in a park swing, rocking back and forth. Suddenly, "it came

to me that I really didn't need to be upset about all these things, because God had probably made a mistake, putting me in this family. I just had to learn to deal with it. It was only supposed to be a learning experience for me. If I got through it, I would be okay." She smiled as she recalled the spiritual balm of that early epiphany. "I just remember being lifted somehow, filled with this incredible feeling of 'okayness.'" Laurie's ability to stay serenely above "the fray" infuriated her family. But she never lost the sustaining power of that childhood revelation, "that it's all right, I'm *supposed* to be learning from this situation but I don't have to be a part of it."

Laurie credits that first experience of spiritual empowerment with helping her reclaim her sense of self in adulthood after her divorce. When she was growing up, she knows it helped her resist a series of "absolutes" that would otherwise have shaped many of her decisions — including what she made of the relationship with her problem-ridden family. "I didn't grow up to be like them. I didn't marry an alcoholic. I didn't stay poor. And I have this sense of sureness, now, about what I can do." As an afterthought she said, "I guess I really always thought I could do anything I wanted to." A scholarship at a local denominational college involved Laurie with a group of young idealists who were "providing volunteer service" in the area, and her first real love. A young man from a Mennonite background seemed to represent the stability of an immense family and the emotional rootedness for which she had longed. He also encouraged her idealism and budding dissent against the local view of patriotism. "We both felt... pretty anti-American at that point, during the Vietnam War... and we needed to go somewhere and serve other people in the world, besides Americans." They married during her junior year and, after graduation, joined other college friends in a kind of Mennonite "commune" in France. There they all studied languages in preparation for volunteer work in Africa.

France was "complete culture shock" for this "kid from the Plains," Laurie recalled. "I remember being numb, my brain just being numb." That first plunge into another culture was almost an amnesiac period in Laurie's history. "The climate itself was depressing. It was damp and gray all the time. When the sun finally came out, it looked like a sixty-watt light bulb. There was just never any bright, clear, Plains sunshine." Africa compounded her sense of alienation. "First of all, it took two and one-half days to get to our village, by boat and then by rutted, impossible road. There was no way to go back, so you were trapped — couldn't leave if you wanted to." She felt at the edge of desperation all the time. "Mobutu had just won the revolution; in fact the country's name changed from the Congo to Zaire less than two weeks before we got there. There was this militaristic climate permeating everything, all these people walking around with guns, and yammering at me in a language I couldn't understand. Here I had gone there to be *useful* — I was supposed to teach." But women there didn't even go to school, "let alone teach school, so I had to teach adult males. I felt the students were terribly hostile toward me. It was just a terrible experience." Her husband, in contrast, loved his teaching. It represented liberation from the world of the Great Plains to him, which further reinforced her isolation. "My religious experience there was ... almost desperation. I was like those people put into prison who become converts as the only way to save their sanity." Laurie found herself reading the Bible desperately, praying, trying to bring some coherence to her circumstances. The Bible was the only thing that represented anything familiar, something she could grasp. "Now that I look back on it, most of the time I was on the edge of suicide."

What made the second year better was finding an American missionary colony in a nearby town. "They had Wednesday night hymn-sings.... You could actually talk English to other people. You could say, you know, 'Pray for me,' and feel that you had ... not only your own connection, with this Higher Power ... but that others were actually with you, supporting you." Meanwhile her young husband, dealing with his own culture shock (though neither of them called it that at the time) moved in the opposite direction — to a complete denouncement of faith. "He had become agnostic, so I couldn't even talk with him about my need for religion. He would make fun of me. He'd stopped needing to believe in a God, so I couldn't share where I was. Actually, after that time, I never could." She thought a minute. "It was ironic, because it was our interest in developing and deepening our religion, our idealism about activism, that drew us so close, originally. So when *I* would go to those evening hymnsings, he wouldn't go with me and really scorned it. But I always went anyway. I was able to say to him, and to myself, 'I need this, and I'm going to do it.' "

When I complimented her for her strength, Laurie explained, "It's not so much that I was a born feminist as that my family system just didn't have any clearly defined male-female roles. My father was the dependent, my mother the breadwinner. So I seem to have started out with no preconceived notions of what I could or couldn't do." Additionally, she credited God. "This probably sounds terribly simplistic, but I grew up feeling that God had really chosen me for some special thing. All I needed to do was make sure I lived up to it," she said. Her certainty wasn't accompanied by a "punitive feeling, as if I would be punished by God, if I didn't. It was just that . . . that He was paying special attention to me, and I needed to respect it. I tell you, it kept me . . . I just didn't do some of the things others were into, like drugs and drinking, and sex. [Being kept from] that was pure grace, nothing else."

When the "commune" returned from their two-year volunteering (the others had been at different locations in Zaire) they moved together to the state university. Her husband planned to study law; the others had other degree goals. By this time Laurie was mother of year-old daughter Christina, so it was up to her to get a job and support the others who would be studying. Her first assignment was to locate the student aid office and pick up the forms they would all fill out. Entrepreneur Laurie found she could generate the necessary income by getting a study grant to "work with behavior-disorder kids," so she earned a master's degree while supporting the group. "Of course, none of my career choices have really been mine. I had wanted to go to law school, but my husband said no — he was going to. That's how I moved into psychology." During that period, "I did nothing but work. I didn't watch TV. I didn't read a book other than my texts," Laurie recalled. "I didn't even take care of my child very well." After one semester her husband found law school too confining and wanted to leave but Laurie was once again able to resist. "I absolutely refused. I wasn't going to quit until I finished my master's degree."

When they returned home, Laurie taught. "I think I have a real gift of working with the Special Ed kids nobody else likes," she explained. "I can see past their behavior. . . . They can say anything and do anything, and I can still respond in love. And it's turned out to be very effective. I've really liked it, both because I felt I was really good at it, and because it is an important work." Finding her "calling" thus gave her a new, adult sense of fulfillment. "On the way to school, I would pray for the love that I would need to get through that day, and I prayed a lot during the day. For the patience and the love . . . for God to help me learn how not to lose my touch." These weren't spoken prayers as much as "a kind of consciousness."

Meanwhile, her husband worked in a family business and cared for their child. But still unsettled and angry with himself, he began insisting they have another child — in effect, that they suddenly assume the "normal" family roles. "I didn't want it. I was perfectly happy with one, and I didn't see any reason to disrupt our life," Laurie recalled. "But finally under the threat of divorce, I agreed to quit my job and take care of the kids so *he* could to go to work. I was sick for nine months. I threw up every day." Tensions multiplied. They tried marriage counseling for two years.

Laurie was designated the 'enemy' by her husband's church community, which she had joined when they married. "Though I was not, and could never be a Mennonite, really. You have to be born into it!" She amplified her sense of foreignness in that church. "Those people go to church, all right, and are very involved in Good Works. But they never have any religious or spiritual experience associated with it that I can see." Their extreme emphasis on words, on "the Word" and on external behavior, offered her nothing but legalism and judgment. "They certainly never talked about what I call religion." At the time it seemed to Laurie they worshiped ancestry and heritage — history! — more than God. "They would talk about their migration as a people. They recite the family tree of Hostetters or Detweilers — *when* the family arrived from Europe, those kinds of things. It may have been religion to them but it was far from anything spiritual to me."

The real cause of their disintegrating marriage, Laurie began to see, was the psychological dependency into which she had let herself sink. An entrepreneurial, self-directed young woman had allowed herself, beginning with her junior year in college, to "become extremely 'meshed' with him. Totally unable to make decisions on my own. He really was so intelligent . . . so intellectually superior. And I was so in love with him, so impressed with him, that I simply melted into him, gave up all my thoughts. If he said a certain thing had to be, then it must be right." Within that domain, of course, "I felt protected, acting under his decisions, because he was smarter than I was, and he knew better what to do than I." Laurie now recognizes that this trajectory of postponed autonomy is typical of many white middle-class women, though more often found among women from more privileged economic background. "But then, as I got into more responsible positions in my work, that kind of dependence wasn't so functional anymore." She began to see that the reason she had no say in the marriage anymore was because she had changed so much: "He really didn't like me anymore. Who likes somebody that just lets you run all over them? He never had time for me, or for the children." Custody of the two children had to be painfully hammered out. "He thought I was totally irresponsible, and incapable, a terrible parent." Laurie began to reassemble her life and experienced some restorative therapy. Then "I went church shopping. I was looking for a place where I could feel a spiritual connection right within the building. A place I could go into, not worrying whether I was wearing the right clothes, or who was looking at who, or whether or not they accepted me. Redeemer is that place. Redeemer felt best. It made me feel the most whole and welcome."

Laurie tried to explain further what had drawn her to Redeemer. "It was the spirituality of this body, of this religion. Here I can talk with people if I want to. Or I don't have to. There's a freedom, a dignity. That's the big difference: nobody here preaches it down your throat, or pushes you to a point where you're uncomfortable." Recapitulating for a moment, Laurie confided, "You know, nobody in this city would perceive me as a 'religious' person. Most people would be shocked to hear that I have these religious feelings. Everything I'm telling you? Even my family — some of them would be surprised." She knows her reputation is one of always resisting external structures and commands. "I don't like being told to pray all the time, to believe that God is controlling *this*, having to thank Jesus for *that*. I don't like any of that pressure. I like it to be from *inside* me, to share it if I want to and feel comfortable. And that's what I found here at Redeemer." She has also found a friend and counselor in the priest. "I feel responsible, internally, in myself, to do things. I want to do something for this parish, give something back. But I don't feel *pressure* from anyone." All her life she had looked for a congregation that was "open" and could free her spirit to wonder, to question, to be lifted and transformed. "Most of our churches are so 'closed,' so cold. You can't feel that deep welcome in them." Finally she has found the structure and spiritual space that "opens" to her and allows her to open within it.

The petite treasurer of Redeemer, Ann, in her late 30s, has three picture-book children and a husband who is a local lawyer and city council member. "I love doing the bookkeeping for the parish, because it lets me in on the action, but also lets me stay kind of out of the limelight." She particularly enjoys the discussions of the major issues confronting Christians today — abortion, pacifism, addiction — because they challenge her own thinking. When I asked if she equated her church work with a kind of continuing education, the analogy made her smile. "Sure. I'm learning about myself as well as the church. I wouldn't trade this job for anything!" Having "married into" Redeemer without attending college, Ann found her "own place" in the congregation through this job.

Ann is the rare female of her generation at Redeemer who says homemaking is her fulfillment, at least while her children are young. "Also, I guess since my husband's life is such a fishbowl, I want to keep our family life private and off-limits." She ponders many deep questions about religion and spirituality. She longs to be "more sure," more intellectually secure about "doctrine, what Episcopalians believe." Ann loves the sense of awe and sacred mystery first glimpsed as a child when she visited a Roman Catholic church. One of the things she hopes to pursue in the near future is a spiritual relationship with Janice — someone who could guide her inquiries, be her mentor. She particularly wants to understand her own eager response to the piety in her new Episcopal identity. "I really don't know what's behind the rituals, why we do certain things, and I want to," she said, " . . . the history of the church year, and saints' days, which I love but don't really understand. I need to, for the children, and for myself."

These young women, each exploring her own life and relating to the congregation in her own way, have not formed any kind of subgroup within the congregation, except of age and newness. They live in a region that valorizes women's domestic arts and homemade products, often treating that as women's only religious role. But they rejoice in a religious space that frees them from such constraints. What preoccupies them, as it does young women in the other three congregations, is a personal quest for meaning and religious self-definition. Their chosen religious home encourages that preoccupation; they respond by wanting to find a way — their own way — to express their gratitude and belonging. They are still relatively free of the organizational work that maintains the church, with the exception of the Sunday school, which is largely staffed by their age group. Having no memory of women's caste-like relegation to the kitchen, the experience of the two older generations of Redeemer women, they wonder why bridge-generation women have turned their back on that way of relating to church. They feel somewhat more close to the older, "grandmother generation" women.

•

The conversations at Redeemer were distinctive, in this project, for their preoccupation with the meanings of "church" — in terms of personal religious identity, and in terms of relating to this particular congregation. Women in the other congregations also explored this theme but not with the same urgency or analytic interest. Relating to one's church is particularly vital at Redeemer because the issue of religious choice and "finding" a church home has often been traumatic.

Both physical and emotional geography must be included as factors in the dominance of "church" as the identity issue at Redeemer. In some obvious and some subtle ways, the terms in which they thought about and became part of Redeemer all evoke a sense of discovery, of safe haven, of having "landed" in the right spiritual location (among the options available). Their contentment is reinforced by contrasting themselves with women they meet at school meetings or civic gatherings. In the Plains setting, the gifts of Episcopal liturgy and its distinctive spiritual culture strike them as singular. Redeemer is to them a biblical and symbolic "city built upon a Hill," the New England Puritan image transposed to the central plains of the continent.

The congregation's profound contentment, however, does not eliminate internal obligation to explore, challenge, and discuss. Because of the lively denominational competitiveness in their small city, nothing about their church or Christian citizenship is left unexamined. In their setting, minority status as Episcopalians provides an oddly secure place from which to think about changes, in practice, polity, and theology. Exploring "the new" might well have been more threatening to the congregation's unanimity if they weren't so well protected by their sense of being unique.

The younger women's phrase, "church shopping," has often been given pejorative overtones and equated with "pick and choose" religion, another derogatory expression.[7] A person exercising congregational choice has been seen as revealing a facile, self-indulgent spirituality without denominational depth ("brand loyalty") — the religious equivalent of consumerism and shopping malls. But the women at Redeemer belie that implication. They make it clear that choice stems from a conscious rejecting, or being rejected by, another religious identity, not a desire to find an "easier" God. Their process of choosing involved them in discovering a place for themselves in the web of a faithful community of worship.

The middle generation of Redeemer Plains women rebelled against the type of church involvement once expected exclusively of women because they didn't want to be valued *only* for the ability to generate income. One woman's recollection was that women in the older generation had been "allowed" only to "raise the money that men then spent!" They needed to reject everything associated with that kind of past "success."

But they continue to view the Altar Guild positively. This organization, a part of every congregation in the Episcopal church, no matter how tiny, persists as a locus of "background" work for women who join it as a way of relating to their church and expressing their faith. Until the ordination of women in the late 1970s, Altar Guild work offered women the nearest association possible with the worship function and priest-controlled "sacred things." Today's churchwomen assume that the Altar Guild has "always been" gender-segregated, because in their lifetime it has been.[8] Few are aware that altar work had been discharged by sacristans (by definition, male) until the beginning of the twentieth century. It became the "territory" of women only at the turn of the century, when laymen were no longer volunteering for that role.

The Altar Guild remains an interesting anomaly as women assert that Redeemer no longer has a "real" women's organization. What Altar Guild women do — set the table (arrange the chalice, paten, and altar vessels), open the large Service Book (to the selected pages for the celebrant of that liturgy), decorate the altar (with the appropriate seasonal hangings and flowers), and clean up (bleaching out spots of spilled wine, vacuuming up errant bread crumbs, washing and polishing the vessels) — is "women's work" in the most ancient understanding. Those tasks, however, are exempt from the general negativism toward traditional women's work. An older-generation representative from Advent South pondered why it was primarily women who devote this "very special attention to a major function of the church, almost invisibly." She thought the secrecy and piety of it appealed especially to women. "You give this gift [as caretakers of the Holy Table] in a very secret way; that's what makes it so precious and so deep." Private acts that are a kind of prayer, work that is a form of devotion,

caring for the most sacred part of the church building and providing the objects of sacramental corporate action (without which
Eucharist cannot take place) — all these hallow Altar Guild work,
ritually and actually. Even in today's changed view of spiritual self-
expression, Altar Guild volunteering escapes the opprobrium of
"women's work" that attends cooking a parish supper. In contrast
with the private devotion it offers the older-generation women,
the young feminist Laurie chose it for the "camaraderie of other
women, to do something that is just with women." This "serving"
is legitimated as being holy in a way that kitchen work cannot be.
Altar Guild women are able to ignore or rise above its implications
of subordination by hallowing them.

For women of the bridge generation, however, the new possibility of assisting in the Eucharist is the ultimate way of relating to
the spiritual center of the church. Dorothy's words form a benediction on all the seekers who have ended up at Redeemer, bringing
all their explorations of "Church" to this sacramental union. "It's
very special to serve at the altar, to administer the chalice. Some
of the times when I'm there, and I've been holding the chalice to
their lips — these were times as . . . connected with the divine . . . as
I've ever been in my whole life. I have a sense of being in the direct
flow of Knowing . . . of participating in the gift of the Spirit."

Chapter 4

NATIVITY NORTHWEST AND "FAMILY"

*T*HE WOMEN OF NATIVITY NORTHWEST and their iconography of "family" presented us with the biggest
puzzle among the four parishes. We found no single
interpretation of their use of "family" adequate, though several
were at least partially helpful. "Family" as a metaphor appeared
in all our conversations. On the one hand, there was dismay that
women still live in the stereotype of white middle-class suburban
family, "unnecessarily in the shadow of husbands." On the other
hand, there was anxiety at the actual shrinkage of "nuclear family" units in the church because "health" was still measured by
the Christmas-card image of the "family pew." There was some
sense of loss of the old separate-spheres order, as all-female organizations and the "jobs" associated with that division of labor
disappeared. "Family" was also a synonym for stability in verbal
portraits of the congregation's "comfort factor." Yet nuclear-family
imagery (dad, mom, two kids, dog, and station wagon) no longer
reflects the actual experience of members at Nativity or in many
other Protestant churches today, as it did in the 1950s.[1]

The word "family" also substituted occasionally for other theological terms, at times evoking a clear spiritual overtone. Family
iconography burdened women just coming to terms with single-
hood because of divorce; they were forced to confront the hurtful
assumption that families (not individuals) were the truly constituent unit of the parish. It constrained those struggling to align
feminist self-realization with this congregation's self-identity. Even
those who avoided the label "feminist" but were trying to carve
out new self-realization felt the strain. Links between a traditionally subservient female role and the idealization of a "perfect"

101

middle-class family seemed to be still fairly powerful, some at Nativity said. The feeling that one was valued more "as part of a unit"
than for one's "self" was a gnawing subtext. But for women who
were recovering from deep personal tragedy and finding a new intimacy with God, the language of family seemed appropriate. Thus
the word "family" was complex and multifaceted at Nativity, far
more than in the other three congregations we visited.

"We have some really angry women here," one of the bridge-
generation women observed. "Here they've lived out the picture
of what they thought women were supposed to be, and now the
world's changed on them. So they feel misled. And frustrated."
One of the younger women sighed, "There's so much concern
about economic realities in my age group, about paying the bills
and supporting a family, that it's hard to find people with the
energy to be interested in spiritual things — less interested in materialism." Also, in a church consciously trying to embody family,
diversity of human sexuality could represent the ultimate threat.
"What would really shake this parish up would be if two male,
gay Christians showed up and wanted to become members," one
of the men opinion-shapers suggested. "I'd like to see how we'd
respond and if we could encompass that."

Two opposing dimensions of the "family" label often came up:
the issues of single status and a lack of intimacy or community. "If
I were young and single, I wouldn't choose to attend Nativity," observed a long-time member of the older generation who has been
divorced many years. "It's always been a family church, and I've
suffered here because of it, even though I also love it." Its actual
membership had always had a strong component of true kinship
families. A bridge-generation woman said that churches like Nativity could and should foster community — through "family-type
connections," deep emotional bonds. But it couldn't be a policy
or something that was imposed from the top down. "It's got to
be the 'lower level' in an organization; they're the ones who create community . . . telephoning each other, sharing, being involved
in each other's problems." Coffee-hour conversations, the major
arena of exchange, never delved below the surface: "Episcopalians
just don't share their personal lives." But balancing that, another
young woman praised the ethos at Nativity. "This church, as I
see it, is primarily run by women," she said. "And I don't mean
this as an insult to the rector. In fact I consider it a form of
praise: he's not a man in the standard sense of being insensitive

or patriarchal." His freedom from a dominant-male administrative posture encouraged new possibilities in the congregational family, she believed.

The Context

At first impression, Nativity Northwest could be mistaken for a "suburban" church that accidentally landed in the middle of a huge city. A church building with an attached parish hall of the same basic design as Redeemer Plains, it had been given a distinctly northwestern tone. Nativity and Redeemer, both built in the 1960s, epitomize the adaptability of the modified A-frame architecture popular in that era. Topping the rise of a hill, Nativity is surrounded with camellia bushes and flowerbeds, and embraced by nearby bungalow-style houses. There is no church parking area; a few empty lots on the side alley supplement street parking for Sunday mornings.

The two-foot band of clerestory windows, where the steep A-frame roof and the plain cement-block walls of the church meet, is clear glass. This admits a bright blue ribbon of sky intersected vertically by the dark silhouettes of tall pine trees. Two sets of cloud-toned rectangular banners (10′ × 3′) hanging from horizontal iron bars at four locations on the steeply slanted roof soften the peaked-roof chancel interior. The pipe organ and choir loft are at front left. On the opposite side is a large harpsichord, sometimes used to accompany a choir anthem or for instrumental offertories. The acoustics are bright, thanks to the tiled floors and bare walls. The whole sanctuary — light, natural-colored wooden pews, pulpit, altar rail, and a huge wall-mounted, unadorned cross above the altar — provide a Scandinavian-cool color scheme that harmonizes with the thin, dark pines outside the windows.

Nativity's main doors open directly out onto the sidewalk — into nature, instead of into an entryway or hall. The church's most striking feature is the clear glass that fills its entire A-shaped north end at the peak of the roof, above the building's main doors. The span of uncluttered sky thus admitted is vastly expansive and unifies the church with its out-of-doors surround. This makes an interesting contrast with the same basic architectural design at Redeemer, where the church seemed to "hunker down" into its Great Plains setting. Here the church seems to rise into the sky.

Nativity Northwest is situated in a regentrifying area of the city. Young professional families who can afford the real estate are being attracted to the fifty-year-old bungalows coming on the market as their owners age. In 1905 when it was founded, Nativity was literally suburban and, until fairly recently, indeed a family or "kinship" congregation. "Three clans really dominated the congregation, and through them almost everyone was related to someone. You really had to watch what you said!" one of the older women recalled. The founding families, of Scottish-English heritage, had been in the construction business. They had moved "out" from downtown, bought land, and developed housing for themselves, building an earlier church on the present site.

A burgeoning Sunday school and community-run day nursery in the parish hall act as magnets to the new young families, gradually reconfiguring Nativity's historical "family-ness." The facilities for children were one explanation for talk about family. Seventy percent of Nativity's members describe themselves as "living in families," the highest among our four congregations. Young, career-oriented singles and homosexuals, we were told, would choose a congregation nearer the university or a downtown cathedral over Nativity. About 3 percent of its members were of ethnic-Asian (Chinese, Japanese, Filipino) background, the only non-Anglo representation in the church. New members have expanded the uniformly British ethos of the founding generation, thanks to more varied geographic origins, and a wider range of professional, educational, and economic backgrounds.

With 407 members on its present membership list (after a severe downturn during the 1960s), the two Sunday services at 8 and 10:30 attract a total of about 200 people, many from the nearby geographical area. In this sense, Nativity is a neighborhood church, which led one bridge-generation woman to comment on Nativity's freedom from the "kind of suburban conformity" you might logically expect. There were no "standards for what is dressing properly" that one might find in the usual Episcopal church. In fact, "you can amble in here, late, and informally dressed, and people will treat it as just your personal idiosyncrasy" instead of an affront to congregational conformity. In her view, "real" Northwesterners disdain "Eastern preppie" standards for church attire. "I've become the quintessential Northwesterner," she gestured, "wearing my down vest and sandals to everything, including the main [10:30] service."

Relaxed appearance notwithstanding, the members at Nativity want no taint of the negativity associated with California in the popular mind. They pride themselves on representing "the best of Western culture," at the same time acknowledging East/Northwest contrasts. "We have less sophistication in terms of wit or humor; you might have to explain some of your jokes here. But there is a politeness, a 'niceness' here that is an overarching characteristic," said one of the woman lay leaders. The widely shared view of an "ideal member" of Nativity, and of the Northwest in general, involved such adjectives as "active," "open," "energetic," "cheerful," and "pleasant." The latter description appeared again and again among the two older generations of women.

The 10:30 service had good music, a well-rehearsed choir and lively hymn-singing. There was a level of ease in the service, along with the prevailing sense of order; people felt free to look around, smile, and nod; they moved unself-consciously in the chancel. No particular "territory" belonged to a particular age group: parents and children were throughout the church. In fact, during the recessional hymn, children slipped out of the pews and joined their choir-robed parents marching out the center aisle — a vivid enactment of "family-ness." The leadership at both services included women and men as lay readers and clergy. When the rector delivered the homily, he came down the steps and stood informally near the front pew rather than speaking from the pulpit.

An older woman described the congregation's current "flowering" with the analogy of "a tulip bulb just starting to open up." Another rejoiced that the congregation, formerly with a majority of its members "over 60," now had an older generation that was only "maybe a third of the membership, or less." A young middle-aged senior warden assessed the congregation anxiously. "Every stage of parish life here at Nativity is at a critical point right now," he said: the upsurge of new young families and how to minister to them; the need to revitalize the adult education program; a more egalitarian representation of women in congregational leadership; and "better marketing," a clearer sense of mission.

One bridge-generation woman identified a new and encouraging ethos of openness, especially toward women's participation. "Women can initiate anything here," she said. "For example, since I'm remarried, I could start, if I decided to, a support group for second marriages." But the opposite side of this new generativity was a lingering sense of inadequacy. Somehow Nativity was "always disappointing, never quite living up to the ideal." One person interpreted Nativity's self-perception as a parish that "never quite makes it. We expect to measure success by large numbers, and that's exactly what we can never get in this congregation. We're just too fragmented for that." He was a spokesman for the mobile late twentieth-century urbanites who recognize a sense of displacement from the cohesion of their hometown settings, an invisible contributor to their "disappointment."

People today acknowledge, at some level, that churches experience "cycles" of decline and revitalization related to changing neighborhood demographics. Parishioners at Nativity are clearly energized by the perception that they are in an upswing of renewal. Still, they gave more actual credit to their "young" rector for the new vitality in the parish than to impersonal economic factors. "He's the new generation [of clergy leadership]," one reported admiringly. "What he's about is empowering individuals! He's not just duty-bound to maintain the overall congregation." She obviously enjoyed a leadership style that affirmed, in her view, the importance of the individual member rather than the institution, noting that such an ethos had not always prevailed at Nativity. In fact, during the period when the parish was in its down-cycle, visitors had often received the impression that if they couldn't fit into the existing framework of relationships, they wouldn't be welcome.

The rector, in his early 40s, is a serious "educator" and effective pastor. His view of program development, expressed in organizational language, is "if I can just bring it off, to be able to call out of this congregation the right kind of leadership." Interested in biblical studies and the links between religion and psychology, he has made the congregation feel he is a fellow-learner along with them. At the same time his view of priestly and parish administration is surprisingly traditional. He was one of the two chief pastors we visited who still "did" pastoral calling in people's homes. Several of the newer members pointed out that his style of "old-fashioned" attention — calling on people — was one thing that drew them to join. They had been thrilled to discover a rector who visited so promptly after their exploratory Sunday morning visit, while their interest was still fresh.

The paid staff at Nativity includes a full-time parish secretary/administrator and the organist/choirmaster who puts together a full-time salary by combining it with the job of sexton. Recently they have been augmented by an ordained female. Dot, as everyone calls her, previously employed by the diocese, worked in a series of outreach programs before coming to Nativity, most recently as a street minister in the downtown slums. She has elected to remain a deacon (rather than become a priest) because she had her fill of managerial experiences — running her own business — before she pursued ordination. "I made that choice in order to be free to concentrate on pastoral, rather than administrative, responsibilities," she explained. A dynamo, a good preacher, Dot is opening up the "suburban" sensibility of Nativity to more awareness of their part in urban problems such as homelessness, drugs, and hunger. Many of her sermon illustrations are located in that previously "unknown" part of the city. She is also helping re-energize the remnant ECW (women's organization) by nurturing along what may be its new form for working women — presently called "Mother's Night Out."

The early-50s senior warden identified two distinct "elements" that would have similar reactions of dismay to "male homosexuals seeking membership," who would see that atypical member as a challenge to Nativity's self-image of church-as-family. First would be an older generation possessive of Nativity, because it's "the one constant in a world that's changing like crazy. 'It's always worked well before, let's not change it now' " is their position. They'd want to "put up the barricades" and keep enemy Change at bay. From an opposite position the many new members, many of them new to Episcopalianism as well as Nativity, would be cautious about anything "that might seem controversial" or interfere with their putting down solid roots. However, he himself seriously wanted Nativity to be more adventurous. "We should adopt a 'program church' approach and develop programs that are challenging; of course it means risk. It means stirring people up. What I really dream about seeing here is an 'action theology' centered in the liturgy. We need courses on AIDS . . . on radical theology." Revealingly, however, the best attended adult study group in the past few years was on church history and "what it means to be an Episcopalian."

Another background interview presented a different kind of impatience with Nativity. Marty, a single parent in her early 40s, had been given the specific congregational assignment of developing lay leadership. She discovered that previous attempts to reshape attitudes about leadership had not really replaced the "dependent, subservient" clericalism developed through Nativity's history. She had hoped to bring about a pattern of shared collegial leadership, lay and clerical. But she was disappointed. "Some of us see this congregation as still essentially unwilling to give authority to lay people, especially laywomen," she reflected. Then she said, "I'm sure if I'd been a man, I'd have been ordained long before this. I would have been pushed into it, since that's all we Episcopalians know to do with anyone who takes theology seriously. If you love your religion, if you take it seriously and try to study and grow in it, supposedly that means you really want to be ordained."

Marty came to the painful conclusion that women were the worst opponents of other women in new roles — the ones most likely to "withhold authority" from fellow laywomen. "I guess I have to say this," she began, reluctantly. "We women are often our own worst enemies." Awakened to feminist self-empowerment after a painful divorce, Marty understands women who still see themselves as "shadow people in the church," because they "have been shadows for so long. I don't mean to sound real militant. It's just that I'm seeing that we, many of us, *choose* to be oppressed in our marriages, and in our church." She understands why: "It's safer. You don't have so much responsibility. But it's as if we haven't been really quite 'in existence,' somehow; we carry around something in our solar plexus that knows about, even clings to, invisibility.

When I said she sounded like the kind of feminist one might characterize as "relational," rather than individualistic and career-defined,[2] Marty exclaimed, "That's it. Thank you. 'Relational' is what my theology is: you can call it 'relational theology.' What I care about is relationships. Actually, I'm just as moved when I hear a male priest who knows enough to put in the names of Rebecca, Sarah, and Rachel [in Eucharist Prayer C where their spouses — Abraham, Isaac and Jacob — are named] as I am when I see a woman celebrant behind the altar. What counts is that the person *doing* the celebrating honors the relationships — and doesn't pretend that men did it all by themselves." The King James translation of patriarchal lineage, "all those 'begats,'" traced Jesus' relatives through father and son only, "as if a child could be born without a mother!"

Marty's view of change in the church went beyond women as priests. The new female leadership, ordained women, must have substance behind the symbol: "A woman has to preach with inner authority." Seeing a woman celebrate the Holy Meal was still very moving, but "authenticity in the church is not solely determined by gender, for me."

"What we're talking about here is an entire style of spirituality or consciousness," said the male head of Nativity's Christian education commission. "Men today want what women have — relationships," he said, echoing Marty's perspective. Ideally, the religious side of their lives should open that sphere of emotion for them," but from his experience as a therapist he believes men church members are unconsciously threatened by women's anger. They can recognize the "unfairness" of power in church structures but they don't really understand how to change. "I see the challenge facing the church as one of promoting increasing *relatedness* among both men and women in the face of these deep primordial angers," he observed.

Nativity's socioeconomic profile is quintessentially "middle," a membership that is mostly college-educated (over 55 percent) but not wealthy. Only one-third of the parish has a combined family income above $50,000. "Lots of nurses but few doctors" was the slogan. Instead of great community activism, members focused what they thought of as their religious volunteer work within the parish itself. One person explained that, while some individual members are indeed committed to "outside" causes and concerns, there were "only small numbers on any one issue" because few were "willing to risk involvement in larger ideas." A bridge-generation woman gave a different explanation. "This congregation doesn't need its own peace activists because there are so many in the area; there's one knocking on your door every evening."

Nativity's bulletin boards revealed little social-issue orientation. "Oh, some of us do lots of marching. There's a high level of political awareness," a bridge-generation woman responded. Then, qualifying that, she said, "We like to think of ourselves and our neighborhoods as racially and culturally mixed, but we know that realtors discriminate in terms of the houses and the areas they are willing to show to blacks. And we have bussed schools." Nativity's part of the city had "no real private schools," except Roman Catholic parochial schools. "Let's face it. Black kids in our white school system are unfairly treated." The "*most* mistreated minority in this city," however, is the Native American. "We don't have much cultural awareness of Indians beyond their drunkenness as a public nuisance; it seems we can deal somewhat with the homeless, and other racial groups, but not Indians; our state is 47th in its rate of spending on mental health. American Indians are the really lost people in this city. Even the homeless and the street people are mostly white."

Those interested in causes and outreach were likely to join some church other than Nativity. "If you wanted to be really active in social justice," one woman said, "you'd go to the cathedral or some other downtown parish. This is more of a family parish; people here would rather go to their kids' soccer games, or camping or hiking... something outdoorsy." Another said, "I don't think a family focus in this congregation interferes with the *numbers* of church attendance, but I do think it interferes with 'causes,' like Shalom Groups, or Amnesty International." And the factor of how one distributes one's time. As in the other congregations, Sunday is now the only day people give to "church business." What can't be fit into a Sunday will suffer low commitment and attendance. Even the Sunday hours traditionally considered sacrosanct for church now run into the outdoor mania of the Northwest. "A beautiful Sunday will just about halve this congregation, with people taking to their sailboats or going camping," observed one of the wardens.

A small core of committed laity attend the adult education class offered between the early and family services on a busy Sunday morning. Nativity's main outreach effort is a once-a-month Sunday dinner cooked and served to about a hundred or so elderly and/or homeless "neighbors," many of whom come from a distance by public transportation. There is a remnant ECW organization; a vestry; commissions on pastoral care/parish life, buildings and grounds, and Christian education; and a women-only Altar Guild. An experimental gathering of younger women meets for a monthly "Mother's Night Out" — doing handwork, munching on apples and cheese, and sharing soul talk with Dot (the ordained woman). This group was initiated for young women employed during the day and unable, even if they wished, to participate in daytime meetings. Even this new configuration is too "nuclear family–oriented" for some of the single-parent women, however, the conversation too narrowly centered on couple concerns.

A sizable Lutheran church was their only close ecclesiastical neighbor. The larger religious context around Nativity is a "New Age" consciousness. A number of women at Nativity reach outside for educational or spiritual nurture — Bible study groups, women's professional groups, and courses exploring New Age or other religious systems. The titles of courses available at a variety of retreat centers reflect the range of religious perspectives: "Vipissana Meditation"; "Sacred Places: The Spirit of Place"; "The Creative Nudge"; "Solstice Ritual and Fast"; and "Desire, the Egg, and the Royal Pair."

The heritage of women's secondary status at Nativity persists at a frighteningly basic level, noted an observant young Sunday school teacher in an essay she had recently published. "The girls in my Sunday school class are already denigrating themselves," Jan wrote. She had found herself saying, half tongue-in-cheek, to one of the 10-year-old girls, "If I hear you put yourself down one more time, you'll have to stand in the corner!" It grieved her to realize that her bright girl students were full of "ways to show that we love God and our neighbors" but drew a blank on ways to show how "to love ourselves." The boys in the class had no such problem, she noted: " 'I'd buy myself a Porsche,' one announced. Material objects symbolized 'rewarding' and loving themselves."

A second example of female passivity confirmed her worries. When the class discussed the big Exxon spill in Alaska, the girls seemed unable to suggest what they as Christians could do. Once again the males had no hesitation: "Nuke Exxon," they offered, and "write Congress." Her third awareness was even more startling. In the class sessions themselves, the girls seemed to respond equally to their coteachers, Jan and her husband, while the boys treated her, Jan, as invisible. They listened primarily to him, addressed him rather than her. Had she unconsciously contributed to notions of women's invisibility by not being aware of this and letting it pass? Was Sunday school itself reinforcing the religiously sponsored subservience of the female? Ten-year-old boys at Nativity had already learned, perhaps, that they "didn't have to take women seriously." What they weren't "old enough to have learned," she concluded, was "how to conceal it."[3]

The multifaceted ethos of family at Nativity contained its own conundrum. There, in a progressive northwestern location, on what many called the "open horizon" (geographically and psychologically), women of all three generations seemed somehow more "traditional" than women in the other three congregations. Many seemed very concerned about the opinion of others — more anxious to "please," less comfortable speaking forthrightly. One bridge-generation woman, a former warden, reported an adult version of Jan's Sunday school observation. "When I call on the telephone about church business, the wives want to know why I'm calling, why their husbands need to talk with me." That suspicion stemmed from a lack of self-worth on their part, she believed, and offered her own prescription. "If I were starting a group of women in this parish, I'd focus on helping them recognize their own worth, raise their self-esteem. Some of them are still operating on some old image of what they're *supposed* to do in church. And some of these women will even say, 'No one ever told me that I could really believe in myself.'" To the suggestion that perhaps there were layers of unhappiness to keep in place underneath the required "pleasant" exterior, she replied, "There are a lot of angry women here, still, who've lived their whole lives in the shadow of their husbands."

The potency of family symbolism for Nativity was clear in the senior warden's opinion that openly homosexual members would upset the parish self-image, the female lay leader's discovery of "women opposing women" in leadership roles, and women's inability to take themselves seriously or be "taken seriously." Scars in the consciousness of the older generation helped explain some of a retrogressive internal focus. One older woman wrote me a description of the incident epitomizing their feeling of being besieged — violated — during the 1960s. Only a night or two before the Christmas Eve service, the two tall Christmas trees decorating the sanctuary "were stolen right out of the church." The shock of it still reverberated in their collective memory. Then one of the senior businessmen in the parish was murdered by an addict during a robbery at his drugstore. These horrifying tragedies turned Nativity's location "on the frontier" into a place where defensiveness and a deep-seated sense of vulnerability were functional; for a long time after that the congregation turned inward on its own pain.[4]

The oft-repeated casual information that Nativity had "always" been a "family church" signified the protean quality of "family" as congregational icon. Recent information revealed that it was indeed more myth than fact. An analysis of Nativity's present membership demonstrated numerically that those who actually lived in "1950s-style" nuclear families were the smallest percentage of the congregation, Dot had found. She had decided to analyze Nativity's self-image as "family" statistically. Over half the membership consisted of unmarried adults, nearly a quarter of them managing single-parent households. Those up-to-date numbers show Nativity's composition to be similar to other big-city congregations of all denominations, and further challenge its preoccupation with family imagery.

At least some at Nativity were consciously beginning to combat the perception — the truism — that "families [are] more the truly constituent units of this parish than individuals."[5] Meeting schedules tried to demonstrate awareness of the working woman and the demands of time on single parents. Nativity's education commission was consciously designing programs to nurture a multigeneration, nontraditional church family. Although the rector dramatized old-style family symbolism by walking up the aisle hand in hand with his own small son at the close of the main service on Sunday, he also promoted new ways of thinking about family. In 1989, about a hundred members in three-generation groups of twenty to thirty met in each other's homes for four potluck dinners. The conversation was organized around a theme to which all ages could contribute — for example, "experiences of high holy days, Christmases, and Easters" — and the evenings ended with a table Eucharist. Participants reported a new awareness of relating across generations from this venture.

The Older Generation

The older women we spoke with were primarily those who had joined Nativity when it was indeed literally kin-dominated. Claudia is a retired teacher, divorced, who now volunteers full-time as pastoral visitor in a nursing home; Gladys, also divorced, is a career executive secretary, approaching retirement; Vinora, wife of a retired military man, basks in "traditional" churchwomen's activities and relationships and has come to Nativity within the past decade. Ruth, a long-time member, is a full-time volunteer at Nativity along with her husband.

For Claudia, a woman in her late 60s, family and church became interchangeable in childhood. Family was sacralized for her by a beloved English grandmother, "the kind you'd crawl into bed with, so you could watch shadows from the oil stove flickering on the ceiling, right from her arms," and whose afternoon tea "was laced with a generous dose of religion." In Claudia's early adult life, she experienced a cruel and wrongful divorce. Although divorce was still rare at Nativity, the congregation had rallied to her support so completely that she was astonished to discover later that other women — in congregations that "weren't there when you needed them" — had been less fortunate.

For Claudia and others of her generation at Nativity, emotional and religious bonds were also the fruit of an early formative relationship with a woman, no longer living, who was mentor and role model in their adolescence. "There was this wonderful volunteer 'director of religious education,' who was related to one of the three main families here. She was just marvelous! So creative, so inspiring, and so beautiful. And so much fun! She was the kind of talented person who wrote her own curriculum and set up exhibits all over the diocese; she had us involved in every conceivable kind of exciting church thing, so that's how we got the idea that religion could and should be alive."

Around the time she turned 60, the onset of severe arthritis forced Claudia to reorient her personal compass. Physical limitations suddenly imposed a sharp redefinition of what she could take for granted, "things I'd always done: no more skiing, no more hiking, no more serving tables at parish dinners." Then on an upbeat note, "But I'm learning not to worry about what you *can't* do anymore, just worry about what you *can*." A personal ministry emerged out of her new limits. Her career had been working with mentally disturbed children so she had imagined that it would continue as her retirement "calling." In a recently completed pastoral counseling degree program, she interned in nursing homes to meet a course requirement, and found, to her surprise, "what I need to do is to be at peace where I am," with the elderly and infirm. "What God means for me to do is just show love to other people. It doesn't have to be with children. And I don't need to rely on education or degrees or anything else; to rely on God is good enough."

Claudia was deeply moved by her contact with stroke victims. "Though their speech centers have been affected and they can't actually talk, you'll see them mouthing the words of the Eucharist along with you." She also related an "almost miraculous experience": seeing "the amazing, calming effect of the Eucharist" on the heart-monitor screen of an elderly woman to whose bedside she had brought communion. As she watched, the mechanical tracing of the patient's agitated heartbeat evened out; her entire body and countenance became soothed, relaxed. Claudia thinks that "to have it pictured on a screen" is technological confirmation of the Spirit's healing power.

She actually loves "being the Church" to people in nursing homes. She feels strongly about church jargon, though. She thinks theological language is "a stumbling block" to real "heart religion. What's in the Bible is what's important. Needing to know who said what, when, its history, in what words? They call that theology? It's all just background. It has nothing to do with religion." She is equally clear about "how full of love this place [Nativity] is." She attributes the disappearance of a once-divided "older church versus younger church" and the revival in "genuine family feeling" to the rector, to the many young families he attracted, and to the prayers of her own group of long-time women members. She is one of the rare older-generation women who acknowledged that, had it been a possibility, she would have sought ordination in her younger days.

Claudia's approval of family image at Nativity Northwest contrasts with the experience of Gladys, the career executive secretary also in her 60s, also divorced and also with no nearby family. Gladys had also grown up in this congregation, though she, unlike Claudia, had winced at its "family" exclusivity. In her psyche, family and church were blended in childhood, as for Claudia. Gladys's childhood image was sitting on the piano bench with her little brother and singing hymns — "In the Garden," "There Is a Green Hill Far Away," and "The Old Rugged Cross" — while their mother played. After all these years the memory can still bring tears to her eyes. "I always felt, even as a child, that my mother knew who God was, and was close to Him." Gladys and Claudia had both loved the same Christian educator, "that wonderful woman who was 'a mother in the church' to so many of us. She really was my 'church mother.'"

That beloved mentor expanded horizons for Gladys through enlisting her in an organization called the Girls' Friendly Society, a kind of Christian "Girl Scouts" flourishing in many urban Church of England (in Great Britain) and U.S. churches from the 1920s to the 1940s. That organization took her as a high school senior all the way to New York by train, as delegate to the first-ever national conference of Episcopal youth, an experience that opened her eyes to the larger church and its mission. "It wiped away my provinciality. It gave me confidence, and an experience of the holy. It also provided me with...the only racial awareness or internationalism to which I was exposed as a girl." Gladys is the one woman at Nativity who remembered, and expressed, emotional outrage over the internment of Japanese Americans during World War II — many of them fellow Episcopalians from the locality. "One of them, a leading American-born-Japanese church historian today, couldn't make it to my wedding in 1942. He was arrested trying to get here, for violating curfew. Imagine! This scholarly young man I'd known in youth work had to spend the night in jail in this very city, just because he had Japanese features."

The advantage of having ordained women leaders, in Gladys's view, is tied to the "sensibilities and concerns" women just "naturally" and efficiently carry into leadership. "Do something for the homeless? Women instantly come up with something practical, like 'let's furnish a room.' Their response to a crisis is always at the practical level, you know. Women are always the first to respond to [Jesus' command to] 'feed and clothe.'" The tragedy that had precipitated her divorce years earlier, and sent her into the working world, was a prolonged kidney illness that killed her young daughter. "How does anyone survive the death of a child without God?" Yes, Nativity has in some ways excluded single women from its programs and concern, but she remains loyal, "though I've also suffered here."

Vinora, the spirited 74-year-old wife of a retired Navy officer, "didn't become an Episcopalian" until she was 55. Her husband's career moved them so often that "church" meant only the interdenominational chapel at military bases. She, too, recalls the immense importance, in her youth, of an older woman, "someone I looked up to as a saint. She was very poor, but she never felt sorry for herself." Her aura was "almost divine, in a way. I don't mean she was a prude, or anything like that. She was just a person who had lit up your life with her smile." This spiritual godmother was "truly an angel on earth, if anybody is. She had nothing materially, but she was incredibly rich inwardly.... Every life she touched was richer for it. You don't experience that too often. So some of it, thank God, rubbed off on me."

Vinora is one of the women at Nativity to speak glowingly about the remaining ECW circle of her contemporaries as "family." "Of course, young people here aren't very active in the Circles, because they work at jobs, you know; they have such busy schedules. We don't seem to have many young women in the Circles. Those of us who're still here meet the last Tuesday of each month, bringing a sandwich." The ECW is still important for women in their 80s, she believes, because "the Circle is their only social thing. It means

a lot to them, and I enjoy it because they do. Last time, for example, we each shared Thanksgiving memories from some period in
our past. It was wonderful for all of us! In my car I had a 92-year-
old, an 87-year-old, an 85-year-old, and a 77-year-old. I was the
'baby' at 74!" A family label illustrates her view of its youngest
member, the only one under the age of 50: "She's certainly got a
lot of mothers!" In an impersonal modern world, the Circle and
Nativity itself embody the work of caring and assure her God is
really "in our midst."[6]

Vinora sees women's ministry of outreach as totally practical,
the aspect of female spirituality she most values. Women think in
"concrete material terms" about any task such as "fixing up a
building" for homeless mothers and children — "the people society has totally let down." She enumerates lovingly the items she
and other women have contributed to furnish "their" room in
a diocesan-purchased family shelter: "Towels, sheets, lamps, curtains, a rug, a Boston rocker — we just gave everything. There was
absolutely nothing but bare walls when we started!" Her pleasure
in the coffee hour "flea market" put on each Sunday by her Circle
was another occasion for the pleasure of list-making: "Our young
Circle member makes the most adorable baby-size little sweatshirt
and pants, with ribbed cuffs and all; and I make lots of orange
marmalade that these Brit-Episcopalians just seem to love. And
the most beautiful knitter in the parish, Vera, makes darling baby
sweaters, and beautiful vests."

For Vinora, the congregation is family in explicit ways as well.
"People here are so wonderful. This church is where all my friends
are. I have no kin here, you know, so we have to depend on other
people, and this really is our family." She is not alone in this, she
added. "A lot of people in this church feel that way. The only ones
who don't are those who'd be miserable anywhere you put them!"

A fourth woman of the older generation, Ruth has belonged to
Nativity over forty years, has served as ECW president in both parish and diocese, and on many local political committees. Presently
she is librarian for a remarkably well-equipped and professional
parish library. For Ruth and her retired husband, the volunteer
treasurer for the parish, "church furnishes all our social life." One
of her pleasures in the library work is contact with young mothers
as she helps them decide on religious books for their children, for
example, or — going much further — helps them find babysitters
or the nearest clinic. They have become her pastoral "job." An

old-line political liberal carrying vivid recollections of the abuses during the Joseph McCarthy era, Ruth nevertheless aligns herself with a conservative "old-fashioned view of the issue of male-female equality." Her explanation is complimentary to women and protective of men. "All through this congregation's history, the women have always done more of everything! So I think there has to be — we have to reserve *something* in the church for men, some job that is only male." If they weren't given sole responsibility for some specific task, she fears men would end up doing nothing or withdraw altogether.

Vinora enjoys her late-in-life discovery of religious fulfillment through a churchwomen's organization, while Ruth turns away from twenty years in the ECW to a more self-defined ministry; the two women of this generation who were employed full-time adjust in differing ways to its family iconography. Their perspectives were less problematic than those surrounding the women in the next younger generation, the children of the 1950s' nuclear family idealization.

The Bridge Generation

Church and family imagery are again interwoven here — leading some to yearn for a deeper familial "community" within the congregation, others to redefine and free themselves from its confining stereotypes. Lydia, a former church organist who was occupied with school-age children, presently is not employed outside the home. Beth is emerging into a professional career from being "submerged" in flesh-and-blood family. Barbara, now divorced, is employed part-time in a school for emotionally or physically handicapped children; and Esther is a nurse in a cancer ward. Each looks at Nativity through the "lens" of family and sees it in a distinctive light.

Lydia, slight and quiet in manner, is beginning to looking for a paid job. She is in her middle 40s and her husband is currently out of work, so he is job-hunting as well. Her primary spiritual concern is "the lack of a feeling of closeness in this parish." She suspects that Nativity could never be a real "family" for her but wishes it could. "Community is really important to me. I really struggled over it when we first came here." She explained: "You see, this is not a 'neighborhood' type church. People live all over the city, you don't see them from Sunday to Sunday. There is just no place where . . . your paths cross, except at church." She talked a lot about the "ways a church can foster that community," a subject to which she has given much thought. The kind of community she wants is not something artificial or mandated from the top but a genuine interrelatedness that could allow the self to enlarge and deepen. "People are the ones who must create it. There has to be real conversation, sharing, being willing to be involved in each other's problems." Most conversations at church, before and after services, remain superficial. "Episcopalians just don't share their personal lives," she said regretfully.

Since Lydia's high school years had included a job as organist in her Episcopal church, she "knew all the words" of worship and prayer by heart. But she discovered as an adult that she had "no *real* understanding of the meaning of the liturgy" or anything beneath the words. A lifelong Episcopalian, Lydia suddenly realized that she was "illiterate about the Bible, and about prayer." Involvement with an ecumenical Bible study group, one that had chapters in many neighborhoods of the city, changed that. She now feels a "secure knowledge of closeness to God, the only One you can really depend on." Lydia trusts that, in time, "if I rely on God, He'll lead me to find those people in this congregation that I am to know and be in community with."

Lydia is still amazed at her previous lack of spiritual self-awareness. She had been a person who "used to put other people at the center of my life rather than God." Spelling it out, she said, "I used to idolize my family, my husband, my children, my parents. They were always much more important to me than God. In effect they *were* my God, and I was worshipping them." Presently, her life in the congregation is "really better, because now God is at the center. I no longer feel that I am a divided self." And though she is still disappointed at what she sees as the shallowness of the congregation at Nativity, Lydia has "no need to leave my church" and look for a different one. "I need to stay, and find out where it is I am to be. I want to help, to contribute to this congregation, in my own behind-the-scenes way." She has kept this personal renaissance mostly private, but has joined a small in-parish women's prayer group that helps fulfill her need for closeness.

Another bridge-generation woman, Beth, in her 50s, is disillusioned with the understanding of family on which she had grown up and married. A handsome, well-dressed speech pathologist, now completing her public school license, she stated the nuclear-family idolization that she and other white middle-class women of her generation had brought to marriage several decades earlier. "*Family* was going to be my personal 'high priority.' " She now knows that what she had meant was "looking to him [her husband] for everything — companionship, direction, and decisions. There was no 'me.' " She accepted the unqualified wife-as-auxiliary role, but he was married to his job. "He worked fourteen hours a day at his profession." Beth discovered she was bereft of the very things she expected him to provide: companionship, direction, decisions. "I married with the idea that I was his handmaiden, you know — whatever he did, I would help him do it better...that kind of thing." Her life was based on a series of "if onlys": "If only I have a child," that will solve everything; "If only this or that will happen, then I'd be happy!" After the child arrived and her husband continued his single-minded career pursuit, "I realized I was feeling like a single parent. Finally, I went back to school! The whole family profited by it, because I was going crazy." Salvation from idolizing the nuclear family saved her and them.

Beth began graduate school, still believing it would remain secondary, "allowing me to keep my family first — in the center. But at least, I thought, I would have a strong interest with which to *supplement* it." Her interest instead turned more and more toward a rewarding career. Now, because she has her own interests and priorities, she is coping with "lots of the resentments that husbands and wives have to live with." Learning how to resolve them has meant "a gradual coming back together" in her marriage. "These resentments really could have pulled us apart." A fresh perspective allows her to supplement and recast her original assumptions about family. "We find ourselves, my husband and I, much more...dependent, now, on somebody besides ourselves — on talking with our minister, for example. 'Family' is really more a series of experiencing 'ins' and 'outs' that are ongoing, rather than...any one central event," Beth summarized. Actually, that isn't a bad image for Nativity as a church, she thinks.

Beth has always kept herself somewhat removed from the family-ness of Nativity. "My church involvement is not very deep. Oh, I've nearly always had a finger in one pot or another — a day's help at the bazaar, putting on an occasional dinner — but not as deeply as I assumed I would, following my mother-in-law's pattern." Then she checked herself. "I've always said to myself, '*When* I get married, *when* I stop working, *when* I get to this age, then I'll do something more; I've always been thinking that the next stage will be better." Tuned in to the fallacy of "next stage" thinking, Beth is trying to free herself from the need for "neat closures." She has finally accepted, through therapy, that viewing a problem as "being over and done with" isn't the only way to deal with change. She admires Nativity, the church of her husband's family, for its ethic of caring, but having just carved out a new way of being in her own family, she is not going to become enmeshed in *its* family.

A third member of the bridge generation, Barbara, comfortably casual and jolly in her mid-50s, is highly positive about Nativity's family image. "We're trying to meet a lot of different needs, and really doing a pretty good job. We have this young rector, new young families, young [adolescent] kids — all the really worthwhile things. And we have a nice balance of all ages, of men and women, of young and old." She is another member of Nativity who survived the trauma of a marriage dissolving under her nose at middle age, another whose sanity and spiritual equanimity have been regained through one of the neighborhood ecumenical Bible study groups. "That's a wonderful experience, for which I'll always be grateful. It's very different from having only a casual acquaintance with other women. You get together for a real — the only — purpose. It's a group that promotes spiritual strength, even activism — but sends you back to your own church to express it."

The surface harmony of Barbara's marriage to a successful workaholic lawyer had for years lulled her into assuming that everything was okay. "I did everything I thought I was supposed to: be a good wife, cover for him when people phoned, protect him." He had never been "communicative," a code word applied to marriage in the 1950 and '60s. He, on the other hand, always "refused to talk," even when she confronted him with irrefutable evidence of infidelity. Recalling her desolation at the moment of confrontation, she asked, "How do people who don't have the Lord in their lives get along when something like this happens? Because it was just *devastating*. I'll never forget that night." Then she added, "But even so, I just had a real sense of . . . that the Lord was there. No, I didn't ever feel betrayed by God." Her inability to "blame" God, Barbara thinks, might have been because she wasn't deeply enough connected, at that time, to "really know Him." Perhaps people "closer to God" would have experienced this tragedy as divine betrayal also. She knew hers was purely human — forced unwillingly into her consciousness as she emptied the pockets of her husband's suit for the drycleaner.

Barbara recovered, thanks to the Bible study group, and looked for work. She found the channel for her energies in working with retarded children. "Nurturing is just one of my ministries," she said calmly. "I love doing it not for the money but for my mental stability. I need to be needed." She is also training to become a court-appointed special advocate for victims of child abuse. An occupational outlet for her unused "family" emotions makes her especially appreciative of "what's happening" in the Nativity family.

Esther, a dark-haired, dark-eyed woman in her early 40s, married, with two college-age children, is a deeply committed and articulate Christian, a nurse who quietly "prays over my patients." Esther was "born into" membership here, a great-niece of the beloved director of religious education who so profoundly influenced many of the older women, and a descendant of one of the three founding families.

Her earliest recollection of God was a sense memory: breathing in the fragrance of freshly ironed choir cottas, a little girl held in her father's arms for a moment as the choir lined up at the back of the church, ready for the processional. "Even as a child, the smell of white linen [vestments] always seemed really holy to me." She also sensed very early that "there was something holy and set apart about church; you did special things when you attended here." She created a corner for this specialness at home. "I set up an altar in my bedroom, when I was in the fourth grade, with a picture of Jesus. I would change the flowers, and arrange things on it, reverently; I would kneel and say the Lord's Prayer and the 23rd Psalm. I had my own 'holy routine,'" she smiled at employing a monastic phrase for her childhood sensibility.

Marriage also brought her a direct experience of the divine. "God was present at my wedding," Esther recalled. "Here we were: my dad was crying, I'm crying—and one of my friends sang an anthem that said it in words: 'Lord, who at Cana's wedding feast / Did as a guest appear.' I knew He had....I could never deny that I had been married in the sight of God. The marriage ceremony itself was not something I could ever put lightly away." The recollection made her tears flow. "You'll have to forgive me," she explained softly; "my tear ducts are directly connected with my spirituality." When I asked if she thought tears were indeed a language of the soul, she admitted that tears were often more eloquent than words, at least for her.

After her husband returned from serving in Vietnam, they faced the adjustments of starting a family and "growing up." An emotional crisis with her two infants sent her to a pediatrician who was "smart enough" to direct her to the ecumenical Bible study in her neighborhood. As a practical matter, that group offered, along with its sociability and spiritual nurture, the best and most inexpensive child-care program available. Her children needed it, the doctor prescribed, needed time away from her! "Oh yes, I was a real mess. Very overweight, smoked all the time, cried all the time, and I'd bleached my hair absolutely platinum." Her experience with that women's group and its intense study of the scriptures produced the inner confrontation she needed to take herself in hand. "I began to ask how could God shine through me, if I'm clogged up all the time?" After her physical reclamation, she was challenged to join the leadership program and began to lead the study sessions. This was a big step for a young woman who had not attended college, who was basically an introvert. During her first attempt to lead the study group she had a moment of blanking out, but also another experience of God's presence. It was "like a big white wing had come over me. I'd been protected, during that moment of going blank. Then I was able to go on." She even recognized an accompanying smell of freshly ironed white linen, her childhood scent of "the holy." Gradually she became free from the disabling shyness she had thought could never be overcome.

Next Esther finished college, as an adult, and entered nurses' training. The vocation of nursing in turn introduced her to the hospice movement. She felt God leading her toward that work "because I feel so tuned in to others' pain — the sick, the deformed . . . I just have to, I am able to see that . . . I'm bathing the broken body of Jesus." Her "sense of being hooked up to a Source, a life-sustaining source . . . an alive relationship with the risen Lord" sustains her as she cares for the dying. She finds similar nurture in the worship at Nativity, where she is lay reader and chalice bearer. "Giving people the chalice is a sense of being in the direct flow . . . just knowing . . . knowing God is flowing through you and into people's hands." Esther's words about this kind of service echo a woman in the same generation, Dorothy, from Redeemer Plains, an unconscious reaching for a similar image to articulate an awareness that is all but inexpressible in words.

Esther now feels some ambivalence about Nativity and its closed-off internal visage. In spite of the "many, many wonderful people here who have a deep faith, we don't share with each other, so we don't know. Our faith is simply an unknown quantity." She often prays about "how to make sharing one's faith and insights a genuinely lively ingredient" in the congregation. "Your talking with us about religion is going to help make us more aware of what we actually have here." And she wonders about a merely "casual use of the Prayer Book. . . . Sometimes I fear we experience the words and the ceremony, but not the Presence." Since Nativity is literally kin for her, Esther questions whether she and her husband might not benefit from attending a different congregation, now that the children are grown and gone. Another congregation might help her discover how much of her religious experience is, or is not, family.

The Younger Generation

The younger women provided a graphic illustration of this generation's quest for religious certainty. As children and adolescents of educated middle-class families in the late twentieth-century culture of "bureaucratic individualism," they have pursued individual paths strenuously.[7] Their almost torturous narratives reveal a complex, painful, often lonely, struggle toward selfhood. Each of them, similar to the younger generations at Redeemer Plains and Advent South, dramatized the burden (as it seemed to them) of having to work out one's own religious identity — her own "salvation"[8] (a word they did not use). A parent's path — religious, occupational, marital — was nothing they wanted to imitate, more a trap to be avoided. Independent of generational guides or models, each of these young women has undergone real trials, especially the sense of being utterly alone in a harsh world. Their quest has been fulfilled by arriving "at a church home" at Nativity.[9]

Arlie, now in her early 30s and "back in the Episcopal church," sought religious community during her college years in a variety of forms: first in a Christian Missionary Alliance church, then in a fundamentalist Baptist church, then a charismatic Episcopal congregation. "I always felt the pressure to be nothing but good" in the Missionary Alliance congregation. The ever-present sense of unworthiness and judgment appalled her; the literal approach to scripture among the fundamentalists was equally foreign. In her third experiment, "I found that *I* was the only one singing the actual words of the hymn. Everyone else was speaking or singing in tongues!" Being caught up in group religious ecstasy, however fulfilling to her fellow worshipers, seemed to come between Arlie and God. "I never got that sense of sacredness I was looking for, which is what finally drew me back to my kind of Episcopal roots. Especially the ritual of communion, just submerging myself in the fullness of it. None of the others [churches] had anything like it."

Arlie's personal life also involved traumatic efforts at self-discovery. She made an early, disastrous first marriage that ended in divorce after only a year. Reeling from that, bewildered and rejected, she entered into a relationship with a physically abusive man who left her with a further diminished sense of self and an out-of-wedlock pregnancy. Thanks to the help of a physician-employer who was "a wonderful Christian," she was enabled to "get strong enough" to surrender the child at birth for adoption by a strong, loving family. "It has taken years, and lots of therapy," to achieve some spiritual serenity about that. But Arlie meanwhile completed her college education, rejoiced in a strong second marriage, and enjoys working with teenagers through her job in social work. "Giving something back" to young people, in her congregation as well as in other work, is important because in her own teen years she loved the Episcopal Youth Fellowship. "I really enjoy trying to help make it a great time for kids today," she explained, one of the few women of any age who expressed an interest in working with adolescents in our conversations.

Arlie begins now to comprehend the self-destructive passivity in which she was trapped for a decade, where she "let life just happen" to her. "I went through long periods of my life, making decisions by *not* making any decision. But now that awareness seems to really help me. It equips me to really listen to kids." Her favorite hymn, "Amazing Grace," a national popular favorite in her youth, now speaks theologically to the thorny path she has walked. Nativity as a church family has been helpful in personal peacemaking with both her birthright family, from whom she had been estranged, and her birthright church. She can now enjoy thinking about her biological child in a strong and loving family. Although it must be forever separate from her, she can pray and "let it go" in her new spiritual location.

A second young woman, Betsy, had also experimented with fundamentalist and charismatic Episcopal congregations. Before that, during her student days, she tried some Eastern religious cults that flourished on the campus. Now in her early 30s, she has arrived at a satisfying Anglo-Catholic-Episcopal identity that finds a home and church family at Nativity. Tall, lean, dressed in a faintly "hippie" style, she commented, "In some ways, we really don't fit in here. It's not an Anglo-Catholic parish like I thought I needed, and at the same time it's not as evangelical as we had tried earlier on. There are differences between us (my husband and me) and a lot of things here. But it's a place that feels like a real supportive community to us. I can get my spiritual direction from an Anglo-Catholic priest elsewhere, and here at least we are encouraged to 'try out' lots of things." At this point in her quest, church solidity has become a magnet rather than a repellent.

Betsy and her husband actually "shopped" for a church. "We got out the phone book, wrote down all the Episcopal churches within reasonable commuting distance by bus — we didn't own a car on principle! And then we just tried them all out." What they discovered at Nativity, besides its ethos of family rootedness, was "the freedom here to initiate things." An example was "our taking a booth, downtown during the Merchants Fair, and handing out Bible Society tracts. Something never done by anyone at Nativity before! Oh, some parishioners might have looked a little askance at it," she thinks, but nobody actively opposed it. In fact, one of the "real patriarchal families" that "used to run Nativity and think they owned it" actually "came down and took a turn at our booth. They came back feeling really interested and challenged. They discovered they felt good about that kind of witness, instead of thinking it was weird and 'un-Episcopal.' What I like, what I really give them credit for, is not putting us and our idea down before they made the effort to see what it was really all about."

Betsy and her husband hadn't designed this street-witness to "test" the flexibility of their church "family." This kind of public service with the American Bible Society has been one of their personal projects for several years. Unfortunately, "when we wanted to give it up, after two summers, no one from here picked it up," so that was disappointing. But even so, by that time "we just felt like we needed to stay someplace *solid*, so we've been at Nativity since then. You never feel 'tied in' [obligated] here — other than the fact that there are lots of nice people you really want to be with, and a rector who is open to lots of creative ideas. That was one of the things that was important to us."

Betsy believes she was "led" to Nativity. It had long been important to her to feel "a holy Spirit" in her life. Hers had been a "very *rational* Episcopal family," an academic father and an author mother, both of whom "distrusted emotion" and left her craving a religiosity with more passion in it. Her youth was lonesome. She thought of herself as a "John Wayne" type. Dutifully attending the Episcopal church in her Western mountain hometown, she envied the boys who could be acolytes while girls couldn't. That irrational gender barrier brought to mind another set of images that still infuriate her: the Flintstone cartoons of her youth. She hated the wives who were stereotypes of self-effacement and subservience to their boastful, juvenile spouses.

Betsy had an adolescent experience of conversion, a powerful awareness of God's presence. She was in a football stadium under an immense starry sky, all alone. The image that remains vivid is her own infinitesimal being in a vast universe, at the same time intensely related to it in every pore of her being — a "Oneness with the universe." An important theological "interpreter" of Jesus' life in her adolescence was the Broadway musical *Jesus Christ Superstar*. She listened to the original-cast recording over and over, identifying with "the Judas character who kept trying to figure out who Jesus was, and making all the wrong choices!" By herself, keeping it a secret from her parents and sister, she then began to read the Bible from start to finish. "Suddenly I realized what all these people had been trying to tell me, all these years," in Sunday school classes, and what she heard in the preaching of radio evangelists. "The light came on, like 'aha!' I finally saw it."

A summer exchange program sponsored by the interdenominational organization called Campus Crusade for Christ lifted Betsy from her "small town, small world" for a summer in Germany. Then she won a Rotary scholarship for a year in a high school in Mexico. Those tastes of other cultures made her determined to attend a "big university" and major in journalism — to get herself out into a larger context and away from her restrictive "home" forever. At the university she spent more time in religious experimentation than study, eventually "rescuing" from a religious cult the fellow student who became her husband.

Both Betsy and her husband took their spiritual search extremely seriously, becoming wholeheartedly involved in each of

their church "belongings." They first "tested" a strict, evangelical
Christian para-church group. "It was anti-evolution, antifeminist,
anti-intellectual. It emphasized conforming, a chaste style of dress,
and the submissiveness of women," she recalled, almost in disbelief. They fit that community ideal in at least one dimension, she
laughed: they'd remained sexually chaste before marriage in part as
a way of distinguishing themselves from the destructive promiscu-
ity on the campus. Marriage "was a total commitment" for them,
their wedding "a real entering into a covenant." Even so their time
with the fundamentalists was brief. They then joined a "standard"
Episcopal Church (not yet Nativity) but continued to be evangelical volunteers for the Billy Graham Crusade and the American
Bible Society.

Next they tried a charismatic Episcopal congregation. Betsy said
they were "grateful to have the experience of praying in tongues,"
but were "turned off, once again, by the doctrinal rigidity and conservatism toward women. You know, the picture painted by *Acts
29* [the newsletter of a national Episcopal charismatic "renewal"
movement]. Of course the Episcopal Renewal Movement itself has
only men leaders, no women!" Too intelligent and too feminist to
be content for long in that congregation, Betsy had a genuine spiritual awakening in the next church they tried, a socially committed
Anglo-Catholic parish whose rector became her spiritual director.
She basked in that ritual-rich congregation, having the experience
of formal confession and absolution for the first time. Finally, she
and her husband decided it was time to make a permanent commitment to a church, as a step toward building a spiritual home
for the biological family they wanted to begin. That's when they
were "led" to Nativity.

Even though Nativity is not Anglo-Catholic in its worship, being more "low church and informal than St. Barnabas, my high
church spiritual home," its ethos of "family" (a term she used in-
terchangeably with "solidity") was the magnet for Betsy and her
husband. Wanting to be on the cutting edge of change toward more
egalitarian participation of women, and still in the evangelical view
of personal discipleship, they have found here what they sought so
long and hard. Betsy's narrative summons the image of a seeker
who feels one must "invent" a self, as if from scratch, the message
many in her generation have received. She is grateful, now, to be
"at home" in her church identity, recognizing that she has come
"full circle."

A third young woman, Eileen, a professional singer, had always found her "church center" through music — starting from the text of the childhood hymn "All Things Bright and Beautiful" (whose first verse is "All things bright and beautiful, / All creatures great and small; / All things wise and wonderful, / the Lord God made them all"). She, too, loved the musical *Jesus Christ Superstar* in her teen years. "Actually the choir in which I sang professionally, at a huge New York church, really became my family," she said, because in many ways her own parents couldn't. An alcoholic, temperamentally unstable father marred her early years. A mother emotionally unable to cope with being a single parent and wage-earner became addicted to medications during Eileen's late adolescence. Amid the kind of stress that continued into her adult life and marriage, "spiritual things have become almost a luxury." To this point, her deep hunger for religious and emotional nurture has been better fed by Eastern mysticism and some "gurus" than by her "own [Episcopal] church." That has often seemed too literal, too flat and text-bound, too lacking in mystery and spirit.

Eileen and her husband, wanting a place where they could "worship together" and have their son with them, "church-shopped," like others in her generation. They looked for a congregation that would "mesh with who we are as a family. Now that there's a 'baby boom' in this church, we're going to stay. We really couldn't find another church in which we felt more comfortable." A warm relationship with the rector and his wife was the convincing experience: "They're very family oriented; they have even helped us in a crisis with babysitting."

Raised to be idealistic, Eileen has always wanted "to do something that will make the world a better place." What that will be, she isn't sure. She mentioned ecological and peace crusades, concern over Central America. "I'd like to work through the church, but I've kept myself . . . held myself back. Because — I have this mentality that says I have to get my own life straightened out before I can take time to do that! Recently, I've had this 'revelation' that maybe I'm never going to reach that point. That if I'm ever going to do this kind of work, I just have to start doing it . . . fit it in with everything else I do. So now I'm trying to find a way to do that. We both are, my husband and me."

Given her deep uncertainty about the world in which her child must survive, it has been spiritually crucial and affirming to Eileen that "this church really loves my son. People in the congregation look for him every Sunday; they watch him — see everything he does, as he develops. They all come up and talk to him, and hold his hand, and talk to us about him." Such explicit, enveloping concern symbolizes the kind of family closeness lacking in her own childhood. "It's so dear of them. He's really a favorite with the congregation, has been ever since he was born. He's got a big following here."

Additionally, her approval of Nativity has another element. "This church, as I see it, has the energy and vision that is congenial to women." The rector "has a lot of sensitivity. He comes across as a father, and a person, but he doesn't have a lot of those big, scary, masculine-authority-figure things like the clergy at the church where I sang, back East. He's very down to earth; he's a really good person, a low-key California type...an everyday person." His lack of distance from the congregation and his empathy with young families made this church family safe for her. "Most rectors have an 'image' they project from the pulpit, so that it's hard to know who they really are. But not our Father Jeff!"

Apart from her positive view of the clergy leadership, however, Eileen avoids women's organizations — the ECW circle, the Altar Guild. Despite her longing for religious companionship, her views are still shaped by those of her mother's generation: women's tasks are "boring," their work has no real status in the eyes of the congregation, or for women themselves. Worse, it puts women in a situation of forced intimacy, gendered segregation under the imprimatur of "religion." She expressed a distrust of women's groups as "mere sociability," not spiritually credible. She "steered clear of them" because she doesn't want churchfolk to have "the kind of information" about her that becomes church gossip, "gets passed around." Yes, she had examined the idea of seeking ordination. "Doesn't everyone in my age group?" But she held back, out of fear that women priests will still be "only second-class." Ordained women will never be accorded the same respect as men clergy, Eileen declared. The church will probably just settle for "token acceptance of women's leadership." Her cynicism has been tempered a bit since Dot joined the clergy leadership team at Nativity. "Women have strengths that men do not. They can serve in different ways that will...perhaps they [women] *will* be able to make the church something that people will come to, will want to return to...because they now find something in the church that they really need." Underneath her hope in that vision, she remains cautious, having made Nativity her "family" home.

Two other young women, from non-Episcopal backgrounds, found Nativity by differing routes and had still different responses to its "family" ethos. Brigitte, a divorced mother with two young children, joined because it was located "in the neighborhood," one of her major principles. "I believe in going to the church nearby." While it offers the "constancy of ritual" she needed, she wants church to *be* family as well as neighbor. She wants it to help her "be a good person." Still occasionally prickly in relation to the "authority" and mores of Nativity, she maintains a somewhat wary relationship with it. For example, the "Mother's Night Out" group is not helpful to single working mothers, she thinks.

A career environmentalist nearing 40, Brigitte found that her first-generation immigrant-German background equipped her with a different language and worldview than the dominant "English mentality" at Nativity. In a way she is used to being an "outsider" — it heightens her idealization of church as "something special, a place that the kids want to go, where there's a special kind of interaction." Previously she belonged to a small charismatic congregation in Texas, "the closest church I've found that is like a family." There, because it was a new mission-congregation right in her neighborhood, church services held in the homes "made it very real, very exciting, almost primitive." That shaped Brigitte's view of church as nurturer and support group. "In that congregation, we could just let the kids run. There was lots of land, nowhere they could really get in trouble. Also, each Sunday school teacher would round up the kids and take them off to class." It had literally functioned as extended family for her.

Coming to Nativity was a shock. This congregation has more hierarchy and expectations about demeanor, though unarticulated. "Here, I realize, I've come to be perceived as incredibly lax with my kids." Transplanting her earlier experience, she had expected that "when I come to church, I have the feeling I ought to be able to say, 'Well here, kids, here's home; you know what you can do, what the rules are, now go ahead.'" But she ran smack into different ground rules. "The people here are different, the kids, too." There is more formality. "Kids are not to run around; *you* take your kids to class, *you* make sure they're in their class. You are the one. Kids themselves are not given as much freedom, and as much responsibility here. I'm supposed to be with them, have them under my wing constantly!" Although Brigitte finds this confining, since she had no one to sit with her children if she sang in the choir, she is trying to assimilate. It comes down to a different type of church family.

"I do know a lot of the older members in the congregation are uncomfortable with kids zipping in and out. I don't blame them; kids can be unnerving if you're not used to them." Actually, she mused, "Kids are a concern in this church, an issue. People want to be open and friendly toward children, but there are just some who are uncomfortable with them." Age, ethos, and habit contributed to a hurtful exchange when one of her sons, still very short, stood on the seat in the pew in order to be able to see what was going on. "I didn't see that as a problem, if his shoes aren't muddy. But people here tend to disapprove. 'He's standing in the pew,' they mouth at me, as if I didn't know what he was doing. It's a different culture! The priorities here have all been for older folk, till now."

An attempt to align herself with Nativity's self-understanding led Brigitte to volunteer as the coordinator of the four cross-generational supper groups taking place that year, and it had helped. "The most important thing for me is that my kids be able to feel that church is a home, a loving, caring environment they can go to and know they're accepted and loved. Of course, there are some problems in any home, in any family." The concrete aspect of church-as-family is strong motivation for Brigitte even if these ways seemed somewhat foreign.

The recent "homecoming" of Marcia, a medical technician, came about as theological and ritual recognition of this "family" as part of "the church universal," the part of the Body of Christ that is the Episcopal Church. Needing to find a church identity for an only daughter, now aged 6, Marcia was another who deliberately "did my research" — visiting, reading church bulletin boards and parish newsletters. She was well past "considering going back to the Roman Catholic church." Her fervent working-class father had imbued his many children with his own impassioned Catholicism *and* his disillusionment after Vatican II. That rupture demolished his personal idols — regular attendance at mass, idealizing the authority of clergy — and his religious hold on Marcia.

Marcia thinks she must have been "a typical female religious fanatic as a kid," one of those romantic Roman Catholic girls who "gloried in self-denial and masochism." Adopting her father's religious extremism, she so idolized nuns that when she visited a real convent and met "real sisters" she could only be disappointed. She recalled luxuriating in the sacred aura of "those huge dark churches" to which her father "dragged all five of us kids." Her mother was "a sad, defeated Protestant who got overruled" at every turn. "I always knew God was located in that little red light in those big dark sanctuaries. I enjoyed giving myself bad dreams about it." She yearned to be an altar boy like her next older brother: "Why can't I?" she remembers asking. "I'm just as loving of God as he is; I'm as smart as he is." She joined the Navy to provide herself with an education, and to escape from her family. As a college student she "converted to other fanaticisms: militant feminism and atheism." During her Navy years she married a fellow officer, studied her science, and simply "shut God out for twenty years."

Her first experience of a woman priest (Dot, the ordained deacon) at Nativity "was so refreshing. It was like I could finally say 'Yeah, hello, women are human beings! God created us, too!'" Also, since she has given birth to a child, she appreciates biological male/female difference more than her feminist mindset had previously admitted. "Okay, so I am a woman. Still, I can accomplish things." In fact, female distinctiveness might be good for the world. "I don't see anything wrong with an 'emotional' female perspective in leadership.... Just look, historically, how men have screwed it up trying to keep emotions out of leadership!"

Wrestling the relics of her childhood faith into unity with her present self has been difficult but rewarding. Marcia enjoys being an agent of her own spiritual identity rather than a passive recipient. "This time, belonging to a church I've selected, I'll be fitting God into my life on my terms, knowing who I am." The personal autonomy she had struggled so long to find emerged as she shed her antireligion armor. "I'm no longer a child who blindly accepted what I was told, and had this bizarre fantasy of becoming a saint. Nor do I have to be, any longer, this cold, cynical adult who couldn't admit there was a God because it was too awful to contemplate. Finally, I think, faith is going to be really *real* for me." Nativity Northwest as her place and the place for her child is a chosen religious family replacing the one she had inherited.

For Marcia, it was important to find the theological "safe harbor" of Nativity because it "gave me back my rituals," along with a church where she could worship. Her father, a layman who "never had a chance at higher education," had tried to authenticate his own paternal role by "almost *worshipping* the Catholic hierarchy and structure. That's why he felt totally betrayed by Vatican II." He and one of her brothers died of alcoholism; her mother and a sister suffered emotional breakdowns before dying. Only one brother remained. Family trauma "marked all us kids. You know, although I was part of a large family, five children, I'm sure I survived by thinking of myself as an only child a good part of my childhood." Her atheistic stage, she now sees, was crucial in freeing herself (psychologically and religiously) from the destructiveness of her biological family.

Ordinary human friendliness was a kind of heavenly omen during Marcia's search for a church home. "Yes, believe it or not, you can tell a lot by the way the phone is handled! The way the secretary here answered the phone, and my questions, convinced me." The last of Marcia's twenty-year religious resistance disappeared when she came to know the rector and found that her Methodist-reared spouse could also be comfortable at Nativity. "These are intelligent, thinking people who — in spite of that! — still find that God has validity in their lives." The struggles against her childhood's anti-intellectual faith and family "authority" had left their mark, but "this is not a religion that just blindly accepts things."

Although comforted by the liturgical similarities between Episcopal and Roman Catholic worship, she is still bemused by the congregation's informality before the service begins. It is a sharp contrast with the rigid, enforced silence she remembered — eyes straight ahead, no looking around or whispering. "And here at Nativity they are tolerant of so many different kinds of people . . . and of feminism. Here I can really believe that all of us are equal in God's sight, that *all* of us have gifts to bring. Here and now I see all the issues I was marching about, back in the '70s." The ideologies of atheistic individualism and feminism, substituting for her lost Catholicism, have sustained her psychologically during her spiritual homelessness. Now she is re-integrated within a Judeo-Christian framework that provides a new kind of "home." The earlier pieces of her life have come together and she "no longer feels like an orphan in a storm." Her story and those of her peers at Nativity illuminate the many identity-quests of late twentieth-century Christians. Their place in organized religion is hard-won.

•

Although kinship family was a major factor in the lives of these women — none were single by choice — nowhere else was the concept "family" as provocative an element of religious self-definition. Women at Grace New England took family for granted in calculating what work "counted" for their church, especially among the younger generation. The theme of work itself was more problematic. At Redeemer Plains, family had been a source of religious trauma so "church choice" became the focus of their anxieties and identity. And as will be evident in Advent South, family as a theme in women's spiritual identity is a significant factor. Still, only in "suburban-seeming" Nativity Northwest is the language of family such an interesting mixture of anxiety, satisfaction, questioning, and exploration. This surprised us, because we hadn't expected it.

Perhaps as visitors to that location my colleague and I brought overly romantic assumptions about "frontier" and "freedom." That became evident while we were there, and clearer in the transcripts, as many facets of "family" came into play in their reflections on church, secular life, and spiritual experience. Three lines of potential interpretation are (1) a look at the "comfort" factor, something many of them identified as a reason they chose Nativity; (2) the overlapping, literal and symbolic, of two institutions — family and church — in Nativity's own congregational history; and (3) the ways in which the language of "family" can be invoked to substitute for other theological or spiritual vocabulary in modern-day religious consciousness. At various times "family" imagery seemed to be used to describe experiences that, several generations earlier, would have been referred to as "salvation" or "transcendence." Today those traditional holy words strike many mainline Christians as pretentious when applied to one's own everyday experience.

"Comfort" was employed as a negative by the social scientists who first used it, a disapproving term signifying church members who sought self-indulgence rather than moral standards and challenge to self-improvement in their congregations. Church members, according to this view, were supposed to want ethical challenge; they should choose an organization directing their consciousness toward social justice. During the civil rights era, many congregations avoided the political difficulties of confronting their own racism by invoking the rubric of "moderation" or "fairness to all sides."[10] In a textbound interpretation, the word "comfort" signified only something bad. Despite the fact that Christians in any congregation often act as individuals with passionate moral conviction about an issue (homelessness, or racism, or hurricane relief), even if their fellow members don't, the idea that a congregation might or could provide *spiritual* comfort to its members was not considered. Comfort signaled only a failure of Christian commitment, a damaging rather than empowering "goal."

In the words of Nativity women, the factor of "comfort" has both positive and limiting functions. Clearly related to the reassurance of "family" and the symbolism of home, "comfort" may in fact strengthen members' desire to improve the world and the plight of the sufferers in it. It can also insulate people against the pain of the world outside. Still, the "revival" of family-type relationships among the members — such as the older women expressing grandmotherly love to the infant son of the young singer — constitutes a cross-generational "comfort" at Nativity that cannot be dismissed as merely negative. In a city on the far edge of the continent, where the legendary ideal of "rugged individualism" still flourishes, a congregation that maintains an interwoven fabric of human relationships against impersonal worldly tensions is living out one meaning of its designation as a local "body of Christ."

A Jungian psychologist, head of the group responsible for planning Christian education at Nativity, named "relationships" the key issue affecting both men and women in an era of sphere-confusion and role-shift. Some men may be unable or unwilling to assimilate the new definition of community and "comfort" when it involves accepting women in new areas and participation. Some women remain trapped in the traditional male-female hierarchy, unclear about how to achieve a more profound spiritual life. Somehow family symbolism both assists and hinders the "comfort" at Nativity. Members value Nativity's family-type relating at the same time they want such a network of emotional and spiritual relationships to be more inclusively Christian. Those who fall outside a sentimental "in-group" definition of family — singles, people from nonwhite or ethnic heritage, those living in "invented" or nontraditional family groupings — find it hard to be drawn in. The religious paradigm that idolizes the comfort of a limited, self-protective religious family has to be recognized as an obstacle to the authentic comfort of a genuine "family of faith."

Second, the broad societal patterns known as institutions, here particularly "church" and "family," occupy overlapping realms

in the physical world. Home and church are the two most intimate institutions in human life, in that sense part of the "private"
realm, their standards expressed in emotional values and language
rather than in commercial or political terms. Family and religion
operate powerfully but often unconsciously via invisible attitudes,
values, and mores. The congregation at Nativity has some psychic
residue from having been literally a family church; it still carries the
message of church-as-family in its current identity. This presents
newcomers with a haloed aura of "caring" that people can actually see and experience. But the styles and demeanor of caring are
idiosyncratic, a captive of its own congregational culture as the
young scientist from Texas found. The historically undemonstra-
tive style of Nativity's founding generation still exercises a defining
influence on the way this congregation expresses an understanding
of church-family and "what caring really is."

In our four congregations, women are the ones who do the
connective work of caring, who make the family-church conjunc-
tion a concrete reality. The secretary who ministers to strangers
on the telephone, the librarian who helps with a babysitter or
a clinic, the knitters whose products pay for the nursery curtains — this intracommunity "caring" embodies Nativity's historic self-image and values, and supports women employed in
the professional occupations of caring: nursing, teaching, mothering, visiting. The interrelating of "church values" and "family
values" has generational dimensions, however. When the younger
generation interprets the work of caring as public evangelizing,
feminist self-discovery, or environment crusading, they challenge
Nativity's self-understanding perhaps more than they intend. Older
and bridge-generation women at Nativity seem so anxious to
avoid self-promotion that they fall back into past patterns of self-
negation. A cultural equation of family and church can be as
confining as expanding.

Many at Nativity bring to the "public" realm of the congregation their unspoken anxiety about physical and psychic security.
Even as "biological family" is constantly disrupted and re-forming,
they want a religious "family" to help them survive and make
everything "all right" there in an urban context. The icon of
church-as-family has overwhelming appeal. "A home-centered belief system," carrying the suggestions of a happy-ever-after halo,
is a powerful magnet to the homeless, even those vulnerable to
"homelessness" in only the symbolic sense.[11]

A third interpretation centers on the use of language at Nativity, particularly the ways in which "family words" were used to convey religious emotions or experiences. The kinds of insight that people expect to experience religiously are hard to articulate, often impossible to express in words. Sophisticated, educated Christians today fear that they will sound fanatical if they use old-fashioned religious terms in conversation or even in private, personal prayer — anywhere out of the context of formal worship. Such language seems to have lost resonance with the spiritual realities or states of mind it came into the language to express. One young woman said breezily, "God isn't dead, but God-language sure is." The vocabulary in which seminary students are taught to categorize and write their sermons has become separated from the language of laity in the pews by a vast chasm.

One interpretation of the avoidance of "church words" is that women have come to associate "theology" or formal "God-talk" with the intellect, rather than heart, spirit, soul. They have been made to feel that what they have to bring to religious expression — a kind of wholehearted or whole-souled offering of self — is less valid than a loftier, more abstract realm of meaning found in "church words." A young clergywoman said, "Laywomen have been taught in a clerical church — at least nonverbally — that you're supposed to separate emotion and intellect. They have come to assume that theology and theological words belong to the world of the mind and that they must keep their emotions out of it. Their emotions might be negative about them, anyway, since they don't identify with them. Theological terms don't express anything 'real' to most women." She thought a moment and then added, "But how about the statement, 'I believe in God'? That's not an intellectual statement, it's an *emotional* one!"

Deep spiritual longings or insights may be more comfortably couched in words that already contain emotional overtones: brotherhood, mother, sister, father God. "Family" is the audible icon[12] in the distinctly reserved Anglo-Protestant ethos bestowed on Nativity by its founders (and its Episcopal culture). Some young people are indeed drawn to this religious formality in their quest for stability and rootedness. But limiting the expression of religious emotions to family words contracts and reduces the vital associational possibilities in a "family of belief."[13] Each of the voices here expressing something about congregational life in family language also hoped, in some way, that those words encompassed their personal evolution in the larger currents of historical and societal change.[14] Equating the language of "church" with only "family" metaphors, while "comfortable," is narrowing.

Beverly Wildung Harrison suggests a more subterranean motive for constraining the expression of religious imagination to family images: "Family" language can become a mask for undealt-with feelings. Feelings — emotions — are not right or wrong, moral or immoral; only actions may be weighed in that way. Because modern-day church members are schooled to exclude or mask strong feelings (they don't "know what to do with them"), she sees contemporary Christianity "impaled between a subjectivist and sentimental piety that results from the fear of strong feeling, especially strong negative feeling, and an objectivist, wooden piety that suppresses feeling under pretentious conceptual detachment." A feminist moral theology, she argues, welcomes and accepts "feeling" for what it is — "the basic ingredient in our relational transactions with the world," especially in transmitting our religious experience. The heavy burden placed on the concept and language of family in churches like Nativity has to be considered in this light. It must be prevented from congealing into a "wooden piety" or a fearful "avoidance of strong feelings."[15]

Members of congregations in an earlier era undoubtedly felt more connected than women today with the orthodox religious formulae of their church vocabulary. They undoubtedly felt less pressure to turn into "their own" words any conversation about religion and spiritual life. Perhaps what we saw and heard at Nativity is an example of the adaptation process — the ways a multifaceted imagery of family moves into and modifies (or even expands) other ways of talking about God.

Chapter 5

CHURCH OF THE ADVENT SOUTH AND "INNER LIFE"

*A*DVENT SOUTH produced this study's most intense and comprehensive conversations about women's inner life. While women here also employed the symbols central to the other three parishes — church as a family, work as an expression of community, "church" as the symbol of individual religious quest — words exploring the timeless yearning to connect with God and fellow human beings dominated in this parish.

On the surface, the images of work, family, and church explored in the preceding chapters seem more self-evident, less in need of contextual narrative. By definition, "spirituality" and "the inner life" bespeak a state of mind with questions rather than answers. They focus on the interplay between a person and her choices in dealing with inexplicable events or forces. "Inner life" is apprehensible only through reflective reminiscence — women telling their own stories and interacting with our responses to them. Narrative is the chief way we try to make sense of existence and reflect on our experiences and, hard though it may be, speaking about the spiritual self is crucial. In this congregation the language was personal and relational — concrete, lived reality — not speculative or theoretical. Remembering, retelling, their narratives often countered what they had been taught, by "official" religious voices, as "official" versions of reality. These women described "coming into relationship with reality," Carol Ochs's definition of female spirituality.[1] Fewer voices are quoted here, but at greater length. Even so, this chapter is asymmetric with the previous ones.

140

More forthrightly than in the other three congregations, at Advent there was an unabashed focus on God. "All I really want," confessed a young woman, "when I dare let myself admit it, is that Spirit inside me...the gift of praise, the gift of survival." A bridge-generation lawyer said, "The kind of support I'm talking about isn't something I get from individual people. My 'support group,'" she said, gesturing upward, "is elsewhere." An older woman experiencing severe physical limitations expressed it this way: "I'm beginning to get a different view of the Kingdom of God, and what it means to have it *within* you." Women at Advent saw their congregation as a place that contained all the confusion, diversity, and darkness of the inner city and yet profoundly nourished their inner life. Their language conveyed the spirit, not the duty, of sharing and giving. In ways similar to the New England congregation's hallowing of "work," or Nativity's of "family," the ethos at Advent imbued concrete acts of service with a numinous quality. Their attachment to this congregation and its inclusive spiritual community was not something abstract but the reason they were there.

One male congregational leader described succinctly the "two threads that are big life-givers to this congregation. For one, Advent is the center of Anglo-Catholic worship for the city — though many new Episcopalians have no understanding of the old "high/low" controversy and don't really know or care about Anglo-Catholicism as a church 'party' (or faction). And two, it's the center of Social Gospel — a genuine old-fashioned sense of mission in the inner city, with the best possible sense of commitment." Anglo-Catholicism as a religious mindset emphasizes the "catholic" and symbolic elements of worship over the Reformation or Protestant elements, springing from a nineteenth-century movement that reacted against the Enlightenment overemphasis on rationality and intellectualism to the neglect of ritual and sacrament. Anglo-Catholicism often, though not always, implies an authority pattern more like the Roman Catholic understanding of priesthood and the corresponding disempowerment of the laity. A Social Gospel theology accompanied the emergence of British Anglo-Catholicism, establishing mission work in local cities as well as foreign lands — at that time a new emphasis in Anglicanism.[2]

Advent's Anglo-Catholic identity provides worship adorned with "high church" ceremonial such as sanctus bells (rung at the most sacred moments of consecrating the Bread and Wine) and incense (to augment a sensual atmosphere of the holy). Advent

South's location on a hilly mound is also symbolic. This congregation has made that location, now part of the "inner city" ills, its central reason for existence. The "inner life" theme, phrases and thoughts about praying, religious visions, and other direct experiences of the holy, emerged naturally there, without embarrassment or special effort. Two explanations of this relative openness to sharing "private" religious experience are: Advent's geographic location, and the intrapsychic influence of Anglo-Catholic worship and worldview suffusing its congregational ethos.

Some women themselves offered the regional truism: "The South is more openly religious than other regions; people still go to church here, more than they do in other parts of the country." While that may be true, churchgoing by itself has never been a guarantee that speaking openly about spiritual matters would be easy. And while Anglo-Catholicism is a form of piety that often finds expression in visible gestures of humility (such as genuflecting or crossing oneself), those do not signify a more substantive inner life, much less a willingness to talk about it openly. The aura of solemnity that may accompany the inner and outer reverence characterizing Anglo-Catholic practice is not oppressive at Advent. There, theology and worship blend in a distinctive mix of modernity and traditionalism among both ordained and lay members. The "Catholic" hierarchical style of authority often assumed by priests in this cast of churchmanship has been elasticized and humanized. Both male priests, for example, were most often called by their first names rather than the honorific title "Father."

A tension being explored during our visits to Advent South confirmed their idealization of shared authority and responsibility. Some of the women were planning a day-long diocesan meeting to be held at Advent, during which they proposed to have one session open only to women. The chief pastor, as well as some of the women, were opposed to scheduling a gender-exclusive session in a "public" conference. The rector declared he would not arbitrarily resolve this disagreement, as a priest in a more authoritarian parish would have, but wanted "wide input" about it. The importance of unity in Advent's image and reputation — unity out of diversity — was the concern. "We've fought so hard for inclusiveness that the idea of divisiveness, even in a just cause, is anathema," sighed one of the older women.

Advent is an anomaly in both its geographic region and ecclesiastical tradition. Its "otherness" from the usual mainline church consists not only of its blend of high church practice and low church "shared ministry," but also the range of social class and racial backgrounds from which it draws its members. Differing liturgically and demographically from the other non–Roman Catholic churches and from its fellow Episcopal churches, it was the most inclusive congregation in our inquiry and its own region. Its verbal badge, in fact, is "Inclusiveness." The inclusiveness at Redeemer Plains encompassed a pluralism of religious backgrounds; inclusiveness at Advent South is sociological and keeps it from looking like "your typical Episcopal congregation" because of such visible externals as skin color, demeanor, and sometimes "poor" clothing.

A modest brown-shingled church building with a steeple bell, relieved on the outside only by fire engine-red Gothic front doors, Advent looks across the street to a Methodist church of equal size. Downhill is a part of the university campus. On its right is some decrepit "temporary housing" left from World War II. The neighborhood has survived urban decay and is in the cycle of regentrification. A two-story parish house, recently added, provides much-needed modern facilities for parish offices and their social service programs, including a modern restaurant-style kitchen.

One woman explained that Advent isn't "really a neighborhood church anymore." "I'm always surprised how far many of our members come," she said, "especially since such a high proportion are employed and commute into the city all during the week to work." On a Sunday morning approximately 140 worshipers (an average total of both 7:30 and 10:30 services) are there, through personal choice and considerable effort. Nearly half drive past two or three other Episcopal churches on their way, though a few live within walking distance. The tone of worship at Advent is dignified. An all-volunteer choir sounds professional and meditative. In contrast, the hymn singing is energetic. At the 10:30 service the psalm is sung (rather than said), the initial line chanted by the Jewish organist/choirmaster. This is a liturgical sophistication for a parish of Advent's size, one usually found only in cathedrals or parishes with a hefty music budget.

Built as an end-of-the-streetcar-line, all-white "suburban" parish in 1904, Advent's interior is various shades of brown, a lighter hue than its exterior. Even the fourteen plaques of the Stations of the Cross, newly bolted to the walls against theft, are a metallic golden-brown instead of polychrome. The windows are opaque gold-brown glass; the hardwood floor is varnished brown; the carpeting on the sanctuary and its steps is a deep, light-absorbing red. The contrastingly bright and open parish house hosts the university Episcopal chaplaincy, bringing in diocesan funds. Other programs located in the new facility are a daily noon-meal program for 75 to 100 homeless citizens, a counseling service called the Street Ministry, a foundation that administers group homes for developmentally disabled adults, and "in-parish" activities like the thriving Sunday school. Each accounts for the slow but steady absorption of a few new members.

This congregation of 250 communicant members manages to maintain these varied ministries by attracting both funds and volunteers from wider circles — diocese, foundation, and ecumenical. But the congregation itself assumes significant responsibility for each of them. The language used about Advent reflects its lively sense of Christian "mission," and their personal investment in it. Thus while physical effort and finances are somewhat augmented by outside sources, the congregation itself "carries" these programs in its own rhetoric, prayers, and giving (time and money).

Various opinion-shapers reported Advent's history, the most venerable being Miss Fannie, now in her 80s. She has "stuck through all the changes," the only one of her family to do so. Her commitment also represents a degree of independence for a well-brought-up Southerner trained in conformity. "I'm usually not one for change," she admitted. "Roots" and faith helped her endure. She gradually adjusted as "formality of worship" became the norm at Advent, but "it [took me] a couple of rectors! Never did learn how to cross myself," she confessed. "Oh, I learned how to do a little genuflecting by watching the lady in front of me ... couldn't ever really do a deep knee bend, though."

According to Miss Fannie's estimate, about half the congregation engages in "high church" gestures — genuflecting as they enter and leave the pew, making the sign of the cross when they receive the sacrament and at the words "Father, Son, and Holy Ghost." One of her peers, an exuberant woman in her late 70s, suggested that Advent's uniqueness is due more to its style of ministry than its style of worship. "The reputation of this parish? Outreach! Diversity! The identity of doing all this work for others! When you say 'I'm from Advent,' it instantly conveys something admirable, liberal, positive in the eyes of others from this area." The congregation's only "weakness," from this second point of view, is "generational — it's hard for families who have young children to get them really connected." To her, genuine appreciation of Advent requires an adult's mental and moral framework.

Miss Fannie, now retired from a secretarial career, recalled the ups and downs of the civil rights struggle, the adoption of the new Prayer Book, and the battle over admitting women to ordination. "There was a time when people got on and off of Advent like it was a transit bus," she said. "People came and went, came and went, and it was just real hard. Some even went off to join that weird group, the breakaway Episcopals [who formed separating congregations, particularly in opposition to the new Prayer Book and the ordination of women].... We really were about to go under, financially. But the rector at that time kept telling me, assuring me, 'God won't *let* Advent die.'"

It was during the most dire financial straits of the 1970s that Advent's leadership (lay and clerical) made the decision to become the high-church outpost in this low-church diocese. One of the young congregational leaders, Peggy, characterizes Advent's Anglo-Catholicism as broader and more substantive than mere churchmanship. She sees it as "a continually negotiated opposition to the status quo within Southern Episcopalianism" rather than a theological commitment to ritualism. "New members may be attracted, some of them, because it's 'high church.' But most of us come here because of the 'outreach' reputation, and then we make our peace with the style of worship."

The paid staff is large and varied. Full-time staff includes the rector, an associate rector responsible for the university chaplaincy, a social-worker coordinator of the street ministry, and a sexton — the linchpin of the parish because of the constant use of Advent facilities. Part-time staff includes the organist/choirmaster, the coordinator for the community soup kitchen, a director of the group homes program, and the bookkeeper/parish secretary. She, in turn, has a daily "staff" of volunteers, older retired women and men, who answer the phone and help with multiple office tasks.

The other side of Advent's watchword "diversity" is "unity." Both descriptive nouns were continually cited as *the* reason for being there. Its "more truly Christian attitude," as many in the congregation believe, produces a mix still rare in many (Episcopal or other) mainline churches in the South or anywhere: up to a quarter of the congregation who might be considered "not typically Episcopalian": African-Americans, "street people" or others in "un-Episcopal Sunday garb," many who identify themselves as homosexual, all in a variety of ages (high-schoolers in the smallest numbers). Women as lay readers and chalice bearers are taken for granted, as are women priests, one of whom had served on the staff till just recently. Such topics as homosexuality, women's ordination, and racism, often politely "not discussed" in other congregations, are not taboo here, though also not an easy thing to include in the prevailing public discourse. Residents from a group home for mentally retarded adults and members of Asian-American or African-American background are comfortable and welcome. While Advent consciously encourages the widest possible spectrum of humanity, an unspoken covenant operates to shield from public debate the actual constituents of its diversity. It was as if actions spoke louder than words and contained less potential for upsetting each other. Talk about their diversity was also easier in conversation with a visitor than in a parish meeting.

Some congregants said they deliberately "escaped" to Advent South from the all-white middle-class conformity of their previous congregations. One young mother, a professional civil servant speaking in her soft, deep drawl, said, "I didn't want my children growing up in a church where they would get to know only carbon copies of themselves." She chose Advent South because it advanced "a perspective other than materialism. Here all social classes are visible. Here externals are not the most important thing." Having admired the class difference visible in terms of clothing, however, she laughed at her own contradiction: she still insisted that *her* little daughters "dress up for church"! About half the congregation consists of families; the other half are singles — young professionals, widows, never-marrieds. Few at Advent fit the proper *Wall Street Journal* Episcopalian stereotype. Only one of the parish, an African-American businessman, is a financial pillar of the city. The rest are "idealists" from many backgrounds, making relatively modest incomes in service professions, holding liberal social and political views. One of the men on the vestry bemoaned, in jest, the economic limitations that accompany Advent's high-mindedness. "The kind of members we *need* are a handful of wealthy, successful businessmen. Please, dear God, don't just send us more of the teachers and social workers we always attract!"

In response to a request for the description of an ideal member at Advent, two generationally contrasting views were presented. Miss Fannie instantly named a dedicated talented layman "who has held every office from senior warden to chairing the building committee, the kind that leaps into everything from the most menial job to the largest undertaking. To me, he just symbolizes Advent!" Peggy, a young executive in her late 30s, pointed instead to the small group of faithful older women including Miss Fannie, the "Monday morning group, who've lasted through all the changes," as the authentic image. "They seem to be the river that just flows through the life of this parish.... Of course, they're not as constantly visible in what they do as a senior warden is. But they're the foundation. They're 'the faithful,' in terms of praying and attending."

"We are about as 'mainstream' as a deep-South Anglo-Catholic parish can be," a Southern-born bridge-generation woman declared. "Which, sometimes, is *not* very mainstream! From time to time, though, we do get the feeling that, far out as we often are, the rest of our diocese is slowly catching up with us." She meant in terms of liturgy (in a militantly low-church diocese), not Advent's zeal for inclusiveness and outreach. Against the stereotype of white Southern Episcopalians as worldly self-indulgents and implacable opponents of change, Advent's "social stands, different ministries, and diverse congregation" (as member after member described it) are a unique part of the religious dialectic in the city. A professor of French literature at a local college summarized what to her made Advent unique — its gospel commitment. "The South may have more churches and more churchgoers than other parts of the country, but not necessarily more religion."

Only a few separate organizations currently exist within Advent's corporate life. Undoubtedly some of the energy presently channeled into outreach programs would have been, in an earlier era, devoted to and through specific women's organizations. The ECW is nonexistent, having been voted out by the present bridge-generation women — most of whom are professionals. Its remnant, the ten or twelve women in their 70s and 80s, meets on Monday mornings for Eucharist, fellowship, and lunch. The rector values this group for its "continuity with the past" and also because it is "a group that is very skilled in taking care of each other." Some of the Monday morning women are involved in reactivating a denominational women's prayer order known as the Daughters of the King. Altar Guild work at Advent is shared with male sacristans, the only one of the four parishes where it is not exclusively female.

The printed parish directory alerts new members to its participatory structure. Membership names are divided among thirty-one pages so that one page each can be included in daily prayers, covering the entire congregation over a month. Various congregational "functions" and names of associated organizations are listed on the inside back cover with a "contact person" for anyone interested: "Worship-related Activities" include the Altar Guild, Acolyte Guild, readers, greeters, and ushers; "Outreach Activities" include the peacemaking commission, and the boards of the community outreach ministries; "Religious Fellowships" include the Order of St. Francis, and Daughters of the King; and "Hospitality Functions" suggest assisting at the parish house with phone answering and clerical tasks, helping with receptions and potluck dinners. An old-style fundraising bazaar fell somewhere between the departments; formerly run by the ECW and still essential for parish finances, it is now a congregational activity, although the older women (the ECW remnant) still assume a special responsibility in its organizing.

No jobs in the church are exclusively "owned" by one gender, thanks to Advent's moderate size and ideology of inclusiveness. "If the job is done right, no one cares by which gender," one of the older women said. The senior warden, Arlene, was the only female in that official role we spoke with. She had earlier managed her own business. She attended graduate school in her late 50s, and presently works for the city government. Now in her mid-60s, Arlene had been active with her recently deceased husband in a variety of leadership roles, in a previous parish and in the diocese. They transferred to Advent a decade earlier "because we were bored with our suburban, all-white, conservative, 'successful' parish."

Arlene enunciated the unspoken covenant protecting Advent's diversity: avoiding, as much as possible, open debate about its diverse elements. "Anything that disrupts such tenuous, precious community is scary." A man on the vestry agreed that it is "too bad when any one group, in such a diverse congregation, upsets the balance." That "surface harmony" produces an equilibrium he called "the Southern ethos." A younger man expressed this social convention in other terms. "We seem to believe that it's okay to conceal reality under appearances, if thereby we keep the peace," he remarked, "but of course otherwise it's called hypocrisy, compromise, or what have you. Still, for everyday functioning —

people actually getting along with each other and getting things accomplished — this method has its merits."

Forty-three percent of the women responding to our questionnaire at Advent had graduate degrees. Among our four parishes, women at Advent had the largest number of advanced degrees. Yet the basic maintenance tasks some of these highly educated women contribute reflect an almost Benedictine spirit, a hallowing of the menial and unglamorous by spiritual consciousness. One business executive chooses laundering the altar linens as her "ministry." She loves its contrast with her occupational world: "Ironing is so peaceful, and it makes no noise; besides, you can *see* what you've accomplished, and it's done privately. It's your own form of devotion."

Adult education takes place on Sundays between or after the early and later services. Getting anyone to volunteer for any time other than that connected with Sunday morning worship is difficult. Younger members rarely contribute to ongoing congregational maintenance, though many rally to special-event volunteering, such as the bazaar.

Advent South had the largest nucleus of Christian feminists among our four congregations. Most are in their 30s but a few are found in both the bridge and older generations. Peggy, the young executive, rephrased the question about how she is able to reconcile her feminist worldview with a patriarchal religion. "For me, the issue is how I relate to a patriarchal *church!* I'm not convinced our religion is so patriarchal, but the church really is. One of my feminist friends sees it — the church — as exercising almost a kind of violence against women, and so do I; women take a kind of psychic battering from the institution." Then she added, "At this point, I feel I'm almost more a Christian by birth than by conviction."

Feminism is spiritual as well as an intellectual and occupational issue for Peggy. She is very critical of the individualist or career-oriented feminists who dominate the contemporary women's movement. "That kind of feminism has probably hurt more women in this country than it's helped," Peggy observed. "In my corporation alone, I saw an enormous increase of . . . abandoned women — women left to raise their families alone. I knew these women worked in low-paying clerical jobs because they had no alternative. They certainly weren't there because they were 'looking for fulfillment,'" she said ironically. "It was the only way they could survive! And, at least in my experience, at my corporation, there was *no support* coming to them from the professional women. There weren't any corporate officers, women or men, agitating for daycare in the workplace! My company has built five new corporate-headquarters buildings in the past five years, and not one of them has any facilities for child care or daycare. Even the union is so male-oriented it doesn't fight for child care!"

Speaking about feminist advances in church and theology, Peggy said, "I don't think the church has really changed all that much. So there's a woman standing up there in front instead of a man! That's the only real change I can see. Churches aren't changing their stained glass windows, or any other images; the language hasn't changed, the structure of the worship hasn't changed." What is her response to the image of a male savior? "I have no problem seeing Jesus as a male, but then I don't equate the man Jesus with the Christ. If God the Creator is not male, then God the Christ is not limited to maleness either. But if God is going to *have* human manifestation, then Jesus has to be either male or female. And in that day and time, they had to make the Christ a male. They had to give Him the real power that only a male could have, so that we could see Him trying to revolutionize that power."

Peggy and a few women from Advent and other churches formed a feminist study and support group. "From what feminist theology I've read, I see that Jesus really aimed at breaking through the patriarchalism of Judaism. He came to break it down, open it up. I don't think Christianity *has* to be patriarchal, even if it got patriarchal really fast after His death." She concluded, almost sadly, "I try to think what the Christ was about; I try to separate what religion was intended to be from what the church has structured it to be. If I couldn't do that, I really wouldn't be here. If I thought our religion was *only* about what the church is about, then I couldn't be here."

Peggy cited her frustration about the historic male blinders of both clergy leadership and church tradition. As one of the organizers of the diocesan women's conference to be hosted at Advent, she was part of the committee that wanted a discussion session "for women only." That part of the plan, of course, "goes against everything an inclusive church is about," she said, quoting the opposition. "All this makes me face my own limitations in terms of any power to change the institution. Until it's worth it to *men* to change, to come together and acknowledge the feminine side of themselves, no real change is possible." Then, more forcefully, she said, "*They've* got to come to it, work towards it, psychologically understand and accept it, because it's important for them — so they can be like and with women. They can't just have all the change come from women. It's important for the future of the planet! And we can't do it for them."

Any overtly feminist organization, like Peggy's support group, is still found outside the congregation. But the issues in the debate (a women-only session at a diocese-wide conference) directly link the congregational metaphor of inclusiveness with feminism and with Advent's public image, according to a male spokesperson. "If anything, this congregation is hung up on participatory democracy. Everyone wants to be part of *every* decision. A single individual's opinion counts too much. Frankly, it's inefficient. And those groups that once wielded power traditionally can't see how to give it up or share it."

The only overt antifeminism we heard came from a woman in her late 70s, widow of a civil rights activist. She was dismayed with the sense of power shifting to women and accused them of "threatening the sense of order." She has always considered herself in the vanguard of change in the South. But having a woman as bishop was simply going too far! "Some women are trying to push themselves to the top, just to prove they can," she expostulated, "without thinking about the good of the church. They don't care that it is being torn, injured, damaged!" An older man voiced another version of fear about women in positions of authority: "People used to go to seminary because they loved God. Now they go because they want power." However oversimple, his view expresses the deep misogyny stereotypically associated with Southern gender stereotypes.

The rector's spiritual self-understanding is key to the interesting blend of worship and social action at Advent. For example, he questioned whether or not to continue daily Eucharist (masses in some congregations). For the present, he keeps the schedule because Advent is the only non-Roman church in the area that has it (though attendance is minimal, often five or less). A rigid Anglo-Catholic would not consider dropping it. The most positive function of a daily service, the rector pointed out, is that it provides a congregational occasion at which to pray for the entire membership of the parish, so many names per day. Praying audibly, in the context of Eucharist, for its own members, is a rare public ritual in most contemporary congregations.

A veteran civil rights activist, the rector has no patience with "the kind [of Anglo-Catholic clergy] that enjoy wearing skirts and lacy vestments, and have lots of problems with women." He nominated sexuality or gender, however, as *the* issue confronting Advent during the period of our visits. "This congregation can now cope better with racial things than with sexual," he said. How about homosexuality? Public programs about AIDS have certainly "loosened up" the topic of homosexuality, thoroughly taboo until the mid-1970s. Of course, "there always has been the Southern pattern of gay young men who squire the old Southern ladies around." The carefully preserved ethos of Advent could be deeply ruffled, challenged by the idea of a women-only meeting, he thinks. "The vast preponderance of this congregation would say that since the ideal of inclusion at Advent South has been such a struggle, let's not let *anything* break it down."

The kind of inclusion promoted at Advent encompasses race, class, and homosexuality. Nothing about gender had been confrontational to this point. One vestry member "offered a resolution at vestry meeting," he reported. It would "equip me as rector to not *allow* any exclusionary meeting. But a lawyer on the vestry, African-American, said, 'Well, you can propose something like that, but I'll vote against it.'" From their experience in civil rights, both rector and lawyer understood the motive behind a women-only meeting: "Time for the oppressed group to catch up and pull themselves together," the rector said, "without any white male oppressors present." Instead of deciding this issue arbitrarily, he is promoting active debate, "because I want the widest possible address on the topic." But he worries that talking out this or any in-parish conflict could threaten the precious self-image of unity within diversity. His political and religious commitment is always "against *anything* that excludes." Experiencing vilification and persecution during the 1960s and '70s — as a white clergyman actively working for desegregation — had only strengthened his conviction. "I vowed I wouldn't let *that* drive me from my church. Yes, the Church is corrupt. But it's also the mystical body of Christ. And if they think I'm going to leave *that*, 'they've got another think coming.'"

The rector's own first exposure to feminism had come through the civil rights movement. "I'm aware of my own resistance and anger at these women today," he reflected. "I suffered for them when they were still in diapers, and now they come along and tell me...this, that, and the other!" He sighed. "But I sense, well...it's *their* definition, their right to 'name' their own issues. Where I am is...I'm having to learn to 'pronounce it,' whatever the 'it' is, their way." Then he added, "Like I had to learn how to say the word 'Nee-gro' instead of the word I used as a child, 'Nigra.' I was raised to think of *that* as the polite word for race. Now it's an insult."

Paul, a child psychologist who was head of the Christian Education Commission, said Advent's diversity "hooked" him from his first visit. He was inspired "to see mentally retarded people so well accepted in the congregation, to realize that there was no apparent stigma about the poor or the street-people in their disheveled dress." He approved. "This congregation is far more socially conscious than anything I experienced in the Roman Catholic Church where I grew up." And he appreciated the far greater doctrinal freedom. Although Episcopal theology at first seemed to him "too rational and intellectual," Paul grew to love its particular reverential spirituality. "Besides, Episcopalians are now discovering and using the mystics a lot more, something Roman Catholics have always been more appreciative of." As a congregation Advent could sometimes be "a little dogmatic," he thought, "always consulting the rubrics." But Paul interpreted such constant "referring to the rules" as "not using them to circumscribe but to see how they can be loosened up. This congregation seems to view 'Law' as permission to expand, not to constrict."

In his role as educator of the very young, Paul favors "arts and crafts theology. We take scripture, what they hear of the Word, and do an activity related to their lives — infuse it with prayer and God's presence." As a "feminist male," Paul chooses to do "more 'God stuff' with little children than 'Jesus stuff.' Jesus is a potentially limiting concept for children, I think, since most people move imagistically from Jesus to God. Part of my attempt is to avoid stereotyping their images of religion as masculine, especially because the language we use about them is male. I see it as easier to turn Jesus into God than to turn God into a woman. My concern is to avoid the logic that goes: 'Jesus is a person, Jesus is Son of God, Jesus is God, God therefore is a man."

Paul supports Christian education that "opposes the zap theory" in favor of "long, slow nurture and experience."[3] He also promotes the idea that everyone has a "ministry," not just those who are ordained. He wants children to understand that "the holy Spirit is as concerned with someone who's a dentist or a waiter as a priest." "We bring the kids in [to the 10:30 service] for part of the actual service, so they'll know they're part of the Christian community." But "the tenor of our service is solemn and...that makes it hard for 'kids to be kids' in it. Our worship has this kind of subdued tone. So one little girl wondered aloud, 'Is God sad?' " Advent as a congregation "is definitely interested in education, because of its own educational level and sophistication. But the actual *practice* of nurture doesn't come as easily." Our culture devalues nurture, which is the most important aspect of religious education, Paul concluded, "because the whole structure of higher education in the U.S. makes it hard to encourage people's souls the way we do their heads."

Did any of these background conversations help explain the relative openness about the inner life and spirituality at Advent? A parish sprinkled with yeasty, well-informed laity is undoubtedly contributory. The link between women's personal spiritual commitment and Advent's deep involvement in social outreach seems even more so, in the end. The work of "spiritual homemaking," in practical tasks such as healing, feeding, welcoming, and comforting, gives women (and men) at Advent an expression of discipleship — a way to view church membership as a genuinely connective, creative act for their souls.[4]

The Older Generation

The older-generation voices are those of Cassie, a member of the Monday morning subgroup, reflecting on her inner life obliquely and by indirection; Abigail, a divorced professional artist and modern-day "mystic"; and Adele, a retired secretary and enthusiast about "all the changes going on for women," in and out of the church.

Cassie, a spare, white-haired, fragile-looking widow over 80, described her Southern family as very large and "humble." She'd been drawn to Advent long ago "by the women's circles and bazaars. Because those were things I could do to help, financially." In those earlier times, "I seemed to know so many people." Sighing, she explained: "Well, we knew each other's problems, and we were close from working together. Today, I can see, as I walk into this place, I can see (in my mind, you know)...people I have been close to here, walking." She is surrounded by her own "communion of saints": "They're here, you know. You're never alone." The group that gathers for the Monday morning Eucharist and healing service is her spiritual community. "Oh, sometimes we are fortunate enough, when one of the younger women gets time off from work and joins us for a while, you know. But mostly it's the older group." That predictable weekly gathering gives the group a means of solidarity. It takes on added significance in their eyes because it receives the full attention of the clergy. "We have communion together, we lunch together with them, then we talk, and we help fold the Sunday bulletins," Cassie recounted. "And the rector, if he has something special in mind he wants us to do, that's when he'll talk about it with us."

"When women began to work harder in the church, [to be more visible in formerly male-only roles], an earlier rector thought we'd no longer need any separate group [the ECW]. Women would now be on the vestry and all. Women would meet *with* the men. That is, we'd all meet together *as a church*," Cassie emphasized. "That's how we got away from having the different circles for women that I loved." She hesitated, not wanting to sound critical. "Well, we older ones still need a daytime women's group," even if "the young women working can't fit anything in, unless it's in the evening." That time constraint automatically raises barriers that exclude her. "I can't see to drive at night." But she shines a cheerful light on the whole problem. "There's nothing like activity with people your own age, all getting in there and doing something together! I think it's wonderful." The annual bazaar is the big excitement for Cassie, symbolically and actually. "The Monday morning group is usually lucky enough to find some woman who's interested in that type of work, who will head up our efforts. Handmade things, that's what sells. You can make money on them because you can ask a really good price!"

One change Cassie loved was the woman priest who had been at Advent until recently, "a wonderful woman. She was a better preacher than most of the other ministers. She was a person you could be proud of, in her position." Other changes are harder, like "getting the meaning of all the things that happen [changes in the worship service]. Those are explained at the various seminars, and so on, that we can't attend," because they were often evening meetings. "Oh, we get a copy of what they study, but we don't get to attend the classes on what has *brought about* the changes that are going on." This prevents genuine understanding. "You can't picture a change in its fullness unless you have a pretty good knowledge of it; you just don't accept it wholeheartedly." Cassie corrected herself: "I mean, you accept it and go along with it because it's what the bishop wants you to do, and after all,... he is our boss, in the ways we run our church." Honoring Episcopal authority justifies both the incomprehensibility of liturgical change and any personal discomfort.

"This parish reaches into your heart," Cassie warmed to her description. "I know it becomes a more important part of my life every year, because... your lifestyle changes so, as you age, so it [Advent] becomes quite a necessary part." She focused on the congregation's handling of funerals. "In times of death, the rector... takes part in the family's troubles, helping to solve them. He even goes right to the funeral home with you, and fights over the prices, that sort of thing. He also started this thing where, the night before the funeral, we have a parish open-house, and people have all their friends come here. They don't want to... they don't really like that cold atmosphere down at the funeral home." She beamed with thanksgiving. "What we do is, we bring the casket here to the church overnight, before the funeral. It's remarkable how much that helps folks, you know. People won't go down to the funeral home to pay their respects, but they will come here. They know everyone is going to be here... all of the family... real nice and close. The grieving is shared. The crying is softer... you don't want to be sobbing or anything, when you're in the church. Our help to the family is the night before the burial, not after, at a wake." Without using any standard vocabulary, and mostly by implication, Cassie numbered the rituals of consolation that would attend her life's end.

A retired secretary, Adele, just celebrating her seventy-fifth birthday, supports most changes in the church, especially those concerning women, with great vigor and enthusiasm. In spite of being badly crippled with arthritis and asthma, she praises the life she has found in this congregation. Raised in the Christian Church in Tennessee — "Yes, I was baptized by immersion," she announced — her childhood ambition had been to be trained for a career as director of religious education, the first professional job in the church opened to laywomen. The Depression wiped out that possibility. Following the pattern of a strong mother, who "went to work for the WPA and pulled the family through," Adele worked for the government and married a disabled World War II veteran. When he abandoned her and their two small children, she fell into a major spiritual and psychological crisis but, like her mother, she "kept going" because she had to.

The Episcopal church was a late-life discovery for her, Adele said. She has joined both the Monday morning group and the Daughters of the King prayer group. "But I guess I'd always been looking for it. Because the Eucharist is in its rightful place. I'm able to take communion every Sunday and midweek days too, when I'm able to get here. I felt I was coming home. And I felt the need for a physical attitude of prayer, like kneeling. There was just something about the teachings, the Prayer Book, the Hymnal." She loves the corporateness of a congregation, "the people here all bowing, and kneeling, and standing together. Also I had a sense of being very much needed, here. And they didn't seem to mind that I was divorced."

Adele follows a regime of personal nurture that includes "*Forward Day by Day* [an Episcopal daily devotional guide], church, sermons, Bible discussions. I find the daily readings something needful to me — as needful as eating or resting." Although in the past her prayers were mostly "lots of supplications," she has come to realize that previously she had had no "deep spiritual view of what that all meant. When I would read the words, 'The kingdom of God is within you,' they didn't have any particular meaning to me. I'd never heard of Jung, or philosophers, or theology." Her eyes misted. "All I could do, before, most of my life, was just hang on for dear life, and try to get as much spiritual strength as I could — because that was what kept me from falling apart. I couldn't afford to fall apart. Too much depended on me." Her remembered loneliness still hurts. "Because...well, I think I felt I had to do it *all* myself. You know, I was raised on 'God helps those who help themselves.' I don't think I ever understood the meaning of...just...real peace, and trust. I always felt that, literally, that, you know...unless I did my part, I couldn't even hope to ask for 'the other part.'" Real tears flowed. "But I've become...after all my experiences, and in these last years, as I grow older...I'm beginning to get a little different view of the Kingdom of God, maybe...What it means to have the Kingdom of God *within* you. To seek peace, and forgiveness and...well..." she shrugged. "To seek the Kingdom of God is just all encompassing." Then, apologetically, she added a generational note. "I guess it goes with age and preparing for another life. Maybe that's part of it." Nothing about her health is improving. But she brightened: "And I do believe in the place of women in the church, [their participation] in all forms of religious life — from doing the dishes in the kitchen, which some might feel could be the highest calling, to being bishop. Yes! all the way through, all the way through!"

Adele even apologized for using the pronoun "Him" in reference to God, but "that's the way I was raised for the first seventy-odd years; I always felt a 'him' relationship with God more than a 'her' relationship. Now I think to myself, 'What difference does it make? that's just a pronoun.' I think of God as being a Spirit and not defined by having a sex, one way or the other." Then she continued her positive review of change: "And I want to say that the new Prayer Book is an improvement! I like the different choices of wording, the different rites....The church, more and more, will just have to move in the direction of offering a wide variety of worship, and lots more opportunities for reaching out." With gratification, she concluded, "I've seen more outreach in the past several years, here in this church, than ever before in any church, anywhere....More outreach to the needy, the downtrodden, than ever before, anywhere, anytime." As if her poor body could hardly contain its vaulting spirit, Adele said, "I'm impatient for the church to get on with its work. I'm like a mother saying, 'We don't have time to fool around, let's get on with this.' I really want to see this church moving forward; I really want us to get a load of steam up and get going, you know. I want to rush ahead *now*." She paused, then added more reflectively: "That's the way I feel in my mind and in my heart, but of course my body would never stand for it. I have to be patient, forbearing, forgiving...take things a little slower. The body wouldn't stand the speed...But I really want to rush ahead."

Abigail, the youngest (62) of the older generation, has handsome curly gray hair and wears striking jewelry of her own design. She is completely at home in the late twentieth-century language blending psychology and spirituality. Highly educated, a professional artist, and long-term participant in a religiously sponsored (extra-parish) women's study group on the writings of Karl Jung, she enjoyed naming her first awareness of God. As a child of five or so, she had been playing in the flowers and tall grass in a field behind her parents' house. She remembers "being flooded with a sensation of just pure joy," an "identity with a higher being and a grand feeling of One-ness with the universe that of course I couldn't begin to articulate, then. Still, even now, the image is so vivid that I can almost paint the scene."

As a girl Abigail found a way to be in God's presence in the devotional labors of the Junior Altar Guild. "I learned early there was something very endearing and mystical about caring for the Lord's vessels, polishing the Cup and the Plate ... the nurturing, the caring, the very special attention the Altar Guild gives to one of the main functions of the Church. Women do it in such a quiet, unseen way ... it's almost invisible." Though in the past few years she is no longer in the Altar Guild, its rituals learned so early still move her, and from time to time she joins in again. "I love to come and sit in with the women who are preparing the church for Easter. I just love to spend a morning, four hours or so, polishing and burnishing the silver and the brass. I think it's because it's symbolic. . . . I like to think that what we're doing is making the setting new — everything new for rebirth from the grave, the resurrection. We're taking off the tarnish, removing the oxidation, preparing for a brand new life." Seasonal rituals speak of the "rise and fall of the church year" to Abigail. She is nourished, esthetically and spiritually, by "the darkness of Lent, then the brilliance of Easter; or the deep, almost somnolent preparation of Advent followed by the glowing joy of Christmas. It's something repeated year by year, something we're part of that is larger than us, something holy. . . . It regulates us spiritually, inwardly."

Abigail's perception of the Holy is linked with an early Sunday school teacher, "though until this minute, I hadn't thought of her for thirty years." She mused, "Her inspiration created that wonderful curiosity in me, you know ... to think about God, and search, and go deeper. Amazing. It really was her." All through her life, Abigail has been "drawn back again and again into the inner life of the church by something deep within the ritual, the liturgy. Also by that sense of legacy and heritage shared worldwide with thousands of people." Then the artist in her spoke: "It's a *beauty* that pulls me by the heartstrings."

Abigail was married for twenty-five years to an alcoholic "who turned out to have a Jekyll-Hyde personality. After the fourth drink, he became violent. I did all the classic enabling things when I saw it coming on, like trying to shoo the kids away, trying to protect him." She endured the terrible helplessness of those who live with an addict. "There were times when talking with him was like trying to reach someone who was in another time zone. It's almost like trying to confer with someone from another culture — we weren't connecting; we were just passing each other."

In the small town where she had then lived, the church was her major support: "You couldn't sneeze but what someone baked a pound cake and sent it over for your supper! I loved it. Of course I was active in every part of it — the Sunday school, the Altar Guild.... It was my bulwark, my stability." A particular memory that drew tears to her eyes was women from the church who ministered to her psychic desolation after a miscarriage. When she came home from the hospital, they "really took care of me, and the children. They cooked, they cleaned, they never asked what to do, they just moved in. Angels, they were. If women can be angels, these were." She wept. "One of them, named Ceil, came into the bedroom and shut the door, and just took me and held me on her lap, in the rocking chair. She said to me: 'Now cry. You never cried once in the hospital. Instead you comforted everyone who came to see you and they ended up crying on *your* shoulder! I don't give a damn how long or how loud you cry, just cry.' And I was finally able to let go — I just bawled and bawled, until I was healed."

During her postdivorce recovery, she learned slowly how to care for her soul, with help from Al-Anon, omnivorous reading, and keeping a journal — something she still does. The journal is both cautionary and an escape valve. "I can look back and see if I had the same problem four months ago, and say to myself, 'Hey! I'm not changing, let's do something about this.'" How did it function as an escape-valve? "What's coming out on the page is real shadow-stuff, pretty horrible. I've told my kids that I don't want them to read it. If anything happens to me I want it destroyed. It's between me and my Maker only! It's totally revealing, because I'm not writing for anything but my soul's solace."

At a Jungian weekend retreat, she came to understand dreams as "God's unique way of speaking to us," and found that she could learn a great deal about her inner self through her own "significant dreams." One of those, a recurring dream, was of "a reconciliation with my mother." It represents work that "you've still got to do, because it's undone. So the dream is the reminder." In that dream, the dialogue is always an asking that brings absolution. To the mother with whom she has a severe breach, she says, "'I forgive you, will you forgive me?' and Mother always says, in that maddening, bland way, 'Well, what on earth for?' " But through it came a kind of benediction. "There is always this deep feeling of peace, and true . . . affection as it ends." Once again the artist used esthetic description. "It all comes together beautifully."

"Yes, I actually heard the voice of God speaking to me, right within the walls of my car. I was driving. I was middle-aged and divorced, it was financially very scary. I had gone to, maybe, twenty-three job interviews, and hadn't got a single offer. It was a bad time in the economy. My age was against me. And then that Voice said, clear as anything, 'You can teach your own art lessons, design your own classes.' " Following that leading, she established a successful "art school." Abigail worried, for a time, that "something terrible would come along and blow it sky high. But at the same time, something in me thrives at living on the edge." Her classes make her comfortably self-sufficient though not rich. Her middle-aged children bring her both joy and sorrow — great companionship with her daughters, differences of temperament and values straining the relations with her sons.

Although without anything like "security for my old age," Abigail expresses confidence. She enjoys a "sense of my place in the scheme of things. The older I grow, the more I believe that there is absolutely no waste in this wonderful plan of God's. He goes on and on — it's not just a theory. I've come to think there really is some kind of reincarnation. I experience moments of wisdom, not just of enlightenment. A light that pours on me from above . . . well, they seem to come from . . . another self. It certainly doesn't come through any experiences I've had in this particular lifetime. But I seem to have tapped into this 'wellspring.' " She paused. "The scriptural phrase that comes to mind is 'seeing through a glass darkly' at this stage of life but at another, perhaps, 'face to face.' It's an awareness of things as yet unseen that may or may not be revealed to us in this short span. . . . Glimpses of something else, of connection with the Host on high. Or with another . . . personality." These last phrases suggest experience of the ineffable, traces of the mysticism in her inner life.

The pre-funeral "feast" would be a homecoming banquet for Cassie, literally and spiritually. Adele's vision for her congregation, and the new possibilities for women she will not live to see fully realized, transport her beyond the limits of her physical existence. Abigail nourishes her soul with beauty and expanding spiritual awareness.

The Bridge Generation

The societal earthquake of the civil rights movement, for white Christians, was central to the bridge-generation women. Everything they'd been taught about ethics and justice was changed when they confronted the horrifying truths of racial segregation. Issues of moral choice and commitment were important factors in spiritual and congregational identity for each of them, though only two cited here were born and raised in the South. Marie, a teacher and activist who is reshaping her former-Southern cultural boundaries, and Harper, a professional musician who has found in Anglicanism both racial inclusiveness and an esthetic and spiritual home, are the two "native-born" voices. Geraldine, a musician turned computer designer, says that her inner life feels "religiously grounded for the first time" through caring for Advent's mentally limited adults; Catherine, a lawyer, balances a deep need for inner solitude with family responsibilities and career, plus the division separating Roman Catholics and Episcopalians; Connie has retired from nursing to "a career of prayer" and is expanding her spiritual horizons through charismatic worship.

One of the youngest, Geraldine, 42, told a story of religion lost and found. "Raised Methodist," she "dropped" religion during college and "basically stayed away from the church for twenty years." After marrying an Episcopalian and joining the choir to be with him, Geraldine learned as a young bride about "sitting, and kneeling, all those gestures. People would just sort of nudge me into the right position, you know: now up, now down." By the time they moved to this Southern city a few years ago, she was ready to look actively for a church home once again. "My twenty years of rejecting the church wasn't twenty years away from religion! But gradually, there was a time of returning to a church-focused interest. I couldn't have done it ten years earlier, I think. And here I finally found a place for belonging, a church that somehow fit within my own personal framework."

Religion and the institutional church "came unstuck" for her at college. "I had more and more doubts. Like the line in the Apostles Creed: 'I believe in eternal life.' I'd have to ask myself, 'Well, do I?' My mother's death, when I was three...People deluded me by saying she was away on a long trip. And when she didn't come back...Well, what is an eternal life? I just had to keep thinking everything out before I could be comfortable in a traditional religious structure. I guess I still kept on believing in a God — but not all the other things. I would still pray to a God — even if it took me a long time to work myself back into practicing religion. I don't think I ever quit praying." Her generation reeled under various aspects of theological controversy. "I was in college when the 'God Is Dead' issue of *Time* magazine came out, for example. I really tried to understand what that was about, but I couldn't handle it; for me, there had to be a God. On the other hand, there was all this doubt — just where was I?"

What Geraldine called her antireligion stance was really antiinstitutionalism. "Around ten years ago, I began a lot of Bible reading and stuff, even though I wasn't involved in any church at the time." Then, she recalled, "I suppose one reason I began exploring the Bible is that I had a job, for a short time, as a church secretary. And there I stumbled on the *Good News Bible* [a modern-language translation]. I discovered it was written in language that I could understand, even at that low point in my spiritual life." A deeply private well of faith had sustained her somehow during the nonchurch years: "I have been always able to reach out, in times of crisis, for help and to receive it. That's one reason why I began to study, because obviously there was something drawing me. I wanted to know more about what it was that I was reaching out to, and finding."

Geraldine and her husband settled on Advent a few years ago, "after we'd visited about twenty Episcopal churches. I just had a gut reaction here; the service was unlike anything I'd ever seen. It was far out of my experience, yet I felt comfortable. I didn't fully understand why they did some of the rituals but it didn't offend me. And I liked the fact that there was a diversity of people, in races and abilities and ages. We'd been looking for a congregation this varied. And we liked the social outreach type of church this is. We were really impressed by that."

The past two years she has taught a Sunday school class for the adult parishioners with developmental disabilities, "grown up children who — though by now they're over 60 — are likely to still think of themselves as the age when they were first institutionalized, say, 24." The "instruction" she devised combines a story — a single point for them to remember — each Sunday, with an activity to occupy their hands, for example, tracing a symbol such as the cross or a palm frond while she talks. The beauty of AngloCatholic worship, to Geraldine, is that it can reach below the

rational level and touch those in a mentally handicapping condition; they can experience at least a visceral wonder and welcome.
In their innocence they sometimes wander up the steps into the
chancel at a "wrong" time — in the midst of the Eucharist or
during prayers — but everyone is careful not to make them feel
awkward or unwelcome. Geraldine's advocacy for these members
at Advent was her first real participation in the historical stream of
Christian caregivers.

"I see the church as going on for hundreds of years, while the
tradition of certain jobs falling to the women and others to men —
that's going to change. The new ideal is men and women together
on tasks." About change itself, "I think the church, whether it
really wants to or not, will change as society changes. A church's
religion is the primary purpose, it's why we come in the first place.
But all the other activities — meeting people, providing stability in
the other parts of your lives — they're also important. I see the
single people here, and think they probably come for a combination of reasons — the feeling of community, being part of the
fabric, warming to a diverse congregation. If I needed help, even
just emotional support, this is where I would turn."

Geraldine was surprised at some of her fellow churchwomen's
intense response to an experimental inclusive language liturgy. "I
thought it was interesting, all right; the new words certainly expand your thinking about God. I wasn't 'pro' it or 'con' it. But
there was a group that met to discuss it, mostly women who had
grown up in the Episcopal Church. They had a lot of leftover resentment about being excluded from being acolytes or whatever —
about growing up female in a church that favored boys. They were
the ones who were adamantly in favor of it! They seemed to see it
as atoning for the church's slight against them in their childhood."
She thinks her youthful Methodism gets the credit for not making
her feel "there were things I couldn't do just because I was female. Some people were so ... so incensed about the new language
they walked out. Others kind of said, 'Well, this is interesting,
but it's not the end of the world ... soon we'll be trying something
else.'" Geraldine made an analogy with her Sunday School experience about receptiveness to change. "Something new opens up the
extremes — but then you do have to go through a period of adjustment. I try to do the same with my class: present a new idea, then
again, and in a new way, again, a third time. Gradually they begin
assimilate it."

Tradition can be positive, as well as inhibiting change, she said. "Of course people want to claim that 'it's always been done' a certain way. But once you see that a woman can be up there in front, preaching, and the walls are still standing, or that a woman can serve communion and God didn't strike the church down...then you can realize it's not so awfully terrible." Geraldine is surprisingly patient with those mourning the loss of familiar customs. "The people who grew up with a certain hymnal...they're still complaining about a new one, how many years later? They're the ones I feel sorry for. The new way of doing things in the service may not be wrong, it just hasn't become comfortable yet. And it's going to take time to change. For someone who's done it a certain way seventy years, that's got to be hard. I have a lot of empathy for people in that situation."

A 44-year-old member of the bridge generation, Catherine, a lawyer, was born Methodist but attended an Episcopal high school and never looked back. "I loved the majesty of the cathedral that was nearby, how just walking into it made you feel very special. I remember how I anticipated being able to take communion, and how the first time it was very much a special kind of experience ...a deepening, I think, of my religious life." She was a child who responded deeply to devotional ritual. "I remember setting up a little altar in the attic, where I could pray, and think about the Christmas story. The verse about Mary 'keeping all these things and pondering them in her heart'...was always so poignant to me. Of course now I think keeping things in your heart, and not doing something about them, is pretty passive! Now I'd say 'don't just sit there, *do* something.' But at that point in my life it was something very special to be like Mary, or to be Mary. Even now I can meditate on that image." She expressed deep sympathy for the first Episcopal woman elected bishop, because having been the first woman lawyer in her corporation she knows "the difficulties of being the First."

Catherine is a person who "always loved to spend time in sacred space." Even today she sneaks time out of a busy day to sit and meditate, in "the mystery of those large, dark Roman Catholic churches." Meditation is her surcease or therapy. "When I experienced a crisis in my job, the first place I went was church — to prayer and daily Communion. I needed it to be a regular part of my day, or at least several times a week — something to lean on like a staff, something to retreat into — a preserve." A more recent crisis happened "last year during Lent, actually in Holy Week. I found I had to have a growth on my thyroid removed. The biopsy came back malignant, on Good Friday. I really had a feeling of Christ on the Cross. I came right to the service and told people. Everyone here was praying for me, and weeping — I was weeping." Daily nourishment has come from "the Prayer Book, having words that I know and that can be repeated — almost a litany I can recite. All that's been real important to me. Actually essential, in these crises, essential!" Her present job in a corporate headquarters "is too far away for me to attend daily mass, and I really miss it. I notice the lack of it. I also miss having a time in the middle of the day where I can pull back.... I need a sense of being able to give up all these cares and responsibilities, put them in God's hands for a while, before taking them back up again."

Married to a Roman Catholic, Catherine and her husband have worked out an arrangement in which they alternate "Sunday by Sunday, at each church." Their two children take communion in both. "I want my kids to learn that God isn't in a box. It's not God that is caught in these artificial separations of Anglo and Roman Catholicism. They ought to be able to experience God in some way that's not carved up! But of course it's taken my husband and me a long time to get to this point." The alternate Sundays routine has meant that Catherine "misses out on the Protestant benefits of being part of the congregation! I'm not as close ... with the congregation as I'd like to be." She quickly qualified: "Not God, but the congregation itself. I just can't be as much a part of the church." Further, she meant: "Not the 'church universal,' but this particular church."

Catherine is a proponent of the new Prayer Book. "Now I really like this new one. It's got a lot of energy for me, even if the language sounds as if it was written by a committee." Her advocacy for it and change in general came up in the context of her bifurcated church attendance — a constant discussion with "others who share my religiously divided household situation. We all ask each other: what do you do about religion? Most of us seem to have settled on raising children in the Episcopal church as a way of preserving the best of Roman Catholic theology, just not all of it."

She is particularly grateful for the theological reinterpretation in the new Prayer Book that allows children who haven't been confirmed to receive communion. Now the practice of Eucharist "lets little children taste communion. My kids love it; I really believe we shouldn't send them away from the rail empty-handed, saying 'Wait till you grow up.' As if that had anything to do with God's grace! We should say, 'We're so glad you want to join in and partake,' as long as they know it's special. My kids know it's God — although their idea of God probably would surprise us."

Catherine appreciates the way women are part of everything at Advent South. "There's one Episcopal church here in the city that still has all-male ushers, though they don't come right out and announce, 'We use only men.' But they're the kind who, when there's a church supper? the women are all waitresses and the men are taking in the money, cashiers." Her only criticism of Advent is that it "doesn't accommodate women who have to juggle demanding careers and families, quite enough." That's understandable, she thinks, because "we're not very organized or demanding, and there aren't all that many of us."

She is conscious of generations in the congregation. "The older women who've lived in the neighborhood for years, who've sort of grown up in this church, are now widowed or by themselves. Then there are the people from the university who are here for limited times, and then younger people, lots of young families beginning now to come. The sense I get is that this parish is still trying to find its way, be open to experimenting. I also think there just aren't enough people to do everything." She views her own limited volunteering as an asymmetrical covenant: she isn't giving as much to Advent as it gives her. "Unfortunately, women in my position are more demanding of the institution's resources than we contribute." However, her true benefit from Advent isn't anything "social" or programmatic. "For me, the support I want and need isn't what one gets from individual people. My 'support group' is elsewhere," she said, pointing upward.

In a long reflection about denominational identity, Catherine articulated her appreciation of Advent's spiritual openness and inclusiveness. "I think of it as a refugee kind of church. Lots of people come into this denomination from the outside, for various reasons," probably because their "other church is just not working for them." She chose her words carefully. "I'm not sure, though, that people outside the Episcopal Church have the understanding that insiders can, of... really why people come here from somewhere else, why they choose it. It's not a subject we discuss very much. If you talk to Methodists or Baptists about why people who are not born Episcopal become Episcopalians, they will probably say, 'Oh, for social reasons!' meaning elite society. But I don't find that true, or adequate." She thought a moment. "I find the opposite. It's people who, for one reason or another, are not able to stay in their own church. They're the ones, we're all ones who find refuge in the Episcopal Church. Because it *is* inclusive, it accepts them and us where our original church did not." The inclusiveness at Advent means "trying not to *ex*clude but to *in*clude people — even the rag-tag, confused ones who don't quite measure up mentally or in some other way." Then an afterthought. "And of course I love the richness of the liturgy, the music, the spiritual depth of feeling I've always experienced in an Episcopal building... that God is there for everyone. You don't have to believe any doctrines or a certain set of prescribed truths in order to experience that."

A bridge-generation teacher originally from a small Southern town, Marie, now in her early 50s, dreams of "retiring from teaching so I could go live, and immerse myself in other cultures, especially the black [West Indian and Caribbean] islands" as "more than just a tourist." Life in "a totally foreign" culture restores her, challenges and upsets her, and is her continual inspiration. "I'm never again the same after that kind of an experience," Marie mused. "I'm not religious, in the traditional sense," yet there are "certain things I would like to change in the way we live and think." Marie's spiritual identity is centered in a deep call to participate in issues of social justice. "My experience in other cultures constantly makes me ask: are we *really* richer, better off, than they are?" Teaching in a private school for nearly twenty years makes her aware of those who are "truly deprived," she said ironically, "the children of the affluent." In that culture, "the coming-of-age ritual is getting your own car! But meanwhile, they learn no skills for dealing with anything else in their lives. These young people grow up in families with no real, lively conversation about anything. Our country is in very bad shape as far as that's concerned." Marie's own children reported back, "when they went away to college," that "they didn't know how atypical our family was. They found out that no one else's family sat down together at mealtime," no one else seemed to have real conversation with their parents.

"I guess I was born a feminist," Marie said. "I never wanted the traditional life, I always wanted to discover, explore, learn. I broke with all the patterns in my small-town childhood — though I still honor my elders. I believe in keeping generations together, little children and old people in the same house." Her husband's father, 94, lives in their household. But being open to the new is almost an innate condition for her now — an article of faith. "I want to take risks, reasonable risks. We can't live our life wrapped in cellophane. Of course that doesn't mean that every time you try something new, it's going to work out 100 percent. But if that happens it doesn't mean I've botched my life; it just means I need to regroup, go in another direction."

Because of her intellectual energy, Marie feels "very young in lots of ways. I have a great deal of excitement about life, for which I'm grateful. I think...not so many people my age feel that way....I think it's from God." Her independence from the church is itself an expression of her quest for the "new." "I have a hard time praying to God in church, in the language of traditional prayers. But I'm totally aware of God in my life, as Love, as a force of love and energy, and as work and harmony." Her inner life has made her optimistic. The words with which she expressed this profound hopefulness imitate the starkly simple affirmation of Julian of Norwich, the fourteenth-century English saint newly popular among late twentieth-century women. "I just have this feeling that things will work out...that everything is all right...that everything will be all right."[5]

Advent, she believes, is a "kind of a beacon helping to promote harmony among peoples, races, gays; this church is no fashion show. It has much more social commitment than most. From that point of view, I love it," Marie reflected, "I who was called a 'nigger lover' as a kid because I dared to take seriously the Methodist Sunday school teaching that we were all God's children." Being the "token woman on an all-male faculty" has reinforced her empathy with the victims of bigotry and inequality. But she dropped regular church attendance "because the rituals that seemed so meaningful to everyone else were not being that meaningful to me."

However, "the outreach program here is great," Marie said. "I feel very strongly about the spirituality in my life; it's just not located in the building of the church, you know. I feel very thankful for my life, the number of people that I know, the huge number of letters I get from all over the world. To maintain all those contacts, to celebrate life with all those people is just beautiful. Makes me wish I could live a long time and do a lot more!" Marie is a member of the National Organization for Women but it, too, is "kind of like church" — an abstract identity for which she is grateful but nothing in which she needs to participate directly. "I feel that I 'do my thing' in my day-to-day life, and that makes a bigger impact than going to meetings. And another reason I don't go to church, or to NOW: It creates fragments: 'a little of church here, a little of something else there,' you know. I don't feel like chopping life up into little pieces like that. Church is only one little piece of the puzzle — over to one side, for most people. Life is glorious as it is, altogether."

A further criticism of the institution is one of principle. "I hate to see the church in thrall to material possessions, to this vestment or that icon, so they have to lock up the building to protect inanimate *things*. Mother Teresa's vision of church is where it's at for me (or where it should be): Calcutta is everywhere." The writer Elie Wiesel is another inspiration and model: "What one individual can do for good or ill is huge. Of course I think the church can also do a lot of good or ill — as individual members and as a group. But rituals here are very hyper-important for some in this church. I know rituals in life, like birthdays, are important so I wouldn't try to do away with them entirely. But simplification is my thing.

"What I most cherish about my religious belief and experience, and would want to see passed on to the next generation," Marie thinks, "is not 'the church' in this little place over here or over there, but the grand principles symbolized by the church functioning in everybody's life, just in a global sense — the way I try to live my life, now. I don't believe there's anything special about being in this building on Sundays. Church, if you live your life in the deep consciousness of things all connected with each other, is with you all the time." She makes the word "church" a euphemism for overarching spiritual vision: "I'm not a born-again-Christian sort of person, but I do wake up in the morning with a certain sense of direction — like 'this is how I need to do something today.' Or 'tomorrow I'll need to go talk to this person about that.' Or, 'I need to put into words whatever it is I haven't yet expressed.' To feel that kind of presence is a gift. I feel very lucky in that way."

A former nurse with a glowing face, Connie, who had only recently turned 50, opened the conversation by announcing good-humoredly, "I was a Sunbeam!" the name of her Sunday school class in the Baptist church. She had responded eagerly to everything religious: she loved church camp, she loved memory work from the Bible. She loved religious images that were spirit-filled, for example, the "ocean . . . its vastness and creative force, an ever-changing part of nature . . . no restrictions, no feeling trapped." The hymn sung when she was baptized by immersion was "There Is a Fountain Filled with Blood." "I still play hymns on the piano and sing a lot. I listen to tapes a lot."

She became Episcopalian when she married into a family for which "churchmanship," observing a certain religious demeanor and pattern, was important. Connie discovered she loved "getting on my knees beside my husband — that type of reverence, just getting lost in the worship." Initially she had found the sacramental words "Take, eat, this is my Body" and "This is my Blood, drink ye all of this" jarring — "it took a lot of getting used to," in spite of her hymn about the fountain of blood. But beginning when she was 22, she responded to "the quiet and the peacefulness" of Episcopal worship though, or because, it was "such a different atmosphere" than she had known. She began the habit of lighting a candle and praying silently in an empty church, a habit that has served her well during many trials and decisions.

Connie's manner of speaking about God reveals the continuing directness of her Baptist childhood. She cited a time of desperation, when she and her husband were feeling hopeless because his job required a quick move and they had "looked at fourteen different houses" without success. When they found themselves sitting in their car, in a parking lot, with the weather as grim as their mood — it was "sleeting outside, and we held hands because we were both in tears. We didn't usually pray openly with each other — we don't even to this day. But right then and there we said the Lord's Prayer together and it lifted us up and over that hump."

A charismatic religious conference gave Connie a spiritual awakening. "People prayed with me and the gift of tongues came; I could feel I had the baptism of the Holy Spirit. I experienced something I've had with me always, since that day." She described glossolalia as "exalted, exhilarating. It wasn't loud, it wasn't long, just...I guess I would call it, now, a 'prayer voice.' I can get into it now, if I need it; I've noticed through the years that it always begins with the same sequence of sounds."

Another occasion of God's healing in her life occurred when their children were teenagers. The discovery that both of them had smoked marijuana, making Connie feel a total failure, precipitated the crisis. "It was just crushing to me. Something within me broke, and I did a terrible thing. I laid a heavy guilt trip on them. I said all sorts of things like: 'I don't even have a profession anymore, I've given my profession up to spend my life on you, and this is what you're doing with it? I've had it.' I went on strike. I stayed in bed. I wouldn't cook, or clean, or eat with them, nothing. It was just a complete crisis in the house. Our oldest son developed terrible hives. We had always enjoyed everything together, but all trust was destroyed." A family that had enjoyed the closest of bonds "since the kids were born" seemed utterly shattered.

On the fourth day of her paralysis, "while I was showering, I just began to pray in tongues, almost a screaming type of thing. You know, like where it says in the Bible that the Holy Spirit will pray *for* you when you don't know the words to utter. The tears and the mucous and the screaming — I came out of that shower drained clean physically, washed clean spiritually. I just threw myself across the bed, exhausted. The burden was lifted from me. I had forgiven them, and forgiven myself. Love was there." The recollection transfixed her. "Then I shared it with my husband, who had been struggling so hard in this terrible crisis, and it began to lift from him, too." She stopped to explain. "He prays, of course, just not out loud. He is less verbal about his love of the church or religion: I say about his type that he was 'born in the rectory,' and they're not demonstrative." Then, concluding her story of deliverance, Connie said, "This was a growing experience for all four of us. It's not that we were trying to be overprotective, or not to let them go and grow up. *I* was the crisis; I just didn't know how to deal with the shame of it, the disruption of my picture of our family unity. And I couldn't tolerate it. I'm still a little cautious talking about it."

Connie loves the visible inclusiveness of Advent South: "The Lord didn't come just to one socioeconomic group. This kind of a blending, I feel it is more truly the handwork of the Lord . . . it's sort of inside-out, or the outside coming in." When she sees a mentally retarded member "going right up into the sacristy" in all innocence, out of place and breaking the conventions of public demeanor, it makes an impact in her soul, a visitation. "Something that touches you in that way . . . just turns everything upside down." To nourish her spiritual hunger, she reads New Age materials, metaphysics, the "Unity Newsletter," and a Roman Catholic devotional booklet that is her daily routine. She has joined the Episcopal prayer order for women at Advent, Daughters of the King, and writes letters for Amnesty International, Common Cause Alert, and individuals on an Episcopal missionary list.

Personal growth is really more important to Connie than "a

structured denominational identity. Through my 'rehab' nursing, I've dealt with people who've had their life changed in a split second," she recalled. "There will always be things that happen, like a sudden stroke, when there is nothing material or physical you can do. Without spiritual uplift, or the capacity to seek it, you are bereft." Connie hopes to let her grandchildren see and know the very "miracle of their own being, a Creator who made you." She wants them to absorb the knowledge of "a divine order in the world, and that they are part of it." She wants them to enjoy something of the spiritual gift she is continually receiving: "I've had the opportunity to wonder. Many women don't, because they're too busy. I didn't, either, when I was commuting and working forty hours a week, and trying to study, and keep a house and family, and be a wife. If I were working now, I just couldn't be as joy-filled! I wouldn't have time."

Harper, a married musician in her mid-50s, began with the importance of Advent South in her life. "You'll hear many people say 'Advent *is* the real world,' and that's how I feel." She listed the dimensions of that image: "We run the gamut here, from middle-class, very family-oriented people, to a sprinkling of upper-echelon wealthy, to academics, to street people and those who can hardly get around because of mental or physical incapacities. People here do God's work; they don't just talk about it, they do it." Harper and her husband, both Southern-born, were active in the civil rights movement, and later became Episcopalian, in her case because of "esthetics." It was inevitable, she thought, since many of her professional music jobs had been in Episcopal choirs.

"We've spent a good part of our adult life trying to re-educate our parents about race," Harper said. "What we really want to do, of course, when they've just said something outrageous is walk out of the room and slam the door!" That whole world has changed, Harper believed, and "the changes in the Southern upper-middle-class are a good example of just how much." She probably always knew that she and black people "worshipped the same God. What we white people just couldn't figure out was how we were going to live together. But then we realized we're not *two* bodies of people, but one body under one God . . . I couldn't believe how I had been brought up so incorrectly." She also knows about Northern race hypocrisy. Her daughters' accents, in their New England colleges, earned them the "racist" epithet from the same white students who were openly hostile to the achievements of black fellow-students.

Harper came first to Advent South as a paid soloist. But at this point in her life, "I no longer want my singing to be a job but an offering — a kind of service, freely given. I no longer want to be paid for what God has given me." Earlier, pay had been important, the symbol of being professional. Harper has always enjoyed a strong feeling of her own worth; in that way she is a feminist, she agreed. But "career feminists, only concerned with their own advancement, not with other women," make her shun the label. Her "worst criticisms of our society overall are that we're killing our environment and we don't really value children." Her most powerful religious symbol is water, because of everything it connotes: something "to be feared if not treated properly," something "to be lost in, something overwhelming, something that is comforting when it is peaceful," something that can be "beautiful, something that links with people all around the world...a sustainer of life. And of course its holy use, baptism."

A women's support group is Harper's other source of spiritual nurture beside her music. "And receiving the Eucharist. It's the ritual, it's the repeated ritual. It's been done, and it's been done over and over again. We always do it again, in almost the same way." She drew back in amusement. "Of course when I kneel, I don't always have such exalted thoughts. I might think, Oh-oh, the rector's beard needs trimming!" She feels a certain squeamishness about the images associated with the consecrated bread and wine, confessing "a little questioning or turn-off in the Body and Blood symbolism. Yet those words convey the unbelievable image that we are able to take the body of Jesus and make it part of our bodies. I love the symbolism of *our* incorporating the body of Christ."

Harper's concluding thought is a kind of benediction, relating her inmost self in the sanctuary at Advent South to the long procession of fellow worshipers down through the centuries. "I wouldn't ever want to lose, I would most want to preserve the link with history my church has. There is no substitute for connecting with things from the past, with tradition — carrying it on, improving in the use of it. I feel it through the prayers, the music, the language, the gestures, the design of the vestments, even the windows and the architecture. That kind of historical expression has been going on for generations and generations, so I can actually touch someone who had a deep religious faith, way in the past, just by repeating the same words they repeated." Esthetic appreciation and deep historical roots surround Harper with "a cloud of witnesses" on Sunday mornings at Advent.

Bridge-generation women here reflect the privileges of high levels of education, professional income and status, and the opportunity to exercise choice in religious esthetics, moral causes, service, exploration. Advent's own unity and inclusiveness, challenging Southern white and Episcopal mores about race, class, and gender, nurture their spiritual roots.

The Younger Generation

The four younger women sharing these reflections were Debbie, a single woman who owns her own computer business; Rosemary, also single and a Northern-born transplant, is a social worker by profession; Annabelle, ambivalent about "religion" but not about her own spiritual realities, was native-born in this city, and is a civil servant, married with two daughters; and Clarey, in her mid-30s, also from the South but rural rather than urban, is a married therapist. Some of their paths have been especially circuitous, and their narratives reveal both the scars and the liberation their quest for spiritual equanimity has brought them.

Debbie's earliest memories of God are Sunday school images: "Daniel in the Lion's Den, Joseph and the Coat of Many Colors, and sticking mother's sweetpeas in the little mite box at Easter," she recalled. In her day children collected their pennies in a "mite box" during Lent, and on Easter they stuck a flower in the box and stacked them into "the big, box-like wooden cross up front, so that it kind of 'bloomed' with flowers." Because of her military father, Debbie's family moved every few years. Being Episcopalian symbolized stability and "comfort, since I was always finding myself in new circumstances. God was always being 'there,' wherever it was." Nevertheless, when Debbie, now in her early 30s, moved alone to this Southern city as "a very young 23-year-old," she felt "very lost. I didn't know what I wanted. I didn't believe I could be good at anything." Then she laughed. "It took me years of being secretary to bosses who were stupider than I to figure it out, that — what the hey! I don't have to do *this* the rest of my life!" Debbie linked her appalling lack of confidence with "the impostor syndrome. You know, there are two people inside: one that says to me, 'All these people are listening to what I'm saying, as if I know what I'm talking about'; and the other one says, 'But really, you don't.' "

In her early life, being able to receive communion after being confirmed at 13 was a first religious landmark. "It was the most important activity that I'd ever been allowed to take part in. Getting admitted to it was a big deal. I got the white dress and kissed the bishop's ring." Ritual has always nurtured a special corner of Debbie's soul. "To me, the formality and corporateness of ritual is what conveys its significance. I don't put down people who like the real casual glory-hallelujah dancing-in-the-aisles worship. But for me, what does it is the solemn ritual and the chanting — trying to make it as beautiful as possible. That says to God, 'I believe,' and 'We're here,' and 'We know we're with You.' "

Debbie's most consistent image of God is of "a gigantic, and slightly amused, incredibly warm, smile. Not a face but an aura, probably slightly above, you know [she pointed up]. Usually when I'm filled with the sense, an almost physical sense, of God's presence, I've been looking up. But that may be just habit." Did the direction "above" imply something about submission? "Oh, I have a problem with obedience, all right: somebody asks me to do something, and I immediately want to do the opposite. It's been a struggle all my life," Debbie confided. But that's where faith comes in, "helping me figure out when to be independent, and when to submit." Her analogy for the way faith operates drew on her cats' reaction when she put them in a box to go to the veterinarian — something they hate. Still, they know she loves them, and she is the one who takes care of them. "God is the biggest intelligence ever — how much greater is God's mind (for lack of a better word) than mine. So in that way, I'm like my cats. . . . I may hate it but I have to know God is the source of all my world and my survival. That's the way I can see my complete, total need for trust in something greater than I. I kind of begin to comprehend obedience when I can make myself stop and realize that I'm not really in charge here — I'm doing my best, but I'm not in charge."

During the Vietnam War, Debbie had to avoid church. Her Army officer dad was there and "the clergy were all preaching against it." That made her angry and confused, "because I knew my father was a good person, so I responded by just tuning out the outside world." Then, eight years ago, "out on my early-morning walk-for-my-weight program, I happened to pass this church and thought it was kind of cute . . . you know: brown stone, with bright red pointed-arch doors." She went home, put on a dress, and found herself rediscovering church. Re-entry was startling because of the changes—the new Prayer Book and a woman as lay reader—during her absence. She inwardly rejoiced. "All this enlightened stuff was going on here; I remember thinking 'Well, well, well! It's about damned time.' Well, actually, I didn't particularly like the preaching of the woman priest who was here then, but she *was* a woman of God. It was just about damn time that all this should have taken place, even if I had missed it." And some adolescent dreams could now be fulfilled: "I'd always wondered why I couldn't be an acolyte; it had looked like it would be a privilege when I was a teenager. So now, sometimes, I can be and I am." Advent has both adult and youth acolytes.

One of the discoveries in her religious reconnection was how deeply she had absorbed the unworthy-female syndrome. "I grew up thinking not very much of myself. It was never very easy for me to ask God for anything that was just for me. Didn't think I was worthy of bothering him. So my present religion has literally been 'Amazing Grace' for me," she said in a pun on the hymn. "It's helped me to think better of myself, and trust that things are going to work out—that I'm actually *worthy* of having them work out. Also that if I get turned down at something it's not the end of the world." What are the factors in a better image of self-worth? "In the congregation, I talk only a little about my own faith and my spirituality. This is a very reserved group of people, so they don't open up a lot. I sometimes say, almost flippantly, 'Well, I'm going to let God take care of that.' But underneath, that's what I really seriously mean and try to live. Little by little, people have come to confide in me, and ask about my faith: 'Is that really the way it works?' So I've begun to realize what an enormous gift I have, this faith. Don't know where it came from, but I agree with that mantra from Julian of Norwich: 'All will be well, and all shall be well, and all manner of things will be well.' "[6] After a moment, she said, "I suppose part of it is viewing my thirty-some years in proportion to eternal time, maybe my tinyness in relation to the vastness of the entire created world. I don't just know how I came by this absolute faith in the immortal soul but I know it exists. Used to take it for granted but I no longer do. Now it's the first thing I thank God for in my prayers."

Debbie was rare in admitting the importance of habit in daily spiritual practice. British writer C. S. Lewis, whose "calm, serene intelligence" she admired greatly, had awakened her interest in habit as well as personal rituals of devotion. "I try very hard to kneel beside my bed every night and say my prayers. I always use the Confession of Sin from the communion service, and the Lord's Prayer, because they kind of sum up the necessaries, you might say. Anything else I put in from time to time is icing on the cake." In addition she has "more or less constant conversation" with God, during the day, "about all kinds of stuff." A further practice is "memorizing hymns when I wash dishes. I have a recipe holder over my sink, one of those Plexiglas things to hold the hymnbook. Right now my favorite is one of the communion hymns: [singing] 'Come, risen Lord, and deign to be our guest; / Nay, let us be thy guests; the feast is thine; / Thyself, at thine own board make manifest, / in thine own sacrament of Bread and Wine.' "

Debbie continued, "Then there's that wonderful one, "Land of Rest," to the Appalachian folk tune "Jerusalem my happy home," another Eucharist hymn. The last verse goes: 'Together met, together bound, / We'll go our different ways; / And as his people in the world, / We'll live and sing his Praise.' That's why I come to church — because it's a community, my community. I need a 'family' that's not family. Right now mine is scattered to hell and gone over the entire world." Having discovered Advent as her spiritual community makes her impatient with people who don't see it the same way. "I get really irritated with people who say, 'Well, just couldn't make it to church this morning!' Because for me it's not just about you, whether you could or couldn't get here, whether you're there to receive whatever you might get from the ritual. When you make the effort to show up, it affirms everybody else who shows up." She summarized her covenant of belonging: "It's not just what you get, it's what you *give* by turning up, by your faith, by being here."

To Debbie, membership in Advent is a gift accompanying her revitalized faith. "It's obvious that ... this little church, located here in slumland — whatever it gets, it gives away. We're a conduit for all kinds of good things. Finally, here's a church that takes the words of Jesus literally: you know, 'visit the sick, feed the hungry,' do all those things. I wanted to be a part of that." Belonging inspires and channels her creativity. "We had just opened the soup kitchen when I joined. I've now been on that board for four years, and also on the Community Kitchens board [an ecumenical feeding program in another part of the city]." She was inspired to give back her own unique gift. "A project I started for them raised $33,000 this year. It's a donations Christmas card that says 'In the spirit of the season' on the front. When you open it, it says 'A gift which will feed — blank, however many — lunches for the hungry has been donated in your name to the Community Kitchens by...and there's space for the giver's name.' People send, at $5 a name, sometimes $250 with one card. I've even received them, because people know how much this ministry means to me. Believe it or not, I opened this Christmas card, and when it said 'So-and-so has donated 100 lunches for the hungry in your name,' I just burst into tears."

Debbie has recently come through the death of her mother from cancer, which turned into a major spiritual landmark. She and her sister were able to care for her mother, at the parents' home, the last days. "Through it, I think I was sort of on 'automatic pilot.' Someone had to get dinner, someone had to give Mother her bath. But after she died, I think I've talked with her more than I ever did while she was alive. We hadn't always gotten along very well, but one night shortly before she died — she hadn't spoken the whole day — I was sitting by her bed, and I thought, 'If I ever want to say anything to Mother again, I'd better say it now. What do I need from her? This is my last chance to get it.' I thought for — it must have been half an hour — going over all the things I loved about her and all the things that made me angry. Finally I realized what I needed from her was affirmation: I needed her to just tell me I was okay. So I said 'Mother?' and she went 'Ummm.' I pressed her hand and said, 'Mother, do you think I'm a good person?' And she opened the one eye she could still open a crack, and whispered, 'I think you're terrific.' "

After we wept together for a moment, Debbie wiped her eyes and said, "It was just exactly what I needed. I've felt her presence a lot more since she died....She would say things to me that I couldn't possibly have made up in my own head. It was like she and I were really talking, finally, for the first time...as if she knew what I was about and understood finally why I did the things that had looked crazy to her when she was still alive."

Silent for a moment, Debbie continued, "She died very quietly one afternoon, out on the porch. The priest was away on a retreat....He'd brought her communion the day before...so he wasn't available to do the little service [Ministration at the Time of Death, in the *Book of Common Prayer*]. So I did it. I got my prayer book out...she might have been dead already fifteen minutes...and I said to the family, 'I have to do this, I hope none of you mind.' I held her hand, and opened up the book and read that service. That was my real good-bye. Part of me was angry, afterward, and sad. Hell, here I did everything right and she still died on me! Part of me was wondering if I should have prayed for a miracle. When she was still lucid, should I have asked: 'Do you want us to pray for a miracle, here? I'm willing to get down on my knees for you, as many hours as it takes, to have you get well.' But — I didn't say it." Debbie wiped her eyes again. "That's my biggest crisis so far. I feel a lot older than just a year ago. This incredible gift of faith — it doesn't keep suffering from me, more than from other people. But I guess what I'm feeling is: my grief doesn't shake my belief. It doesn't depend outwardly on externals so much anymore."

"When Mother's ashes came back from the crematory, I was surprised at how small [she measured with her hands] the container was. I put them on the little table in the foyer, and when we were about to leave for the funeral, Dad says, 'Oh, we can't forget Mom.' I said fliply, without thinking, 'No, she doesn't want to be late for her own funeral!' " Debbie smiled wryly, "If I could sum up what life is, it would probably be God's voice saying [in radio-announcer style]: 'This is a test; this is only a test.' It's a tempering process, like you're...hammered metal. I mean, you get beaten on, and it changes you, it changes your shape. Some of us just seem to have to be beaten on more than others. I know the only reason I've managed not to commit suicide is because of my faith. Even in my deepest, darkest, horriblest hours, I knew that what was going on was eventually going to turn out to be good for me. Somehow, I just knew it."

Annabelle, a civil servant in a second marriage, was the only native-born resident of the city in this generation. Now near 40, she announced that she had "been at war with religion" from the time a lady in the Methodist kindergarten wanted her to use coloring books and crayons "instead of playing in the house-corner." Later, still resistant, "I used to sit in church and count the number of times the pastor would say 'And Jesus Christ said...' in that rotund, pompous voice, instead of listening." She and her husband have two adopted children of mixed racial heritage. When people wonder how a white Southerner with a name like Annabelle and a magnolia accent can "think and act the way I do," her answer is religious: "I still believe the things about race and religion that they taught me in the Methodist Church, as opposed to what they actually did." As a child she was reared to be condescending toward African Americans. The civil rights marches were a nuisance, but she knew they were right on principle. "I knew from my own father that a lot of white people took advantage of, cheated, black people, business-wise. But I couldn't see any way for them *not* to be cheated, except for some white person to protect them from it, when I was young." Her own choice of career — working with teenage delinquents in a city department — is probably an updated form of the same Southern patronizing, she said; there is virtue in "the old-fashioned idea of taking care of people" but also irony, since white people still hold on to the power.

As a child, Annabelle experienced a vision of Jesus near her bed table. He was surrounded by "extremely bright light, not like electric light but much, much brighter, and glowing warm." Tears sprang to her eyes at the remembrance. It was a "very comforting feeling," she said. Her father died when she was 12, leaving her with "a psychotic mother." The maternal grandmother fortunately provided the real nurture she received. "If it hadn't been for her, I would be a real bad mess. She and I were closer than she ever was to her own daughters. I think I must have gotten my religious streak from her husband, my grandfather, who was a minister."

Annabelle was "not a big believer in the Trinity," the persons of the Godhead. "Rather I believe in God the Holy Spirit. That's the 'face' of God I see most. I don't get hung up on conflicting scriptures because I am not a literalist. When I was about 10 — I remember it was the year I had my blue calico-quilted skirt [her eyes glint mischievously] — the teacher was talking about the miracle of Jesus feeding the crowd of 5,000. I just looked at her and explained it. 'Jesus just made everybody ashamed of their selfishness,' I said. 'Nobody would have gone off to a place like that without food, so they all just brought out what they had, and shared it. That's why there was enough to go around.' She was horrified at me, and went and told on me to my mother. But it still makes sense. What's the bigger miracle? Multiplying bread and/or changing peoples' hearts? Changing hearts is what causes miracles, not changing physical objects. Even at that age I never could take scripture literally. I always had a more literary approach to the stories."

Her independent streak has led Annabelle to seek spiritual sustenance in unconventional sources — for example, a seventeenth-century devotional classic, *Holy Living and Holy Dying* by Jeremy Taylor. "I'm not a person that belongs to my own generation" in literary tastes, she explained. "I was reading adult books since before I was 12, big thick novels. I used to check them out of the bookmobile by the armload during high school." Her literary sensibility keeps her emotionally attached to the former (1928) Prayer Book. "It was such a piece of literature, and I do enjoy elegant language. There was a time when I worried that I might feel really lost, about this new Prayer Book."

About the institutional church, Annabelle rejects the notion that there are "women's roles." "There's no such thing as a woman's place, there are just Christians' roles. People ought to be able to 'do' according to their gifts. Here at Advent women can do anything a man can. Of course, someone here once expressed the fear that if women do all the things men used to do, men won't come to church anymore. I say if that turns out to be the case, then men are coming to church for the wrong reasons." Adamant about this improvement, she opposes a proposal being considered at the national church level that would allow conservative congregations to invite a male bishop from an outside diocese so they wouldn't have to deal with a woman if the local bishop happened to be female. "I know the goal is trying to pacify these people who resist change, to keep them from leaving the church because they disagree. But when the talk was about race relations awhile back, there wasn't any effort toward pacification." Remembered inequity made her bristle. "I mean, they just held people's noses and poured the medicine right down their throats . . . until the racial disruptions moved up into Northern cities, that is. Being a Southerner makes me, well, . . . it feels like it makes us second-class citizens."

Annabelle's vision of the ideal church pictures one large enough to have "room enough for everybody, all 'sorts and conditions,' in the phrase from the old Prayer Book. The image in my head is like one of those great big English cathedrals that is nevertheless surrounded by all the little local churches. Also I really believe in an ecumenical church, but . . . " Her sense of outrage returned. "On the other hand, I don't really *want* room in the church for the local 'right-to-life' folks. The Episcopal Church has never been in the business of trying to force its brand of religion down everybody else's throat, which is what I see them trying to do."

In spite of having praised the open-mindedness of her religious identity, some part of Annabelle longs for more doctrinal and moral guidance. "To people who are not in the Episcopal Church, it looks very stiff and formal and rigid. Only when you get in do you realize it's a big gutless blob, without form or fashion." She remembers indignation when she joined Advent. "I tried, before I was confirmed, to get *somebody* to tell me what these pagan Episcopalians believed! Oh I know, there's all the stuff in the back of the Prayer Book, The Thirty-nine Articles [statements of Protestant principle incorporated in the first American Church Prayerbook], and all that. But we're sure not structured like the Catholics: no simple, straightforward rules for you to live your life by." Contradicting herself again, she added, "Of course, religion's not — like — a book of law. It's like a running faucet, water that you can't catch and hold in your hand. It just slithers right out; when you try to hold it, it's gone." She is caught between the life-giving freedom to define her own faith and a yearning for less ambiguity.

Annabelle dismissed her contribution to the congregation. "I do only a bit of the real fine fancy mending for the Altar Guild, the kind with little teeny stitches. It's something I can take home, and work at there." In the past, however, "I've done it all": Sunday school teaching, acolyting, lay reading, flower arranging. Right now, while the children are young, "I do as little as possible. Oh, when we have big parties I like to pour punch and help fix the tables, gather up the dirty dishes. That sort of thing." She tossed off a final self-deprecation: "I'm just a big Martha."[7] Annabelle's femininity is still at war with religion and convention, but hospitality and sewing are a comfortable way to participate.

Rosemary, a young (30) social worker from a Northern liberal, prolabor household, expects activism combined with idealism in her spiritual life. "My father was a very conservative midwesterner, a Republican and an idealist, pro–labor union.... I know that's almost an oxymoron!" Her job deals with human relations in a private corporation. Raised Episcopal, she left it during college, becoming "totally a-religious and pro-science. It was all part of growing up and putting away childish things." Her first job in a Roman Catholic agency exposed her to ritual once again and "a discovery of the sacred and of my own religious dimensions, in a way."

After moving to this city, Rosemary attended a charismatic Episcopal church briefly before finding Advent, its racial inclusiveness appealing to her. A great city ecumenical service that had commemorated civil rights activists epitomized her ideal about worship. "That was terribly moving, maybe one of the most religious experiences I've ever had...the gospel music, and the racial mix." She appreciated the "androgyny" of Advent: its formal ceremonials, its freedom from "hardline masculine leadership." Serving as Advent's representative on a diocesan committee, however, gave her a different picture. The "stereotype that other church representatives have of Advent is: we're weak, impractical, unbusinesslike — no matter how good, how Christ-like our ideas are."

She is still sorting out both her own needs and her relationship to this congregation. Advent members are like "atoms bumping into each other. This congregation is really only a group of aggregates [sic], a bunch of individuals all going their separate ways. There aren't any real subgroups here." And she feels unfed by "overly intellectual sermons" that suggest "clerical insulation" from the ethical questions with which people at her stage of life are grappling. "I would have liked sermons about concrete things like, say, about money: how much to pay for a piece of art, and what that says about your religious choices. Whether to volunteer for several activities, or just one. Things like that, from people who have some experience and insight about them, would be really helpful to people like me."

Rosemary's commitment to Advent is somewhere between "lapsed" and "active," since she is also deeply involved in "trying to put my own life together, make it work. I do a good bit of paid work on weekends now, and...the decision not to go to church on Sunday has become a lot easier." She has discovered, as a result, that "essentially, I can miss church and no one will call me. Maybe it's because they view me as competent, think I want to be left alone." But, "earlier this year, it came to me that if I really need something from them, it's up to me to let them know it." She speculated: "It may be a kind of weird compliment that they didn't want to...patronize me, look after me. I guess I'm trying to achieve some kind of balance between my need for that kind of reaching out, being looked out for, and calling the tune on my own decisions about church."

Outside the congregation, Rosemary's social circle confronted her with another surprise: how she had romanticized 'preacher's kids.' "They have the feeling of an inner circle, a sense of clannishness." Episcopal clergy kids "all rode their first bikes together, they all lost their virginity together, they all got drunk for the first time together at church camp. . . . It's like they're an extended family, great for them but I feel very excluded." She hated being "automatically the outsider . . . the only one at a party who didn't grow up in an Episcopal rectory." Any idealism she associated with clergy kids was also fading in the face of reality. "Most of them are very self-absorbed, really non-churchgoing. Their fathers and their mothers have been activists, urban-ministry types, involved in civil rights and all the important causes. They were born into a really fine spiritual genealogy, you might say." Trying to be fair, Rosemary speculated, "It's possible that the women are going to be the stronger. . . . [They're the ones] going off to seminary, rather than their male peers. They are really the spiritual leaders of this group."

The issue for Rosemary is how to "balance the congregation and its outreach to others with my own admission of what I need and am willing to ask for in the way of nurture. And then to be at ease with myself in that process." Recalling a more simplistic stage, she said, "I guess originally my image of being a Christian was only that I had to conform to a certain set of behaviors. I thought it was a matter of externals — that I should check my style and personality at the door when I came to church. I know now that's not true but I still surrender to a stereotype of 'church behavior.' I have yet to be as outrageous inside the church as I feel it's okay to be, sometimes, on the outside." Yes, Advent "is more relaxed than most other congregations" about conformity of appearance. "You can come here dressed any old way. Still I come in my Sunday school best. It's my training."

Almost wearily, Rosemary said, "If I see myself as more devout than my Episcopal clergy-kid friends, maybe I have to learn, through them, that the stones I want to throw don't really amount to a lot." Almost fiercely, she leaned forward. "I'm having to learn *in every area of my life* that there *is* sense, there *is* order in all the disorder. It's just that I'm not quite able to see it yet." "Life" had just begun to seem more manageable to her when a new trauma shattered her confidence that she had "made it" into adulthood.

A fellow professional to whom she had gone for help made serious sexual advances in the context of the therapeutic relationship. It was shattering. "I've had to work out . . . what I'm going to do," she confided. "I'm still working up the courage. . . . It's really risky business to be a whistle-blower in a city of this size. Maybe in Northern cities women find more support for something like this."

She sighed. "What made it so painful is that this person *knew* I went to him for rebuilding my self-esteem because I had been assaulted before." She wept. "That was my real reason for being in therapy."

Rosemary wiped her eyes and figuratively gritted her teeth. "The whole thing is complicated: who am I going to represent: me myself? me a female symbol of harassment? me a professional person fighting people in my agency? My choice is to determine, proverbially and literally, that I *will not* be a victim. To take myself in hand. And I know God is helping," she assured herself. "The issue is who gets to know about it, who talks with whom. . . . I just have to weigh how much I'm willing to fight, which battles to engage. You know the image I had of myself for a long time? I felt I was crouching, all curled up in a fetal position. That's the way I thought of myself. . . . And I still have so much anger." She tried to invoke lofty ideals: "By now, I find I don't want to retaliate as much as I want remediation. I want to change things in myself." As a wry afterthought, she said, "That man gave me a great opportunity to forgive — something I'm still working my way through." For Rosemary, spirituality is being forged through coming into relationship with agonizing realities.

Clarey's story is a Southern version of the spiritual experimentation and quest pursued by her contemporaries at Nativity Northwest — the most complex trajectory among the younger women at Advent. Her origins were rural, poor, and fundamentalist, in a country town some hours distant. In her earliest religious memories, "God was absolutely real and I wasn't afraid of Him, but it was a masculine God, a very legalistic one. That was okay. Children like rules and a definite knowing of what's right, and not right," she said. Baptism by immersion in a muddy lake left her with a permanent fear of water. But childhood rule-consciousness was one of the first things to be jettisoned in her urban exploration.

"What happened to draw me to the Episcopal Church was accidental, part of my search. This was later, after I'd started going to the university. I had become a student of Tarot cards and symbolism, even witchcraft — seeking something. . . . Not that I wanted to be a witch! But I wanted to study ritual and its relation to the unconscious. From the little I knew, the Eucharist seemed like modern ritual magic to me, so I came to Advent. I sought out the Episcopal church to understand more, to see what I thought was ritual magic in the modern day. Of course it isn't, and it worked on me." She smiled. "Religion suddenly took on more meaning than being only an anthropological curiosity, or just something to save my dreary soul."

What was the actual epiphany? Clarey said, "Eucharist. Just the Eucharist itself; watching it happen, going up, and partaking of it. Then 'the church' in the abstract became this church — Advent South. I came here and started to learn how to worship. It was different from all the rest I'd tried... from the Holy Order of MANS,[8] from the Church of God, from the Baptists, the Presbyterians. My religion became worship itself, not all the other things like beliefs and doctrines. Even all the social outreach here? *That* wasn't what mattered, what drew me." After belonging to Advent for nearly a decade, Clarey said, "I've tried to stay pretty anonymous so I can concentrate on worship, but still — I'm pretty well known now and it's hard to avoid becoming too involved. Sometimes I've gone to other Episcopal churches just for the anonymity, where I can be part of the worship without being distracted by people and jobs to be done here."

She and her husband, a former Baptist missionary in Asia, are both members at Advent, both now in their mid-30s. As a couple, "we live an everyday life that is more Buddhist than Christian — mostly Zen. Like trying to be 'in the moment,' in mindfulness. We try to have a quiet time every morning, to get the day off to a good start. We take time to really *see* whatever happens to be out the window as we drink our coffee, and really appreciate it.... We're trying to be less and less control-ers, more and more live-ers, you know. We both meditate regularly." She interrupted her description to add, "Of course our whole way of life may change if I ever have a baby! But we try to have an attitude of equanimity — to believe life just works this way. Nothing is all good and nothing is all bad."

Because her mother had been committed to a mental hospital, Clarey was raised by loving grandparents. Her father, a man with a violent, almost pathological temper, changed "when he got converted," after Clarey had grown up. "When I was 28, he apologized for all those years he'd treated me like I was my mother, the person who'd betrayed him by getting sick and going crazy." When she was about 12 this father whom she scarcely knew took her from her grandparents to live with him and a new stepmother. "It was like losing two mothers, my real mother and my granny." At 14, she had a psychotic break. "I was hallucinating, I felt crazy —

real crazy and confused, but my father wouldn't let them take me to a hospital." Was she aware that she was mentally ill? "I'd always made good grades and suddenly began to flunk everything. I lost weight — down to, like, 94 pounds or so. I was withdrawn, I had violent headaches. I was just crazy as a bat there for a while. Finally, it was my stepmother who put her foot down and said, 'She's going to the doctor!' " Clarey recovered from her illness after eighteen months on tranquilizers and completed high school.

But two weeks after graduation, her father hit her. "I looked at him and said 'That's the last time you'll ever hit me.' He said, 'Get the hell out,' and I asked my stepmother if she'd 'carry me to town.' So I packed a suitcase and took my $10 babysitting money. She dropped me off here, at the downtown YWCA, and I've been on my own ever since." From that breezy introduction, Clarey's recollections turned darker. "Arriving in the big city I just naturally went hog wild," Clarey said. "I stayed at the Y until I found somebody to share an apartment with me. It was a complete shock. It was ratty, there were window panes missing, and heat only in the bathroom. I lived there five years. My roommate drank and I was wild, promiscuous, doing drugs. I remember telling myself, 'I'm supposed to be like my mother, and *she* was crazy and promiscuous.' " Her first job, selling dresses at a discount house, was as seedy as everything else, but she was soon promoted to bookkeeper because her competence could not be hidden. "I was still wild but I had to work, so that was what pulled me through." She remained in that job for three years.

She had cut herself off from everything: family and religion, even her own emotions. Clarey now sees how much she needed guardian angels and the first came to her through a providential meeting with a member of the Holy Order of MANS. "One day when I had a flat tire on my bike, I met this nice, clean-cut young man in a clerical collar. He helped me change it and didn't try to put any moves on me or take advantage of me. So I was impressed, touched by his kindness. Then his colleagues from the Holy Order began to invite me to meals and drew me in." They became the first of several surrogate families that seemed to watch over her in the city.

A modern, nondenominational religious order founded in the 1960s, the Holy Order of MANS (its full name) brought religious and physical salvation to drugged-out 'Flower Children.' The men and women who joined it lived in community as "Brothers" and

"Sisters," eschewing drugs and investing themselves in inner-city service work. "So after about four years of worshiping with them, and learning about them, I decided I was going to live there and become a full member — actually join the order. By then I'd started taking classes at the university and volunteering at a home for emotionally disturbed teenagers. I was very religious. I was doing everything I was supposed to, including shedding my possessions to become an official member of the order — you know, take their vows and keep their disciplines. But then I found out that I couldn't take my cat with me, and that cut it. They tried to lay a guilt trip on me about not being willing to give up my cat in order to serve God! So that's when I said, 'Good-bye! Don't need you.'"

What Clarey benefited from, during her several years as an associate of the Holy Order of MANS, was that "first taste of religious ritual in their formal, catholic worship . . . the saving experience itself, and meditation. That was the main gift I got from them, and I'll always be grateful for it. I learned that God could talk to me, that I didn't just have to talk to Him, but that I could actually hear this voice — God — and it didn't have to be drug-induced, yeah, and not crazy. I wasn't crazy, I wasn't hallucinating . . . so that was a real gift." When asked about how God speaks to her, she said, "It's meditation. To me, prayer is talking to God, meditation is listening. Me giving God the opportunity to talk back."

She completed college and entered graduate school, training to be a nurse because that was a subsidized degree program. Along with studying, she "got into fitness," and became a vegetarian. "I had come originally from a highly disciplined family, and here I was, without any external discipline — not even the Holy Order of MANS anymore. So I had to impose it on myself." But along with the various forms of structure that she tried out, she was searching for a religious home. "I've always been the mystic in the family. I am attributed to have powers that I don't really think I have. Probably my psychotic break had something to do with making them credit me as more mystical, perhaps, than I really am."

Clarey's choice of nursing was anything but altruistic. "I wanted a degree in something that could earn me a decent living." But she hated its regimentation and endless paperwork. "Writing up a care plan sixteen pages long left you unprepared, psychologically, even technically, to face caring for eight or nine sick people on your eight-hour shift. It didn't teach you how to be a nurse, just how to write scientific language." She stayed in nursing "just long enough to become a counselor," that is, to find a more congenial profession and support herself while earning another degree. She said her shifts in direction stemmed from her fear of "getting stuck": she never wants to stay too long in any particular slot.

The issues that preoccupy her now, as she develops her own counseling practice, are openly, deeply spiritual. "I want to be always involved in the human questions: what makes people tick, how do they become who they are? Where in the dickens do they get the beliefs they have? How is it that something holds meaning for some people but not for others?" Clarey wonders about change itself: "What is it about? How do people change, why do people change, what happens when people want to change and can't?"

How does a person like Clarey, with all her adventures and experiments, perceive the state of the world today? "I think it's gone to hell in a handbag. I don't think it's anything we can fix anymore. I've lost faith that we, you and I, can do anything about it. I think the problem is in this system of government. It's like Bob Dylan says: we've got 'gangsters in power and lawbreakers making rules.' In my counseling with Planned Parenthood and AA, I see many struggling single-parent families. Men have unrealistic expectations of marriage in the first place. And women are just damned exhausted. The marriages are unfulfilling because there's no time for the marriage. Our government gives no support to families, and we are all chasing money as if that would make us happy." Having once held down a job in a big corporation and dressed in tailored business clothes, Clarey was not in awe of financial "success."

"When I was little, I wanted to be a preacher," she remembered; her mother had been a traveling evangelist before she became ill. Clarey's interest in counseling is a generational adaptation of the same calling, she thinks, giving her the satisfaction her mother had sought in leading a congregation. The field of family — rather than individual — therapy makes the most sense to her. "People get sick in groups, and they get well in groups, in families. A group is the fastest place to heal and to work on making changes. In fact, religion is both social and healing." Although she appreciates the power of group-work for her clients, Clarey herself finds it difficult to submit, in both psychological and religious terms, to group situations. "It's not easy for me to be in a group and not have any control. Sometimes a group gets in my way. I'm not very trusting. But I keep learning, going back to it and working at it."

Serious love relationships for Clarey, during her experimenting years, included a graduate student from the Far East, a young medical student who loved drugs more than he loved her, and finally her husband. When I expressed surprise that she and her husband, who had come through so many relatively exotic experiences, "settled down" to something as emotionally staid and traditional as an Episcopal church, she said, "Right, exactly. But that's what we've been seeking apparently. We've been very satisfied here, not just in this parish but in the Episcopal Church. I really enjoy being an adult acolyte, since I gave up being a Sunday school teacher, because it brings me close to my study of magic: the acolyte gets to sit behind the altar during the service and can see what's going on." What does she see in the symbolism of ordained women? "I love seeing a woman behind the altar. Of course, in my fundamentalist childhood church, women had equal religious rights so I didn't understand why everybody we met in the Episcopal Church was so exercised about a woman priest at first." Confident in her own powers, a rural woman like Clarey who "could pick up a 100–pound bag of feed or a bale of hay" dismisses the Episcopal "antifemale stance" as "just plain stupid. And as a person interested in ritual magic, I love to see a woman in the sacramental role. It's empowering . . . very, very empowering."

Clarey admits that a "Higher Power," the phrase carrying great spiritual meaning for her AA clients, is a problem for her. "Sometimes it really rankles me," she said, "the idea that there is a Higher Power conscious of me while I can't fully know It. But submitting is not the difficult part for me. That's the way the world is. I think we just have to acknowledge we're not in charge." Then she interrupted herself. "If you'd asked me about it before I discovered AA and the philosophy that works so well for people recovering from addiction, I wouldn't have been able to say that. I'd probably have said, 'Magical thinking is what works.' Self-control. You know . . . just control your thoughts and you're in control of your own life." She didn't want a "Big Daddy" God to surrender everything to. "There are laws and functions and hierarchies and 'principalities,' St. Paul's term. And 'everything that goes around comes around.' *You* can't control all the variables. Actually a person doesn't need to; it's safe not to have to. That's what's going on; the world is out there and this is the way it works." Reflexively, she added, "Some of why I previously thought that it *wasn't* safe — to admit there was something Bigger than me — was this whole God-the-Father thing. 'Father' hasn't always meant safety to me. Probably subconsciously, I've benefited from having a female priest here; it's made the God-thing 'safer' for me. But I've never really put that in words till now."

What Christian symbols are particularly meaningful? Clarey responded immediately: "I have real conflicts about the bleeding Son, the body and the cross. All I can see...is a magical feat, a transmutation of energies. A major thing that has helped me hang in, religiously, is the Mother Mary figure. That's the other thing the Holy Order of MANS gave me besides meditation: Mary. There's my female image: Mary as another name for God. It works for me." Why do so few Protestant women find nurture in that particular feminine image? "I think it's because there's too much confusing Mary-the-mother-of-Jesus in the Bible with Mary the feminine part of God." She mused for a moment. "We tend to visualize Mary the way she's pictured in beautiful old Renaissance paintings. Actually, I have a painting of her that is my image, a cheap piece of art, valued because it's old in my psyche. My grandmother, who was illiterate as well as illegitimate, had this picture of Mary, the one that shows her with a pierced heart. It always hung on the living room wall, and I never even knew who it was...don't think I even thought about it as a child. But now I have it; it's in my house and brings my two images of Mary-symbolism together. I see it as the two aspects of God: that demanding, legalistic, conditional-love God who is real, but also that unconditional-love, nurturing, I'm-going-to-take-care-of-you-whether-you-ask-me-or-not God. She's there visually and in reality. She's still with me."

Clarey ranked the various aspects of worship in terms of how they speak to her, beginning with the oral. "I tune in less to the art and the visual, and more to the audio part. First, the chants, the singing of the Eucharist as ritual." Then scent: "Incense is important, too; the Holy Order of MANS taught me to appreciate incense. I think odors are a very powerful spiritual stimulant." But finally the visual: "Of course what I love about the visual is seeing the very ritualized movement. Then...the vessels, the cup. That's the most feminine thing, the most femin*ist* thing we have, up there on the altar. It's the vessel into which Christ is poured, and out of which Christ pours into us; and we're vessels, and God fills us vessels. Then we can be shared; we can empty out, and we fill up again." She smiled in benediction at her own imagery.

•

The prism created by the women at Advent illuminates three "generations" of "inner life" facets. Among the older women, church is the chosen spiritual family and "home." The bridge-generation women see deep religious symbolism in Advent as an earthly locus of ideals. Spiritual growth involves them with the work of social justice. Among the younger women, hard-won spiritual self-knowledge helps them deal with old and new wounds. All the women revealed a self-inventing creativity in finding their own faith and dealing with church affiliation. Each finds blessing in certain aspects of worship at Advent and glosses over those that hold less resonance for her. Clarey, for one, focuses on ritual, blending hardscrabble fundamentalist awe and discipline learned from a modern-day religious order with a Roman Catholic pop-art image. Debbie envisions the congregation as "the communion of saints." Rosemary and Annabelle struggle for equanimity and to "realize" their faith.

The reasons any of them gave for affiliating with Advent have little to do with doctrine, theology, or denominational identity. Rather each started from a personal need. They searched for a place that could provide a genuine experience of "the sacred" and a relationship with "the Christ," a saving, transforming experience that could make them want to give and serve. Their spiritual quests traced various "unorthodox" paths. If there is a larger implication in these individual trajectories it is about the way people find and identify a congregation that seems to be right for them. Priest-charisma, Sunday school images, evangelistic confrontations are not what has elicited the personal spiritual response here; nor is family influence. What counts is the inner experience of personal unfolding.

A rekindling of church as family had different overtones at Advent than at Nativity Northwest. Debbie ited family as a community of the like-minded — the congregation as horizontal spiritual bond: "I need a family that isn't family." Many were recovering or had recovered from horrendous crises; individual congregants and the parish as a whole "ministered" to them — congregation as a healing place. Since they took for granted the resource of professional psychotherapy, they wanted Advent for "soul love" more than for personal therapeutic relationships — congregation as spiritual center. Seventy-five-year-old Adele found she was "discovering the Kingdom of God within you" — the congregation as preparation for heaven.

Anglo-Catholicism plays a distinctive role in this congregation's narratives of "inner life" and spirituality. It was apparent in different ways for Clarey, Catherine, Connie, Abigail — women drawn esthetically, to "seek out sacred space" early in life, "the quiet in huge, empty churches." Harper, the professional singer, responded to the profound nonverbal messages in vestments, stained glass, Altar Guild rituals. These dimensions of religious response are always hard to capture in "mere words." Still, the major reason many of these women decided to affiliate with Advent was simply that this "church" let them feel reached by God. Yet the esthetic magnet also operated most powerfully when complemented by the actual work of caring and outreach, the core identity of Advent. "This is a church that lives the Gospel." Without the strong component of outreach to the world outside, without the racial, sexual, and social class inclusiveness that inspires the worshipers inside, the esthetics alone in this undistinguished, humble church building would have been sterile.

Women believers throughout Western Christian history have found their spirituality in the theology and work of caring. Today in some congregations women are actually making an impact on the worship experience itself so that the feminine as well as the masculine can emerge; they are experiencing and creating liturgical links with the unconscious, the intuitive, and the sensory.[9] That is an area in which Advent's Anglo-Catholic churchmanship, atypical as it is, may be less malleable; the women in its worship must do their reshaping only internally to this point. But they remain untiring participants in the never-completed process of spiritual selfhood.

"How do women stay in this church?" Peggy's question implies its own answer: through the emotional and religious insights that enable them to find their own niches within a congregation — their own sacred space. The God in the center of these experiences is not a God of might or conquest, nor a "Lord God, King of the universe," but a God visible in the imagery of "Sophia," the earliest scriptural representation of wisdom and compassion.[10] That kind of God at Advent makes it safe for women to cultivate an "inner life" and channel it into the work of caring and love.

Chapter 6

CONGREGATIONS AND GENERATIONS

Congregations: Women's Horizontal Spiritual Connection

"How *do* women stay in this church?" The answer we have explored in the previous chapters lies in a relationship with a local congregation, the "bottom layer of American religion" estimated by Gallup to number somewhere between 250,000 and 300,000.[1] Ideally, *congregation* is "the family of faith," a group of members that maintains some social and religious coherence amid all "the ambiguity of human association," a structure that tries to live out its "designation as the body of Christ." At the mundane level, congregations are the place where people bring together "their everyday existence and their most cherished aspirations."[2]

Each congregation we visited revealed its own taken-for-granted patterns of conduct, outlook, and story — an overarching congregational idiom — forms in which they express both everyday concern and highest longings.[3] Choir rehearsals and potluck suppers are some of the ways each communicates its particular lore and legends: "We're known for the cooks in this parish!" "We've always rallied for a fundraiser, no matter how discouraged we've been." They provide a public stage where earthly celebrations like Halloween, for example, could be given transcendent overtones. They take practical and ethical leadership in local care-giving, encouraging members' response to "outside" need — most graphically, the feeding program at Advent South. Churches seem to be the primary place and congregations the structure of relationship that legitimates the hallowing of "landmark" life events — birth, marriage, death — and the emotions that accompany them.

When women used the word "church," they more often meant people than building, relationships rather than physical plant.[4] Undoubtedly the historic pattern of "separate spheres" for men and women in congregations, as well as in their daily lives, contributes to gendered modes of relating to one's church. Men take responsibility for the bricks and mortar, and mortgages, of a building — but are often removed from or less at home in relationship issues. Women often concern themselves with "the people element" of congregation and ignore or merely accept the financial and physical concerns. When "no one's there" on Sunday, to them "it's really sad"; the numinous quality of "congregation" is dimmed. From that perspective, the physical realities — building, altar, windows, candles — require a worshipping community to give them meaning. Conversely, when two or three congregants meet, in or out of the building, for example to plan food for a sick parishioner, "congregation" is also being expressed.

In the past, "church stories" — narratives tracing the history of a particular congregation — focused on physical plant or the congregational organization and its ordained leaders. "The people element" was largely absent. Our major focus in these churches was on "the people element," the use of space and nonverbal demeanor to express the wordless aura of serenity and unanimity binding a given congregation.

We often saw worshipers disposing themselves singly in pews that could comfortably accommodate four to six persons — especially at the early, uncrowded service. Men and women in church chose to keep some physical distance between themselves and the person next — except in the case of little children with a parent. Then the physical proximity was emotionally compelling, as if the adult could hardly hold the child close enough. One young mother said she especially cherished "church time together"; she was loathe to surrender that particular hour to congregational babysitters, even if her child might cry or "bother" other worshipers. But adults often seemed to choose spatial isolation as a stance in their communal action.

The synapses connecting individual adult worshipers are, therefore, harder to understand. Yet in and around the unified ritual gestures enacted by each person, almost to herself alone (making the sign of the cross, standing as the organ introduces the hymn), congregants bridge the space with glances of recognition, a smile, an unspoken sense of "oneness." Silent bonds of "companionship" were visually transmitted by a nonverbal reaching out. In our conversations, women identified this perceived potential of shared meanings and religious depth as the horizontal magnet that drew them to a particular congregation, the "bedrock" of community they had been seeking.[5]

Women used many images for congregation-as-community although they did not often speak in those words or employ their grandmothers' phrase, the "household of faith." One middle-aged woman started with individual religiosity. For her, "church" is always in the inescapable tension between the joy of corporate worship, on the one hand, "the richness of liturgy, music, and spiritual depth," and the purely idiosyncratic nature of faith. "You simply can't put God in a box. He's there for each person to experience in her own way." A woman in her early 40s thought "paradox" was the word for congregation. She saw differing, even contrasting, avenues to God in any church, like "the paradox of life. It's complex; don't try to make it simple, or squeeze it down into a little narrow thing. The congregation should just let the Self open up," she said, her out-turned hands making the shape of a shallow bowl. A woman of 30 said simply, "It should be a safe place to establish new relationships." A woman nearing 70 was "sure of one thing about a relationship with God: it's not just a 'heady' idea, not just a philosophy, but a way of life." Reaching for a familiar analogy, she added, "It's the same as a relationship with any member of your family that you really get to know." An elderly Southern woman broadened Christian relationships from congregation to world. "We all live on the same planet; let's not try to shove each other off. Skin color, difference in general . . . God said, 'Love each other the way I love you.' That's what I really want us to be."

Women wanted the sense of participating in "something greater than themselves." They longed for a sense of corporateness, of being lifted in a body toward the divine. "What I want in worship," wrote one on her questionnaire, "is help in finding ways to incorporate faith and Christ in my daily life."[6] "A dignified woman in her early 90s said regretfully, "My 'participation' is nothing more [than attending]. I still think the ceremony itself is beautiful . . . the bonus, you might say. And, sometimes . . . the sermons say something to me." A third woman said, making a wide circle with her hands, "The church building itself, the service, the atmosphere . . . they are all just quieting in my life, sometimes also uplifting." A young woman mused about partaking as part of community. "The Eucharist is just in my soul; it's my favorite part, it's the personal part between me and God. Actually when He is coming into me, when I put the bread and wine into my mouth, I need quiet...you need a quiet time because you've just received the Christ." She added, half reprovingly, "It's not the same as going up and getting a casual snack somewhere!"

Others wanted congregation to enlarge their mental, spiritual, and emotional horizons. "I want the sense that people here really acknowledge God as the center of the church, as the energy that makes us go," said an enthusiastic woman in her early 40s. "What I feel, though, is...it feels more like male clergy are the center." Some saw it as a spur to self-interrogation. A few of the younger women viewed experience of worship as a source of internal discipline, a monitoring beacon to accompany them between Sundays. One confessed, "I like all the scripture reading that we get on Sundays in the service, because I don't do it during the week, though I always mean to." Although Anglo-Protestant self-restraint mutes the open challenging of others' opinions, many saw "church" as the "place where it's all right" to examine issues of moral worth, if only in their own minds. "Church makes one's life and activity, even your intentions, important....It's elevating," said a woman in her 60s. A teacher prayed "that lines would be crossed" in her congregation, "boundaries breached — racially, politically, and in terms of gender." A nurse mused, almost in wonder, "I love that so much of the outside world has come in [people in shabby clothes, social outcasts] and turned this proper Episcopalian stuff upside down."

A younger woman wanted her daily life to reflect her faith more visibly. "I want the Bible to be more part of my everyday life. Scripture can be intellectual, of course, but for me...I want it to be just kind of down-home 'heart' stuff. It's great to know the history and culture of the Bible and all that, and know how scripture can be seen to work in political life affecting all of us. But it's really the heart stuff that's important to me." A bridge-generation woman sent me this multilayered journal entry after being asked about awareness of the sacred in commonplace moments: "I remember, just before I woke, being aware that I was functioning at full speed on many levels at once. A hymn tune kept running wordlessly through my mind, which was not being diverted by my waking plans for a busy day, and my God-and-me conversation.

None of these simultaneous strands bothered the other, each just embellished the depth of this one instant."

The invisible horizontal webbing of "congregation" generated many images that laced together their inner and external worlds. What surprised us was that this talk came out in relational and personal terms, not in standard theological vocabulary — "communion of saints," "redemption," "salvation." Even the word "sacrament" appeared infrequently; more were comfortable with "receiving the Eucharist." As listeners we had to learn that when women were being most inarticulate about a religious insight, they were also striving to be most authentic. That is, they were exercising special care to use words that could honestly apply to their own experience, not words outside the realm of their personal authentication.

A larger issue in their avoidance of standard theological terms was the absence of the church's own language, so to speak, in these conversations occurring in a congregational setting and sponsorship. "It is as though these women have been unaffected by the evangelical, the Anglo-Catholic, the liberal, the Social Gospel, the existential, and the Jungian movements," a seminary professor wrote on reading this chapter. His list named the primary interpretive codes of American church history over the past century. "All of these theological emphases profoundly reshaped the Episcopal Church...during the nineteenth and twentieth centuries," yet women did not mention any of them.[7] The apparent irrelevance to women of that church-history typology dramatizes the gulf between language that communicates to laity and to seminary-trained, ordained professionals.

However conscious of church vocabulary women may or may not be, they have absorbed the therapeutic language that is so much a part of twentieth-century church and religious culture. The word "commitment" served them as a formal religious term: "I was ready to make a real commitment"; or "She had a real gift of commitment." "Needs, satisfactions, potential," even "values" appeared frequently on the written surveys, referring to situations an earlier generation might have covered with language such as "sin, repentance, the fellowship of saints." Once-standard "church words" appeared only occasionally in the written responses, and not at all in face-to-face conversations.

In addition to the loss or rejection of a professional theological vocabulary, there was a shift in attitude toward the spiritual authority of "congregation" and the church as an abstraction. Younger and middle-aged women had no hesitation about challenging "their" institution; they enjoyed a mental freedom in this area that was totally unthinkable to the older generation. In a correspondence some months after our visits, a wise older woman wrote her thoughts about "the cross" symbol. "I hate to blow Christianity's cover... but Jesus did not even *know* about his crucifixion early in his ministry. So he couldn't have said, 'Take up your cross!' I think the cross imagery was an early church device to support its converts in their imitation of Christ during their martyrdoms. Over the centuries it has become a wonderfully powerful, controlling symbol, which has been used to keep the poor-and-humble poor and humble." Interrupting her own train of thought, she continued, "This is not to devalue Christ's death but to acknowledge that it's finished; the work of salvation is accomplished. He is Risen. We are now alive through his life. We have already been 'Christed.'" Then she softened the image. "Suffering humanity is more familiar with the stance of remaining at the foot of the cross, not accustomed to the exquisite pain of joyful aliveness. Launching out into the universe of Christedness *is* a terrifying thought!" She felt utter freedom, even a personal mandate, to examine all orthodoxies on her horizon.

A layman, visiting in one of our congregations, cited the significance of "forum" in a congregation. People need a place and a time to assimilate "church-type issues," he said. "There's just no format in my parish for grappling with new ideas, trying them out to see how we're going to respond to them." He concluded ironically, "The only 'community' we get takes place in whispers after church, while we're walking up the aisle — it's really little more than gossip. And coffee-hour type conversations. We don't develop any congregational glue."[8]

Some women, particularly the younger ones, promoted the idea of argument and debate as a generator of "congregational glue." One from New England even said "arguing" was essential for developing solidarity. Others soft-pedaled open disagreement, as if a lack of unanimity were a judgment on them or the congregation itself. Today's more open discussion of topics that were once taboo (cancer, AIDS, homosexuality, child abuse) is, inevitably, broadening the horizons of church people about new areas of thought, prayer, action. Hearing once-prohibited terms in a sermon or announcement legitimizes them religiously.

However, a demeanor of conformity does not encourage revealing "personal" concerns in these congregations. The wisdom of masking emotion during services is a deeply inscribed inhibitor.[9] A younger woman from the Great Plains congregation put it succinctly: "No one here would be comfortable going against the Order of Worship. No one here would shout an 'Amen,' or think of interrupting what it says on the printed bulletin," referring to hymn numbers, page numbers, and scripture readings.

For many Anglo or Northern European men as well as women, emotionally revealing words about religion are "out of place" even in the context of private conversation at church, except perhaps in the pastor's office.[10] We who were visitors found ourselves having to discern the ways in which women touched on the sacred as they spoke. For many, tears — as accompaniment or sometimes in place of words — turned out to be the deepest, and nearly universal, evidence of profound spiritual emotion. Almost without exception, as they struggled to find words for a God-encased moment or experience, tears appeared.

Since we too were constrained, initially, by the cultural view that tears were (only) sentimentality or ineffectuality, we groped toward other readings along with the women themselves: tears as a gift, a release from the socially required iron cage of "self-control"; as a sign of grace; as cleansing or healing; as tapping a hitherto unknown depth of awareness; as a sense of Eternity breaking into the present. One older woman gave a sacred perspective on tears that she had developed in a women's study group. "I used to cry easily during prayer. Today, in church, I had tears twice: during a special hymn, and during the reading of Paul's letter to the Philippians [3:8–14]. I am always grateful for tears. Weeping may be a sentimental emotionalism, but it reveals a good thing — that my heart remains tender before God." Tears as a channel to inner life emerged as a kind of truism, for us and for them. We came to see tears as the soul's language, an expression of "what the journey into God is all about."[11] By and large, however, Anglo-Episcopal congregations expect a more reserved public face.

Often small groups of close-knit friends dot a congregation, another thread in this social fabric that is not much acknowledged. Such intimate clusters form a subterranean network of support and affinity in a larger congregation, sometimes called cell groups, where "members" bond together for fellowship and deep exchange — plus literally helping each other out.[12] A young widow reported that she and three other single mothers shared long late-night telephone calls over a period of several years. "I couldn't live without that group," she said. "We can cry together; we vacation together. But then — I think our congregation is full of groups like that. There are lots of us who find that closeness here. That's what I love about this parish." For some women the congregation has become the second most intimate arena in their lives.

Besides valuing congregation as "community," as incorporating them into something larger than themselves, and as impetus toward self-improvement, a central congregational meaning for women involved the work and ideal of caring. Congregations were formerly springboards into the "how to" and the "to whom" of that work. Parents wanted children to have the apprenticeship in rituals of neighborliness they recalled — delivering food baskets, caroling bed-bound neighbors. A computer manager in her 40s credited her administrative skills to childhood training in "how to care." "Where I grew up there were lots of women's circles, and do you know, in my Junior Circle that put on the Men's Breakfast (an annual May fundraiser) I, a teenager, managed a kitchen with thirty people working in it? I just ... grew up in that tradition."

In addition to training members in the activities of caring, congregations shaped attitudes about financial giving. As the omni-present grass-roots organization in any town or city, after the home, congregations of all religious faiths have been the "seedbed of philanthropy."[13] Even at the end of the twentieth century, these congregations still represent a platform for naming appropriate objects of charity, and promoting giving as a religious act. Stewardship and pledging programs trained members, year by year, in the organized activity of giving. And congregations are a legal entity that can manage and disburse funds. Many women seem to act on the belief that "philanthropic behavior itself is an expression of religious identity."[14]

However, in our four congregations, the links between women and church-sponsored giving had eroded. Women's giving was shaped by its own female-defined and -managed programs of education, worship, and products until the 1960s.[15] By then, barriers keeping women out of administrative offices and roles in the local and national church were disappearing; the generic women's organization changed its name from "auxiliary to" to "*the* Episcopal Church Women," indicating a changed self-image.[16] Ripples from that name change, plus seminary education opening to women, have gradually reshaped the entire structure of church-sponsored giving. Our inquiry, typifying the denominational ethos of reticence about asking for financial information, did *not* inquire about their patterns of giving — how much money the women pledged per year. Nor did it occur to them to volunteer that kind of information.

We learned about their deep-seated attitudes toward giving, however. Among these women congregants mere attendance at worship was "not enough" for genuine, full membership. They expected to "give" more than "just worship," although the ways that dimension of membership may be expressed are now wide open. We glimpsed some indirect clues, but since women are conditioned to disclaim their own generosity, very little emerged in our conversations. The anonymous paying of a neighbor's fuel bill by one young mother or taking in a family of five after a fire destroyed their home indicate the basic kindness the women in those congregations expect of themselves. Undoubtedly the gift of food to a neighbor was counted by few as a religious activity. Yet such exchanges were taking place all around us. The "natural gesture" of food gifts is still a part of the congregational glue. However, they automatically telephone before dropping in on one another now, to "find out if there's room in the refrigerator." Feeding a fellow congregant may be organized (and legitimated) through the congregation's Casserole Brigade.[17] But we also saw many women quietly depositing cans of soup and tuna fish in the community food bank basket at the church door as they entered on a Sunday morning. None mentioned that secret deposit as "religious contribution."

The most important connection between congregation and benevolence, from the structural point of view, was the congregation's function as a conduit of information about causes and issues — the "to whom" of giving. In each congregation, appeals for the victims of AIDS, the homeless, and battered women were the newest definitions of appropriate "goals" for compassion. In the first half of the twentieth century, the women's auxiliary filled that defining function as well as the fundraising and distributing. Women literally were the denomination's philanthropic work; the same was true of Methodist women. But a related, more long-range contribution of churchwomen's organizations was educational — constantly expanding understandings of need beyond the congregational borders. The women's auxiliary provided an organized connection between women in the pew and "their" distant ambassadors for Christ: missionaries, college workers, settlement-house or inner-city church workers. An older woman recalled her excitement when, as a little girl, "the women's meeting" was coming to her house and her mother laid out pictures and letters on the table from "their" missionary, the person for whom the box was to be filled.[18] No similar mechanism existed to spread the word or channel the funds for laymen. A former missionary in Brazil recalled that it was "the church *women* I could count on, to have a grasp of what I actually faced and of the cultural challenges . . . , not the lay men."[19]

A large proportion of women's church identity came from that unified experience of giving, historically. Home skills, the handwork of quilts and aprons, were hallowed by that usage. The task of educating each other in new topics of benevolence widened their intellectual and moral horizons. Churchwomen's "philanthropy" is the oldest, most continuous thread of personal discipleship. Women who work on a blood donor drive or at a soup kitchen today are participating in "religious" giving. Its congregational underpinnings, however, have been weakened — the rhetorical environment that promoted women's hands-on serving and the church channels through which they responded directly. "Giving" is now perceived as an individual matter, is less a part of congregational consciousness (except about self-maintenance), and is no longer buoyed by its own momentum. The loss of a women's informational network and organization connecting in each parish in this denomination has spread its effects in many directions, but most vividly in the arena of benevolence.[20] The primary vehicle for congregational influence and motivation today, beside newsletters, is sermons. Preaching, while it provides information and motive, does not supply the participatory mechanisms. Women are now independent enough, and have assimilated enough business perspective, to speak of "spending" their time as church members. The verb implies a mental calculus, the sense that they are going to balance church obligations with other activities. "Giving" in these ways has become secularized and distant from "the holy."

Finally, congregations remain, for many, a place that houses the numinous, a hallowed space slightly set apart from everyday uses. The symbolism of the church building is a physical location where people expect the spiritual dimension to be found, the "sacred canopy" people know best.[21] A young woman said simply, "I just never got a sense of sacredness in any of the other churches I tried." A male congregational leader acknowledged the

Anglo-Protestant cultural self-limitation of locating "the holy" in a building. Many things about present-day religion and church life are outmoded and need to be changed, he thought. But "the church building itself is still the place that holds the sacred, in our Episcopal mindset. We can't really just go off and look for the sacred somewhere else, out in nature or whatever, in a waterfall or a mountain, the way the Native Americans can. We may try, but we don't have any real hopes of finding it. It's just not in our psychic inheritance."

In summary, congregations provide women a basic framework, in our culture, for religious emotion, personal spiritual nurture, and a physical place to invoke the sacred. They lead women outward into the surrounding community; they hallow large and small events in life, and they help motivate the activities of giving and serving. As the new field of Family History connects small-scale "local" daily life with the great events of public history, the new field of Congregational Studies illuminates the inner life of such a local "community of memory" and its links with the denominational context.[22] Similarly, an individual woman works out her relationship with the entity of the congregation in some of the same ways. In these and all congregations, women combine universal and home-grown symbols with local self-understandings that, though "as mute as handshakes," to congregational members are "as tangible as doughnuts."[23]

Generations: Women's Horizontal Experiential Connection

The Older Generation

A summary of the generations in our congregations provides an overview of their differing views of change. For the older generation, change generated some resistance but more accommodation. A woman in her early 60s disapproved of liturgical change because it symbolized the entire range of upheavals she had endured since the 1960s: "I sometimes think you reach a stage in your life where you have changed as much as you're willing to...perhaps I've reached an age where I'm just not willing or *able* to compromise any further. My fear is...I just hope my church doesn't change so much that...I...can't stand it." Another, in her late

70s, established her enjoyment of change, particular the ordained woman in her congregation's leadership, by contrasting it with a friend's resistance. "That woman is so against women, it's just terrible. I don't understand how a woman could feel that way against women! I don't think Jesus would feel that way at all, you know."

Women above 60 always identified with their congregations through "work"; they invested enormous amounts of self-worth in "traditional" women's churchwork. Even today their actual labors are substantive. Each of the four parishes depends on a veritable small army of older women volunteers for tasks far beyond stuffing envelopes. The main benchmark of this generation, then, is found in its perspective on work and volunteering. Their model calls for "fitting in wherever needed." One wrote on her questionnaire, "I am one of a small group who is called on whenever a specific need arises." Another wrote succinctly, "When a job needs doing, you just fall to and do it." Stating those self-evaluations in conversation would have seemed too immodest.

They pride themselves on the versatility of their contributions to parish maintenance: making curtains for the Sunday school rooms, cleaning the parish house kitchen, raising money for a new roof. They know they are essential to the congregation but they are used to acting offstage, so to speak — away from the center of attention. A woman nearing 80 from the parish in the Great Plains still "helped out" in the church office when the secretary was swamped. "But I hide it, a little bit. I don't want anyone to think I'm overdoing it.... I don't want them to think, 'She's trying to take over.' I try to stay in the background." Even as they claim the background, they are adapting to the changes in congregational self-definition.

While only eleven out of eighty-seven older generation women openly opposed ordination of women via the written questionnaire, change in words — language about God (less hierarchical and not exclusively masculine) was easier to resist, on the survey and in person. Assimilating change through the eye is one thing, but in the ear it is more visceral, less tolerable. If they didn't forthrightly resist "Inclusive Language" on the survey, objections could be buried under the "No Opinion" choice. As several later explained, they wanted to avoid sounding "too negative." A New England woman of 72 was fully supportive of changes other than language. But altering the verbal images in hymns and worship was, in her view, only a passing and unworthy fad, designed "to meet some strongly held [feminist] feelings."

As a generation they have been resilient and generous. Insofar as older women are able or willing to assimilate change in their congregation, to "go along," they are appreciated by fellow parishioners and clergy. They themselves are determined to remain part of "their" congregation, somehow, even as it changes.

The Bridge Generation

For those between the ages of 41 and 60, "women themselves are what has changed," said one. An aphorism pegs the bridge-generation years as "the old age of youth and the youth of old age."[24] A woman in New England cited the anomaly of being in the middle: "I've always thought that one of the problems in the church has been age exclusiveness. You're either over 60 and active, say, in the ECW, or you're in the nursery. But in between? Nothing counts!" These women literally embodied the shift from post–World War II domesticity to the "Feminine Mystique," into civil rights and then the women's movement.[25] Several recollected living through the romanticizing of family, suburb, and church as a bulwark against world communism. Then the Vietnam War brought further change into their adult lives, often through their children. Change in their churches for some required, finally, almost a kind of conversion.

The most striking characteristic of these women is that almost unanimously they enjoy escape (not their word) from the home-and-housewife status — something to which the older of the generation thought they were committed for life. They are glad to be out of the house. Sometimes the freedom is expressed in pursuit of intellectual or spiritual self-development instead of job and career. What they demonstrate is that they have fully accepted and are fully involved in the many new possibilities for women. They are "experiencing growth" (an oft-used phrase) in career-volunteer work, for example, in gerontology or literacy programs, as members of the city council; or in paid professional jobs, as professors, secretaries, business executives, real estate agents.

When the women of this age group who are now in their late 50s married, after World War II, they expected to find total fulfillment in their domestic and church circles (often overlapping). Many had been schooled to take pride in the fact that they would never *have* to work outside the home: husbands could and should support them. Daycare centers and nursing homes were not on their horizons; achieving the goal of family was to encompass all sexual and relational issues. They were "protected from having to choose a career." Wifehood (and motherhood) was supposed to be their career of choice.

The high-water mark of change here is that "jobs" have become a central feature in their self-identity, if only to contribute to the family retirement fund. Although it wasn't said explicitly, the label of "Mrs." is somewhat devalued. Women like these now feel they must have something more as an identity. Even the act of retirement from a paid job has taken on new meaning, biographical and spiritual.

Meanwhile, the view of "jobs as identity" has moved with them into their churches — where the type of "job" they want is new. A nurse, 44, had seriously "prayed about whether or not I should say yes and become a lay reader," the first female in her congregation. Was it really something women were supposed to do? "The feeling I got from the other lay readers (at that time they were all men) was: 'We don't want a woman.' And being up in front of people hasn't ever been easy for me...but God has proved to me that I could do it and not pass out!" Another woman neatly summarized for her generation the change that opened to women the possibility of new roles in the liturgy. "When I see a woman in a job that has traditionally been male, I don't say: 'Ooooh-eee, we've got a woman up there now!' Nor do I question whether or not she should be there. It's becoming normal, even for people over 45."

A third change for this generation, one unassociated with worship, concerns religiously sponsored volunteering. Their new view of jobs during the week decreases the available weekday volunteer "workers" and rearranges the assumptions around belonging to and maintaining the congregation. Formerly, their volunteer labor constituted a major portion of a congregation's community identity and benevolence. What used to be "traditional churchwomen's work" is drastically reformulated.

Women of this generation matured before the women's movement so they themselves bridged the chasm between previous and present expectations of churchwomen. One used organizational gender dynamics: "Talk about change! Now women are participating in everything but the men's choir. And men participate in everything except the Altar Guild! We don't even have a women's group as such anymore!" Another took a more functional perspective. "Women of this church...maybe in all churches...really hold the church together," she began. "Believe it or not, in spite of all rhetoric to the contrary, *they're* the organizers. . . . In the past, it was the women's group here that raised all the money to do things, and actually did, or paid for, all the housekeeping or maintenance tasks in this church." Another, 49, working full-time, explained, "The women my age and younger are all working now. It's changing the support that the church receives from lay people. Now there's more of a choice. Women will say, 'I intend to do *some* activity, even if I'm not just sure what it will be,' rather than what they used to say, which was 'It's my responsibility to be making pies so that we can buy curtains for the basement.' " In her congregation, the question of curtains — who will pay for, go out, get the fabric and make them — has become "everyone's, and then of course, no one's job." Decisions about something as "unimportant" as curtains become an issue for debate instead of direct action for women. The one-to-one relationship between seeing what needs to be done, from a female perception of need, and then doing it, has been ruptured.

A defining characteristic of this generation, however, is also awareness of and willingness to acknowledge its own spiritual needs. "I really want the sense of being hooked up to a source, a life-sustaining source, not just in the form or in the liturgy, but in an alive relation with the risen Lord," Polly said, a woman at the 40-ish end of the generation. Margaret, nearing 60, later wrote about how she "used" her sitting in the choir during services: "Usually I watch as people kneel at the rail to receive the sacraments, and I bless each person individually, valuing their uniqueness as I know them, and seeing Christ in whatever dimension He chooses to manifest himself, in their life — their being His vehicle. I see their preciousness. I am often overwhelmed by a sense of loving communion, in its richest and most whole sense. But last Sunday it happened that I got sidetracked a lot with my own thoughts."

An example of spiritual attunement came from a description, later sent to me, of one woman's visit to an orthodox monastery. "I was deeply touched. The Holy Spirit was emphatically SHE. Hymns, canticles, and prayers constantly referred to the 'she' of the Third Person of the Trinity. *Shekinah* glory was in that chapel.[26] Everything *shimmered*. It was awesome. The reverence was profound. . . . " Her choice of descriptive language was poetic and theologically sophisticated. "I stood stunned and fascinated by the

ancient music, the incense, the icons, the candlelight, the descent of
the Spirit on the elements [bread and wine]. I ate from that bread
and shared it, for a week."

Because these women are more in touch with spiritual issues
than ever before in their churchgoing lives, they measure the congregation by their own high standards. One wrote on the survey
that she waged "a continual struggle to explain my view of Jesus
as a feminist." Her church was full of "too much busy-work,"
the kind that fills up time and space but "interferes with spiritual
growth." Another wrote, "Caring and love are only rhetoric; doing 'your own thing' seems to be everything." A third recognized in
herself "an inability to open up and get close to others." A fourth
wrote her disappointment at the human measures of value in her
congregation, "that, for example, Altar Guild work is not seen as
important as a regular [paid] job would be. I'm not credited with
doing anything truly 'important' with my time outside the home."

The questionnaire asked each woman to rank the various parts
of the worship service in terms of which activity she perceived as
most important and nurturing. The generational distinction is instructive. While the number 1 choice of all three age groups was
"receiving the sacrament," the number 2 choice for the bridge
generation was "internal individual devotion." Both younger and
older generations ranked the "sense of participating with others"
second in importance. Bridge-generation women come to worship
for themselves more than ever before in their consciousness. "It's
the serenity of the liturgy, and the chance to kneel," sighed a
woman professional. "All week I look forward to it. I love the un-
winding, just handing over to God all the stuff in my mind." They
see church as momentary surcease from never-ending responsibility for others, now including the "parenting of our own parents."
A college professor said intensely, "I just can't wait to get on my
knees every Sunday. It's *my time*, before the service. I have this long
list of people and things to pray about. No matter what's going on
during the week, good or bad, I need that peace. I welcome it. I
crave it."

Conspicuously absent in this middle-aged generation's perspective is emphasis on being a parent. Many of these women have
managed somehow to disengage the topic of mothering from their
sense of religiosity, seeming to think of spirituality more in terms of
accomplishments (like careers) rather than connections with physical humanity. Or they have absorbed the feminist determination

that women define themselves in terms other than parenthood, the way men do. They didn't avoid talking about their role as mothers, but a focus on spiritual self-development was expressed more in terms of their new liturgical and occupational "jobs."

The Younger Generation

The women 40 and under named the upheavals of the 1960s as their ground-shifting experience. For some it had been only negative. A physician from the South wept as she recalled antiwar demonstrations at her college. "I became nearly mute for a while," she recalled; "it was absolutely traumatic for my psyche.... I felt I was always alone, and that people thought I was really strange because I couldn't get with it. I just couldn't cope, I didn't get all involved." Another reported almost total unawareness of the same phenomenon. "I don't even remember Kent State! Only later I thought, Hey, wait a minute! They were shooting *kids* over this!"

What was positive out of the 1960s was the new open-ended view of career possibilities. Even that change for women was below the level of consciousness for some of them; they had never had to worry about whether or not they could actually have a career. They went to college with the internalized premise that the ability to be self-supporting and earn "their own" living was the precondition of personhood — and, in marriage, of genuine partnership. The folksong "Michael, Row the Boat Ashore" brought folk music from the backwoods into their living rooms, a symbol of this generation's dramatic shift in attitude, goals, and culture. That and *Jesus Christ Superstar* were a "generational code" for them.

Religiously, these younger women are carving out "their own ways" of relating to the church. Sometimes it involves re-inventing some of the traditions cast off in earlier rebellion. The distinguishing characteristic of this generation is the importance of choice. Expressions of valuing and approval are all expressed in terms of (one's own) choosing. "It's great to be here out of choice, not just out of other's expectations," one said. For the younger women who answered the questionnaire, "religious gratifications" centered around the maturing of thought and experience that accompanies a first real sense of adulthood. Many associated it with becoming a parent and worshipping in a church with one's own family. One wrote, "I'm more open to others now, incorporating religion into all my daily life." Another wrote, "I'm finally comfortable with the language of belief."

The distinctive way this generation relates to its congregation of choice is again in terms of choice: these younger women look carefully for a particular gift of time or talent they can bestow. It must be something that will give them a satisfying, possibly unique, place in the congregation — nothing taken for granted.[27] It is important to them that their "participating" meet *their* inner needs, not that what they do as a church member simply "fills a slot." They grew up knowing no barriers toward any career for which they could afford to prepare. Not surprisingly, they exercise the same control over deciding how they will relate to their congregation. They have made "choice" a deliberate, internal self-allocation of religious time that would have been literally unthinkable to their grandmothers.

●

An experiential, environmental lens like *generation* is particularly apt for the Episcopal Church, which has historically embodied a stance of mediation — the *via media* between Roman Catholicism and Protestantism. Its self-proclaimed identity has been a denomination with "room enough" for people holding multiple points of view and contrasting definitions of politics and gender, practice and mission. This historical self-image has tended to paper over conflict and disagreement while "change" spreads — in minuscule accretions and without conscious acknowledgment or negotiation, from the outer edges in to the institutional church. Suddenly, it seems, "change" emerges into full view, in a major new arrangement or paradigm. Once that happens it begins to be rationalized historically. In many congregations that takes the form of the protest, "But we've *always* done it this way."[28] Generational perspective offers a meliorative path in congregations — the basic unit of these women's "faith and works."

Chapter 7

UNFINISHED BUSINESS

"WHY ARE THERE so many different voices?" a friend asked. "Is it important to keep them separate?" Her question illustrates "the arithmetic of vitality."[1] One voice, even a few voices, could not have created this aural prism. And no, in spite of their powerful individuality, here they are to be heard as parts of a whole. A living acquaintance with "Episcopal women" requires a multitude of voices, however unique each is in God's eyes and in her own. These concluding reflections discuss what we learned as we went along and some hindsight reflections — topics and constituencies that must be part of any similar future conversations.

Many "first-generation" (1970s–1980s) books about women in American religious history did not have the luxury of focusing on specific women in a specific belief system and organization. The first broad strokes establishing a field of women's history under a collective label "Protestant" meant emphasis on similarities rather than singularities.[2] Here we choose an opposite path, carefully embedding these words in a specific denomination and congregational culture — one itself undergoing "change," religiously and organizationally. The experiences excerpted here may well, I hope, strike notes of recognition in many who are not Episcopalian. My aim has been to provide as vital a composite portrait of this one religious identity as possible, conscious all the while that it has still not included "everybody," and that it is one among many denominations to be similarly studied.

To realize any depth of perspective today, we require specifics about a woman, about a particular religious body. To have any real understanding of her "religion," we need to know her educational level, her social class and cultural background, and her racial or ethnic roots, where she now lives and what books or music she likes. As one historian recently cautioned, we have come to the point in the 1990s where the collective noun "women" needs "a whole paragraph of qualifiers." This complexifying in itself is a sign of growth. "Women's studies" have expanded exponentially, deepening our awareness of the multiple factors needed to account for the immense complexity of women's daily lives, to say nothing of their spiritual lives.[3]

Interestingly, it is only in the 1990s, when multiculturalism is becoming an increasing reality in America,[4] that the experience and worldview of white, middle-class, well-educated Protestant women from an Episcopal congregation can be separated out from "white Protestant women." Only within the past decade are white Christians beginning to examine their own religious and congregational culture, their own experiences as a "race." Until this level of group consciousness emerged, WASP culture was able to ignore the need to be self-conscious or self-analytical. The stereotype "Episcopalian" carried its own assumptions that did not recognize the racial and economic privilege it took for granted in the society at large. It has become a matter of irony, even guilt, for many serious Christian women, that "our own" religious history and its Anglo-European cultural assumptions about God, other humans, and the planet are only now coming to the surface of our own consciousness.[5] Thanks to the context developing from recent studies like *White Women's Christ, Black Women's Jesus*, by Jacquelyn Grant, or an anthology *This Bridge Called My Back: Writings by Radical Women of Color* (by Cherrie Moraga and Gloria Anzualda), we see that no one denominational experience is "standard" for all Christian women, nor can the white experience apply to the theology, imagery, and lived experience of women from other backgrounds and heritage.

Multiple explorations like this one, therefore — specific women in specific forms of congregational religion in the United States — are essential for any composite religious prism. Each denomination must map its own specifics from the experience of the women in its congregations. The portrait I have assembled, with its strengths as well as its shortcomings, has to stand as its own form of "witness." Robert Coles used that term to speak of people whose life stories he collected throughout his oral history career, to honor the gift such listening bestowed on him. He called his collected oral histories testaments of "*lived* moral energy" from which he continually learns.[6] His respectful words summarize the profound indebtedness I feel toward these "witnesses." Anyone who listens seriously to the words of these "ordinary" women cannot avoid the same reflective awe.

My first learning from their "witness," then, is that new ways must be found in which to think about women's experience of religion — new mental categories, so to speak. We haven't had a language that rings true to women's religious experience in general, to say nothing of one that reveals the experience of churchwomen in this particular denominational heritage of theology, culture, and practice. The realization that the "ordinary words" here carry layers of meaning allows us to begin to perceive, for the first time, the women-riches latent in other congregational pews. A second learning is that anyone interested in hearing this type of witness must be newly attuned to the aura of the sacred hovering over these exchanges — over these efforts to convert experience and spiritual insight into words. If I am to grasp or share their depths, I must be freed from listening with flat empiricism and learned "objectivity." To appreciate the "*lived* moral experiences" groping into articulation here, eyes have to see with compassion and ears listen with empathy.

A third learning stems from this new attentiveness. The bonds that became palpable in these conversations I believe were a grassroots version of "womanchurch." Until the patriarchal religious institutional form is modified, theologian Elisabeth Schüssler Fiorenza argues, gender exclusivity (women-only gatherings) is *the* critical setting. Women are the ones who must support and elicit other women's thoughts. Trying to communicate profound religious experience in meetings of both men and women is still inhibiting to most women. Only a gender-specific framework enables women to fearlessly re-read, re-combine, and re-assimilate traditional holy texts within their own inner reality.[7]

A public dimension of that gender specificity is found in the current struggle over language about God, especially whether or not women have the right to name and claim a feminine dimension of the God image, Sophia. Men don't understand why women want or need to do it; many women are not yet comfortable exploring it or using it in worship.[8] In a number of congregations, a phenomenon such as women's spiritual "cell groups" or other study or prayer groups is beginning to diffuse versions of "womanchurch" and enable that kind of self-discovery. Woman-to-woman sharing in small "safe" groups is the most positive context a congregation can offer for *personal* religiosity.

A fourth learning is about language and the two major ideas in our conversations, "change" and "congregation." The fact is that women viewed the major idea "change" in almost exclusively individual terms. First reactions to our inquiry about change elicited new organizational possibilities, roles, or actions open to them. Some enjoyed seeing themselves as participants in a larger stream of societal change also. Only a small number extended their thoughts about change beyond themselves (in their congregations) into more far-reaching arenas: what change might mean in terms of family, where change might affect the worlds of education, commerce, or international politics. The only theme that requested that they think in wider, other-person dimensions was the final one — the question of what about their religion was most precious, what would they want to see passed on to the next generation. In that theme women could pick up on either the reflective or the projective (in the twist at the end), most unconsciously choosing the former.

As we worded the themes, they did not lead women to think beyond personal statements. Our focus, I see by hindsight, was individualist, so it elicited personal, individual responses to the topic of change. The occasional woman who offered a corporate future vision simply illustrated the power of personal witness: she made that her (individual) choice. In retrospect, it is clear that imaginative projection, explicitly encouraged, could be very productive. Asking women to dream and then articulate visions of a truly just world or even of a "whole" congregation is not an activity much promoted in late twentieth-century culture, or in mainline churches. The African-American church, by contrast, has a long tradition of such "envisioning." The theology of many regular sermons in Episcopal (and other mainline) congregations remains securely anchored to texts and documents, largely excluding the visionary in favor of focusing on urgent, here-and-now problems. Yet a remarkable, untapped reservoir of spiritual energy might be released if women were encouraged to explore this avenue of religious introspection.

Language about the second major idea, "congregations," did blend the individualistic and the corporate, because they needed to record their gratitude for being able "to participate in something larger than" themselves. Initial statements about "congregation" focused on ways in which it nurtured one's personal growth. With surprising unanimity, however, both older and younger generations of women expressed profound appreciation of the larger entity, the congregation — an unexpected emphasis from so many self-directed, individual achievers. Women named an almost visceral corporateness, the sense of knowing they were in the midst of people all making the same religious gesture at the same time — kneeling, standing, singing together in unison. But reference to corporate action other than in worship was scarce. In retrospect, the relatively small amount of talk about their own or their congregation's "witness" outside the congregation is noticeable. "Congregational" language was as much about the individual as the entity itself, except at Advent South. Unfortunately I did not register on that realization in time to explore it with them.

Another learning about "congregation" has more gloomy implications for the denomination's future. The reader may have noted, though I did not until I began to craft these reflections, how talk about religious identity was disproportionately local. In terms of denomination *per se*, fewer than 5 percent of the nearly 300 women responding (through written questionnaires or conversation) mentioned any pursuit of personal or spiritual self-development through Episcopal organizations or programs outside the local parish. In the nineteenth and early twentieth centuries, such proportions might well have been reversed. This is a serious disengagement from the organizational paradigm of voluntarism that characterized American Protestant churches beginning in the mid-nineteenth century. If a few women in these four congregations found meaning in a national Episcopal organization, it was because they had somehow as individuals "found out" about it, and got involved in it "on their own." Little interest or influence is currently expended on relating local women to denominational events or issues beyond the local church, the assumption being "everyone's too busy with *their own* commitments." Measured in the formerly significant terms of organization, denominational interest and participation is of diminishing importance.

The most commonly shared in-parish-organization membership, Altar Guild, remains highly local in actions and religious mindset. Since the actual liturgical work in each Altar Guild consists of uniform routines, one might think it could indeed bind its mostly female practitioners together across the denomination. But each congregation views the piety and labors offered under that rubric as specific to that church building and congregation. A woman who has spent a lifetime devoted to the Altar Guild of her own parish rarely develops horizontal fellowship with others doing the same work in other congregations.

Ecumenical or interdenominational interests attract women more. They seem willing to seek out activities and organizations to expand their mental horizons while keeping their denominational identity "at home." Organized ministries within the national church that still attract small numbers of Episcopal women, often in far-flung chapters, are usually special-interest groups pursuing specialized tasks. Current examples are the Episcopal Women's History Project, a small national membership combining scholarly and popular-education goals, including an archive that documents women's experiences historically; ABIL, an acronym for Asian, Black, Indian/Indigenous, Latina Episcopal Women, who have combined to promote awareness and budgetary representation of their presence and works in a dominantly Anglo denomination; the Episcopal Women's Caucus, an advocacy group supporting ordained women and women's causes in general within the denomination; and Integrity, the organization promoting the full participation of homosexual men and women in the Episcopal Church. Each has a relatively small national membership (from 500 to several thousand) and a particular avenue of service and self-expression. No structure today has anything comparable with the former parish-to-parish linkage supplied by the Woman's Auxiliary/Episcopal Church Women network.[9]

Women today who want a corporate experience beyond the local congregation are likely to participate in occasional, single-event regional or national gatherings. The new (1980s) Council of Women's Ministries semiannual gatherings in part fulfill that kind of wider-organization need. But the genre of "church organizations" alters, adapts, or may disappear as younger generations of well-educated, self-directed women join professional and recreational associations instead of church organizations. Women here are likely to direct what church-organization energy they have toward small nonorganizations like congregational cell groups and parish-wide events such as flea markets or Lenten suppers.

The learning that confronted me most forcefully came from realizing the ways our questions had framed — unconsciously influenced — the women's speaking about religion and spirituality.

My mindset unthinkingly limited language about spiritual or interior experience to intellectualized "mental" terms, and that was the language in which women responded. The spiritual *persona* they expressed was primarily rational and verbal. "Conscience" could be talked about, but not physical consciousness. The imagery we elicited was so purely nonphysical it could be seen as almost verging toward the mystical. Episcopalians, however, avoid terms like "inner consciousness," "inner light," or "holy mysteries" except in specialized usage — eucharistic and biblical language or hymns. A further result of this limited spiritual range was that issues of morality or ethics that might have come up also remained largely off-limits.

This leads me to the heart of these retrospections. From hindsight, topics we did not pursue clamor for attention. Now that I have experienced both women's hitherto-unarticulated gifts of wisdom and the openness that "ordinary" laywomen are willing to invest in religious conversation, I wish we had asked them about (1) physicality, "the body," and sexuality in their spiritual identity; (2) the complicated institution of marriage in the late twentieth century; (3) child-rearing and the ministry of care-giving, women's contributions to the theology of care, and care not only for one's own kin but a perspective on families in the world at large;[10] and (4) the range of attitudes about material possessions, especially money.

The way our themes were worded, and the mindset we, or certainly I, brought to these exchanges, remained within the dominant Anglo-American assumption that "talk about religion" involves the mental, emotional, and psychological dimensions of a woman's life but not the body. We politely avoided the physical, I now see, in all our conversation, except when the older generation spoke of failing health. The avoidance of all aspects of physicality in most Episcopal congregations includes even the female voice. Unless women are part of a congregation where a woman's voice and experience are heard from the pulpit, occasionally at least, they hear only men's voices, including scripture that was written down and is still primarily interpreted by men. They listen to sermons that are similarly gendered. Any internal applications women may make on their own remain just that.

A future inquiry has to begin from "embodiment." We all could benefit, women and men, from naming and talking about religious messages we have received about the Body and our bodies in our congregations. One woman mentioned "having struggled with weight *all* my life" under the theme that asked about her experience of God in daily activities. What religious messages had she received about her body? Women who are treated as cultural stereotypes of either beauty or deformity obviously bring profound dimensions of physicality to their spiritual imagery. I wish we had visited women from these congregations who are now confined to nursing homes. How are they and their physical limitations continued in their congregation's prayer and social life?

Intelligent laywomen like these, given encouragement to grope for metaphors with which to express their insights, remain *the* valuable untapped resource for change and institutional reinvigoration. In observations about their own inner lives, a number of the women already used images associating "holiness" with growth and health. Although sexuality is still a conversational taboo among church-affiliated women, reflections about the spiritual dimension of *eros*, "a fundamental life energy," could vastly expand the lexicon of women's religious affect.[11] If women such as these began verbal exchanges of their own learnings and reflections about the body, the topic would lose its aura of forbiddenness and "secrecy." The potential of healing (for both individuals and congregations) toward Episcopal women who identify themselves as lesbians could be incalculable.

A third unexplored aspect of women's physicality — its neglect again demonstrating our unconscious reflection of male epistemology about "religion" — concerns motherhood, as institution and experience.[12] This aspect of female identity was a major preoccupation of church-related women in the nineteenth and early twentieth centuries. Many of the most powerful discriminatory messages directed to females throughout Judeo-Christian history and scriptures relate to this single aspect of women's biology.[13] Among the women here, motherhood was among the most commonly shared, certainly the most time-consuming, aspects of physicality that could impinge on their spiritual identity. If we expand the term "mothering" to parenting and include the care of aging parents, every individual we contacted could have contributed experience and wisdom. Yet this most basic commonality eluded us.

We did not ask them to reflect on their part in the miracle of creating new life. Giving birth is a freely discussed topic in the younger generation today. It is also a female incarnational experience that is unacknowledged in church liturgy except for a few hymns and the Magnificat. Young mothers, if they yearn for a ritual capturing the awesome mystery of creation and new life, might well murmur about the Prayer Book service of baptism. The liturgy emphasizes the biblical concepts of sin and redemption, and the church claiming "its own." "The whole ceremony [baptism] was not about my new baby or the miracle she and I had just been through," a young woman said. "It was more like the church putting its stamp on one more human being." Even in modernized language, the service contains no sense of wonder about physical reproducing, and only partially addresses the awesome responsibilities new parents face with a new member of their human family.

Even when women spoke of congregational membership "for the children's sake," I did not think of asking them to extrapolate that into the arena of "Christian education." This topic occupied much personal and congregational thought in the grandmothers' generation and inspired enormous creativity among women of earlier times. It would have been interesting to hear what spiritual rituals these women observed with their young, in what ways they consciously instructed children in "religious issues." Sadly, this blind spot in our conversations is another example of the devaluation of all dimensions of "embodiment" in thinking about religion — and our unprotesting unconscious participation in it. That particular skewed perspective helps account for the negligible amount of energy directed to the topic of children in most Episcopal congregations, and the small amount of congregational effort often expended on child nurture and instruction. Even when the younger generation women listed "Sunday school" as one of their contributions, I failed to explore its dimensions in their mindset.

Another subcategory under physicality and care-giving could have been their views on marriage, considering the ubiquity of divorce and remarriage among them and women in all U.S. congregations today. The state of being a couple is freighted with hope and despair; it would have been interesting to hear it seriously examined in these four congregations. Given the fact that today's educated, professional men have not fully changed in relation to the changed gender-role understandings brought by today's women into marriage and the family, here is yet another arena deeply impacting on the way women participate in spiritual life.[14] Yet our continuing participation in the culture's view of what may and may not be included in "religion" led us away from it. A contemporary bestseller, *Care of the Soul*, names family and marriage the unarguable basis of most contemporary psychological and spiritual problems. Because marriage falls under the "body" part of the mind-body dualism so pervasive in our mindset, however, I remained unaware that we had neglected to explore it until the interviews were long past.[15]

The hidden reservoir of religious activism among women like these also makes me long to ask what messages their congregations have delivered about justice issues. The entryway poster in Grace New England of a Central American child with an amputated stump in place of her left leg — victim of a land mine explosion — was one form of evidence. What arouses their indignation in a more local setting? An emerging consciousness of Christian stewardship for the planet was also evident in the four parishes, though not much verbalized. Do these women see themselves as trustees of the ecology, "this fragile earth, our island home," the Prayer Book words they hear weekly? Several women, perhaps unconsciously falling into the language of medieval mystics, clothed their earliest awareness of God in a profound sense of "oneness" with all of Creation and Nature. Several were reaching toward an image such as "the world as God's Body," Sallie McFague's arresting combination of ecology and incarnation.[16] A number named gardening as a major direct experience of God in their daily lives. A new genre of feminist theology is exploring the interrelationships between male cultural domination and Nature, women, and the preservation of the planet.[17] If we had raised this as a specific focus, our exploration might have moved further into future terrain for women's religious thought.

A huge topic I wish we had examined directly is money and its place in our daily spiritual identity. Given our overwhelming cultural reliance on financial imagery for calculating and speaking about "value," money is a profoundly significant symbol and "fact" in modern-day religion. Yet women often "leave it to the men" to discuss and manage in the congregations and in the national church budgets. Only a few of the young women named it as an area of ethical concern for them. "Women and money" are important issues in contemporary female self-definition and self-management, but Episcopalians have been too circumspect to discuss in congregations "the things that belong to Caesar" and those that belong to the individual woman, her congregation, or to

God.[18] Perhaps the latter two are not as synonymous as we (and they) have hitherto assumed.

An ultimate institutional issue that also must be addressed more deeply is their experience with ordained female leaders. "It isn't *just* that there's a female up there at the altar, celebrating the mass," one young woman said. Do women see women clergy contributing a new dimension to worship and leadership, or do they see them taking on the patriarchal assumptions that have historically surrounded the hierarchical position of clergy — as increasing rather than decreasing the distance of Episcopal laity from Episcopal clergy? Dare they hope that ordained females will "prevent the spiritual reproduction of patriarchy" and its debilitating effects on women's spiritual potential, or do women priests turn out to be a same-sex version of what prevailed in the past?[19] These are provocative essential questions for a next inquiry. They are also required information if "the church" is to fulfill its calling to be a "countercultural" institution in the world.[20]

All these unexplored concerns stem from change generated by a "feminist religious consciousness," a label that the majority of women here avoided even as they embraced its effects. In Episcopal debates throughout the twentieth century, "tradition" was used to justify resisting all kinds of change, especially any that expanded women's sacramental roles.[21] It was employed as a rationalization for racial segregation in the 1960s, against modernizing the liturgical tools (Prayer Book and Hymnal), and most ardently enlisted to oppose women's ordination. Although I have frequently used the adjective "traditional" for these women, I hope it is clear that, along with its negative functions in Episcopal history, there are positive facets of the label.

The emerging relationships offered here, between "traditional" women and their congregations, clearly open out a new, more complex structure for the church. These women are church members who value "the best," the most dynamic (rather than static and ossified) elements of their religious and spiritual tradition. They see themselves working to enrich and expand it, rather than setting out to destroy it. They are not trying to break down church walls but open doors and windows in them. These churchwomen constitute a growing stream of multiple voices contributing a living "arithmetic of vitality."[22]

We can now see that these women were engaged in remythologizing the spiritual in their lives — trying to come up with words and symbol systems that "work" for them in the lives they are presently living. They use terms of relationship and choice rather than of organization or doctrine, avoiding the "old" church language. Most of them are also in new or modified (though historically grounded) patterns of relating to their congregations. And they refuse any longer to be cut off (or separated from) the historic current of feminine religious piety, buried till recently under "church custom" and official rhetoric. That understanding of our talks was thoughtfully encapsulated by a layman in one of the congregations, a psychology professor. "Our language, the church's discourse, is outmoded. Our metaphors are too small. They reduce our thinking about everything, in this era, to issues of gender. Actually, what we're really talking about here is an entire style of spirituality or consciousness."

Today women draw nurture from a multitude of sources. They are catholic in a sense unimaginable before the 1960s: angels, wisewomen, Sophia, Nature, Native American images, Celtic prayers, Buddhist meditation practices. Such riches of spirit have already freed many spiritually questing women from being confined to rational Anglo-European words and texts for religious insight. In each of the four congregations, an expanded range of spiritual resources was already being explored by some women, bellwethers of wider future assimilation. Some are already creating "multiple metaphors" — a personal spiritual arithmetic of vitality. Because of that foundational expansion, a second development is ensured: women won't and can't leave their church, and its worship, alone. Even if they wanted to, they find it impossible to separate their lives from the congregations that they love and in which they increasingly want to participate actively.[23] They can't by deliberate intention shut off the part of them already beginning to expand and challenge the "orthodox" imagery of the past.[24]

A danger for Episcopal churchwomen here, by their own report, is their present-day distance from the scriptural texts that are the historical source of Judeo-Christian religious insight. Resistance to direct involvement with the scriptures outside of Sunday morning readings and sermons could produce a short-circuiting of spiritual energy. Some realize it but haven't yet found or devised a means, in their own denomination, of reconnecting with the Bible in a way that affirms and accepts their own "lived realities." A few reach outside church walls for special spiritual nurture: interdenominational Bible study, charismatic prayer groups, Cursillo, feminist spirituality workshops, New Age seminars. One bridge-generation woman spent much of the conversation describing how her study of the Bible with this extra-congregation group made "the difference between night and day" in her life. "It's what some people call a conversion experience, though it isn't anything like St. Paul's." Private, personally arranged cell groups could create a "woman church" safety in one's own congregation that would encourage reflecting on scriptures with new authority.

Today, women in Protestant denominations see their individual spiritual life as *the* arena of religious self-hood no one can control or deny them. As Mary Catherine Bateson reminds us in her metaphor of women "composing" their lives, growth in nature occurs at the edges — at the tip of the prickly-pear cactus pads, at the branch ends of a rosebush.[25] Under an article of historic faith and Protestant self-definition that cannot be disowned, no matter how uncomfortably it challenges institutional authority structures, each soul is unique and individually answerable to the divine Transcendent Being. Women are accepting that realization, even unconsciously, and emerging from the shadows of "secondariness" to which their religion in the past consigned them. They begin to trust an unfolding of the sacred in themselves.

Church life itself, the interior culture of each congregation, already evidences growth at its edges. Multiple groups once considered an extra-church (or para-church) component, "self-help" or special interest groups such as Al-Anon, Alcoholics Anonymous, or other "support groups," are now a taken-for-granted part of the larger congregational fabric.[26] There were also a few women in each of the congregations who expressed their religion through local or national political movements such as nuclear disarmament, the environment, world hunger. Some translated their "discipleship" into overt (financial and information-diffusing) support of specific causes like gun control, or citizen-lobbying for peace legislation. They define "Christian commitment and ministry" in societal terms, and consider their volunteer and financial contributions to such "nonchurch" causes the equivalent of anything they might "do" in the congregation. The diversity of these individually defined "missions" was accepted and expected, I noted, even a matter of pride. In each congregation I was told about the unusual crusade for which a particular woman was responsible, or the way a handful of women had raised the consciousness of the congregation toward a special concern — an example of growth at the edges. The burst of daycare programs and prayer groups, in many congregations, is also related to "the spirituality movement," a "movement" largely populated by women.

The generational shift in attitudes toward volunteering and use of one's time raises a basic institutional question. When the present generation of younger women becomes the older generation, how will they view the work of institutional preservation? Maintenance over the long haul requires a different mindset toward physical and organizational structures. A male opinion-shaper in Advent South said, "What we have plenty of is volunteers for a one-shot task — for example, to move the Sunday school equipment or a spring-clean-up of the grounds. What we don't have is people willing to take over the responsibility of lining up the volunteers, or as-suming the ongoing responsibility for that kind of organizing." A bridge-generation woman from Redeemer Plains approached the same issue with a different perspective: "Of course, I understand it. . . . These young women want to *do* mission; they don't want to join an organization that *talks about* mission. They want hands-on service if they're going to invest any time in something; they don't want anything that comes between them and concrete ac-tion." Maintaining the institution's structures is not high on the younger generation's sense of responsibility.

As women share their stories and life experiences, they find "permission" to become attuned to their own sacred imagina-tion. They see significance and worthiness in the inner voice that they (and their churches) did not previously know or feel em-powered to acknowledge. Even if past women assimilated the message that their experience was trivial or "less" important in the congregation, traditional churchwomen today see themselves as significant — to themselves, and increasingly to the life of their congregation. In addition, they are becoming able to "see" and welcome into the ongoing story of God's action in the world — women whose experiences are different from theirs — commonali-ties that contribute to the new arithmetic of vitality.[27]

In the massive paradigm shift remaking our religious bodies, women's creative adaptability is the great thread of continuity with past centuries of faithful women. Obviously each of us in the exchange begun here benefited from sharing these "lived ex-periences" — a concrete example of women spiritually affirming women.[28] Perhaps the great untapped resource for Christian re-newal is in the endlessly questing heart of generations of women.

We uncovered amazing pockets of individual piety and depth among women in all three generations. Regardless of how carefully they avoid standard theological language (and they do), or in what varied forms of service they "witness," their strength remains a common denominator. They are pushing out the boundaries of definition, unfolding the structures and themselves from within, making the prism sparkle. It seems to me "the power of their religious imaginations" is indeed being taken "into their own hands."[29]

NOTES

Chapter 1. "No One Ever Asked Me Before"

1. For a definition of "mainline Protestantism," a rhetorical convention for the major Protestant denominations present at the country's founding that remained influential until the mid-twentieth century — Baptist, Methodist, Presbyterian, Episcopalian, Unitarian, Lutheran, Congregational — see Wade Clark Roof and William McKinney, *American Mainline Religion* (New Brunswick, N.J.: Rutgers University Press, 1987). The recent book *Defecting in Place: Women Claiming Responsibility in Their Own Spiritual Lives*, by M. T. Winter, Adair Lummis, and Allison Stokes (New York: Crossroad, 1994) interviews women in churches who seek out their own nurture in extra-church cell groups or associations.

2. Cullen Murphy, "Women and the Bible," *Atlantic Monthly* (August 1993): 39–65.

3. See Sherry Ruth Anderson and Patricia Hopkins, *The Feminine Face of God: The Unfolding of the Sacred in Women* (New York: Bantam, 1991) as a popular study of spirituality, and Elizabeth Johnson, CSJ, *She Who Is: The Mystery of God in Feminine Theological Discourse* (New York: Crossroad, 1993), a study of language about the divine expanded by scholarly feminism.

4. Quoted from a letter of Evelyn Underhill (1875–1941) to Archbishop Lang, reprinted in *Anglican Digest* (Pentecost 1991): 20–21.

5. Robert Bellah et al., ed., *The Good Society* (New York: Knopf, 1991).

6. Pamela W. Darling, *New Wine: The Story of Women Transforming Leadership and Power in the Episcopal Church* (Cambridge, Mass.: Cowley Publications, 1994), documents the use of "tradition" against women's expanded roles in the denomination.

7. The Lilly grant supporting this research was a corporate project, thus my use of "we." Catherine Prelinger, ed., *Episcopal Women: Gender, Spirituality, and Commitment in an American Mainline Denomination* (New York: Oxford University Press, 1992). I am deeply grateful for

228

many consultations about my interviews and emphasis from Irene Q. Brown, the Reverend Sandra Boyd, Elizabeth Bettenhausen, Phyllis Bolton, Ann Swidler, Rima Schultz, Loren Mead.

8. In the interviews "we" refers to my colleagues, three trained oral-history associates, whose assistance made it possible to complete the fifteen interviews in one congregation within a compact time frame: Nancy Van Scoyoc, Margaret Woolverton, and Margaret Rubel. I am grateful and indebted to them for their collaboration, though they cannot be held accountable for my interpretations.

9. See Mary S. Donovan, *Women Priests in the Episcopal Church: The Experience of the First Decade* (Cincinnati: Forward Movement Publications, 1988); Heather Ann Huyck, "To Celebrate a Whole Priesthood" (Ph.D. diss., University of Minnesota, 1981); and Paula Nesbit, *The Feminization of the Clergy in America: Occupational and Organizational Perspectives* (forthcoming).

10. Jean M. Haldane, *Religious Pilgrimage* (Washington, D.C.: Alban Institute, 1977), 4, conducted the first series of spiritual-history interviews with contemporary laity that I have found. She also documented the common response of laity, "No one ever asked [me] before" about religion.

11. James F. Hopewell, *Congregations: Stories and Structures* (Philadelphia: Fortress Press, 1987), 85, discussing a congregation's "world view." Another way of referring to such thematic identification, a root metaphor, is an application of Victor Turner, *Dramas, Fields, and Metaphors: Symbolic Action in Human Society* (Ithaca, N.Y.: Cornell University Press, 1974), 64; see also Stephen Pepper, *World Hypotheses* (Berkeley: University of California Press, 1942), 91; and Max Black, *Models and Metaphors: Studies in Language and Philosophy* (Ithaca, N.Y., Cornell University Press, 1962), 240.

12. "The culture" of a particular congregation refers to the complex of meanings and symbols that give that particular human, social, and religious group a framework separate from but still reflected, to more or less degree, in their actions. See Gwen Kennedy Neville, *Kinship and Pilgrimage: Rituals of Reunion in American Protestant Culture* (New York: Oxford University Press, 1987).

13. A technical label is "insider ethnographer." See James Clifford, "On Ethnographic Allegory," in *Writing Culture: The Poetics and Politics of Ethnography*, ed. James Clifford and George E. Marcus (Berkeley: University of California Press, 1986), 98–121.

14. See Margaret R. Miles, introduction, in *Immaculate and Powerful: The Female in Sacred Image and Social Reality*, ed. Clarissa W. Atkinson, Constance H. Buchanan, and Margaret R. Miles (Boston: Beacon Press, 1985), 13, identifying the "piecework" pattern as an accurate motif for women's religious experience.

15. See Kurt H. Wolff, ed., *From Karl Mannheim: Essays* (New York: Oxford University Press, 1971).

16. Robert Wuthnow, "Recent Patterns of Secularization: A Problem of Generations?" *American Sociological Review* 41, no. 5 (October 1976): 850–67.

17. Robert Bellah, Richard Madsen, William M. Sullivan, Ann Swidler, Steven M. Tipton, *Habits of the Heart: Individualism and Commitment in American Life* (Berkeley: University of California Press, 1985), 290. Carol Gilligan, *In a Different Voice* (Cambridge: Harvard University Press, 1982). See also Anderson and Hopkins, *Feminine Face of God.*

18. Annie Kriegel, "Generational Difference: The History of an Idea," *Daedalus* 107, no. 4 (Fall 1978): 23–38.

19. Matilda White Riley, "Aging, Social Change and Ideas," *Daedalus* 107, no. 4 (Fall 1978): 39–52.

20. See Robert Wuthnow, *The Consciousness Reformation* (Berkeley: University of California Press, 1987).

21. Douglas Alan Walrath, *Frameworks: Patterns of Living and Believing Today* (Philadelphia: Pilgrim Press, 1987), is another religious report that characterizes church-generation mindsets: the older generation — Strivers — shaped by World War II and the Depression, are committed to hard work, institutions and struggle; the Challengers are his middle generation, shaped by the influence of the Civil Rights movement and the Vietnam War; and the younger generation, the Calculators, were "socialized" in the mid-1970s to 1980s.

22. Personal correspondence, May 23, 1989. Parish and name withheld for anonymity.

Chapter 2. Grace New England and "Work"

1. Stephen Hart, "Religion and Changes in Family Patterns," *Review of Religious Research* 28, no. 1 (Sept. 1986): 51–70, identified *married women being employed outside the home* as the most often cited change affecting congregational life, positively and negatively. Lutherans thought some of its positive effects were: an increase in the nurture, inclusiveness, and tolerance within the congregation; greater equality for women in the churches; and quality of religious participation. Negative effects were seen primarily in terms of "the *quantity* of religious participation," a diminishment of time and energy contributed by women (53).

2. Colloquialism for a place of business that announces a literal religious identity in advertising and public rhetoric, appealing to an evangelical or charismatic clientele.

3. A "Program Church" is one of four analytic types based on size and activities: the Family church, 50 or fewer average attendance; the Pastoral church, averaging from 50 to 150; the Program church, averag-

ing from 150 to 300; and the Corporation church, more than 350 average attendance. Arlin J. Rothauge, quoted in Roy M. Oswald and Speed B. Leas, *Sizing Up a Congregation: For New Member Ministry* (Washington, D.C.: Alban Institute, 1987), 33.

4. Dr. Rima Schultz made a similar observation about Episcopal women in her replication of this study. See *Hearing Women's Voices: A Trilogy 1989–91* (Chicago: Diocese of Chicago, Episcopal Church Women, February 1991), 89.

5. Robert Wuthnow, Virginia A. Hodgkinson, and assoc., eds., *Faith and Philanthropy in America* (San Francisco: Jossey-Bass, 1990), 275, 279, 280, 282.

6. Historical patterns of identifying Protestant women's religious merit through what they "did" is visible in early American funeral eulogies of Moravian women, in books comprising the pious memoirs of exemplary women, and in journalistic obituary tributes, for example, Mrs. Lucia Magaw's July 25, 1790, funeral discourse. She had not *"display[ed] her piety* in a *mere attendance on religious worship* and a regard to the ordinances of God. Her faith influenced her *practice;* she strove to perform whatsoever things were good, true, honest..." (emphasis added), *Columbian Magazine* 5, no. 4 (1790): 263–64. American Protestant women "saints" had to be distinctly different from the mystical, vision-of-God variety associated with Roman Catholicism.

7. See Sara Evans and Harry C. Boyte, *Free Spaces: The Sources of Democratic Change in America* (New York: Harper and Row, 1986).

8. Max Weber, *Economy and Society* (Berkeley: University of California Press, 1978), 1:366–695.

Chapter 3. Redeemer Plains and "Church"

1. Erving Goffman, *The Presentation of Self in Everyday Life* (New York: Doubleday, 1959), was an early observer of the symbolic information transmitted by non-verbal actions or gestures. The first theorist to note the uses to which denominational identification was put, in American culture, was Max Weber in the 1920s, an essay titled "The Protestant Sects and the Spirit of Capitalism," in *From Max Weber: Essays on Sociology*, ed. Hans H. Gerth and C. Wright Mills (New York: Oxford University Press, 1946), 302–22.

2. Which comes first: awareness of one's "refugee status" while still in one's birthright or family church, or discovering an emotional and spiritual connection with a previously unknown religious group and becoming a refugee in order to join it? The women at Redeemer had histories of seeking.

3. Max L. Stackhouse, "Religion and the Social Space for Voluntary

Institutions," in Wuthnow et al., *Faith and Philanthropy in America*, 22–37.

4. Nathan Hatch, *The Democratization of American Religion* (New Haven: Yale University Press, 1989).

5. Designed in 1964 by R. Morland Kraus, a stained glass artist at Washington University, and made in the Jacoby Studios, St. Louis. Pamphlet, privately published.

6. Nancy Westerfield, "Where Have All the Marthas Gone?" *Living Church* (September 30, 1990): 11–12.

7. Peter Steinfels, "Beliefs," *New York Times*, April 13, 1991, 10.

8. See Barbara Gent and Betty Sturges, *The Altar Guild Book: A History and Practical Handbook* (Wilton, Conn: Morehouse-Barlow, 1982).

Chapter 4. Nativity Northwest and "Family"

1. Janet Fishburn, *Confronting the Idolatry of Family* (Nashville: Abingdon Press, 1991), 19, 35, examines the American romanticization of the 1950s nuclear family and Christian meanings of "relatedness" in light of the New Testament mandate to free the concept of family from tribal or kin limitations.

2. Karen Offen, "Defining Feminism: A Comparative Historical Approach." *Signs* 14, no. 11 (November 1988): 119–57.

3. This report is summarized from a church publication. My pledge of anonymity allows specific citation only via written request.

4. Barbara Hargrove, "The Church, the Family, and the Modernization Process," in *Families and Religions: Conflict and Change in Modern Society*, ed. William V. D'Antonio and Joan Aldous (Beverly Hills, Calif.: Sage Publications, 1983), 17–48. She suggests that the social change of the 1960s "was a protest against rationality of modernization," an interpretation that may apply to Nativity.

5. Hart, "Religion and Changes in Family Patterns," 51.

6. Hargrove, "The Church, the Family, and the Modernization Process," 45.

7. The phrase, from Bellah et al., *Habits of the Heart*, describes individualism as a burden on people unconscious of the many ways in which it is impinged upon by a multitude of regulations and corporations. An individual's imperative to define religion *for one's self* is self-imposed (150).

8. Ibid., 65.

9. Wade Clark Roof, "A Time to Seek," summarized the religion of "baby boomers." *Newsweek*, December 17, 1990, 52.

10. Hart ("Religion and Changes in Family Patterns," 53) has given a similar contemporary reading to "the comfort factor" first identified in

Charles Y. Glock, Benjamin B. Ringer, and Earl R. Babbie, *To Comfort and to Challenge* (Berkeley: University of California Press, 1967).

11. Kathryn Allan Rabuzzi, *The Sacred and the Feminine: Toward a Theology of Housework* (New York: Seabury Press, 1982]), 81.

12. Joshua Meyerowitz, *No Sense of Place: The Impact of Electronic Media on Social Behavior* (New York: Oxford University Press, 1985).

13. *Families and Religions*, ed. D'Antonio and Aldous, 309. Stackhouse, "Religion and the Social Space for Voluntary Institutions," in Wuthnow et al., *Faith and Philanthropy in America*, 22–37.

14. Charles Tilly, "Family History, Social History, and Social Change," and Glen H. Elder Jr., "Life Course," *Journal of Family History* 12, nos. 1–3 (1987): 179–99, 319–30.

15. Beverly Wildung Harrison, "The Power of Anger in the Work of Love," in *Making the Connections*, ed. Carol S. Robb (Boston: Beacon Press, 1985).

Chapter 5. Church of the Advent South and "Inner Life"

1. Carol Ochs, *Women and Spirituality* (Totowa, N.J.: Rowman and Allanheld, 1983), 10.

2. Bishop James Malloch and Kay Smallzreid, eds., *A Practical Church Dictionary* (New York: Morehouse Barlow, 1964), 24.

3. He named James Fowler's *Stages of Faith* (San Francisco: Harper and Row, 1981).

4. The Reverend Bliss Browne, "On Being a Christian Woman," *Harvard Divinity School Review* (June 1990): 4.

5. See, e.g., C. Hugh Hildesley, *Journeying with Julian* (Harrisburg, Pa.: Morehouse Publishing, 1993).

6. Ibid.

7. A scriptural image used to derogate a "do-er."

8. Sister Ella Rigney, oral history, 1982 (interviewed by author, personal copy). A life-long Episcopalian, she was a founding elder of the Holy Order of MANS (acronym for Mysterion, Agape, Nous, Sophia). This modern-day adaptation of a monastic order, initiated by a visionary layman and his wife during the "flower-child" era of San Francisco (developing chapters in other major cities subsequently), offered communal residence and religious discipline, a habit of dress, and Christian service in the inner city. One of its best-known programs continues to be a low-cost, high-nutrition vegetarian sandwich-shop called Brother Juniper's Restaurant. In 1988 the order was received in the Orthodox Church and took the name Christ the Savior Brotherhood. Rev. David Lowell, director of Raphael House, San Francisco, telephone interview with author, December 6, 1994.

9. Innovations incorporated in the regular Sunday morning liturgy are

an emerging (if still rare) phenomenon. A creative Anglo-Catholic priest, the Rev. Lois Pinneo, for example, devised a ritual in place of the Prayers of the People to honor the 80th birthday of a beloved "pillar" of the entire parish (see J. B. Gillespie, "St. Giles' Woman of Wisdom," in *Episcopal Women's History Project Newsletter* 13, no. 1 (Winter 1993): 6–7). Such experiments were the subject of a workshop, "Women's History as Liturgy," at the 1994 Triennial Meeting of Episcopal Women, Indianapolis (conducted by J. B. Gillespie and Rev. Bavi Moore). See also "WATERwheel," newsletter from the Women's Alliance for Theology, Ethics, and Ritual, Silver Spring, Maryland.

10. See Johnson, *She Who Is.* Also Susan Cady, Marian Ronan, and Hal Taussig, *Wisdom's Feast: Sophia in Study and Celebration* (San Francisco: Harper and Row, 1989).

Chapter 6. Congregations and Generations

1. G. Gallup, "Trends in U.S. Religious Life Show Considerable Stability," *Emerging Trends* (December 1988): 10. Within the past two decades, the Episcopal Church, among other mainline denominations, has imitated nonreligious corporations in commissioning professional opinion polls (1982, 1983, 1986, 1988). The most recent is "The Spiritual Health of the Episcopal Church" (Gallup, July 1989) which surveyed fifty churches for twenty completed interviews in each, by questionnaire, but with no focus on individual congregations as units with their own interaction. The congregation as reference point was treated as incidental.

2. James P. Wind, *Places of Worship: Exploring Their History* (Nashville: American Association for State and Local History, 1990), 105; Fishburn, *Confronting the Idolatry of Family*, 172; Hopewell, *Congregation*, 10–11.

3. Hopewell, *Congregation*, 12–13.

4. Dr. Rima Schultz, personal correspondence, March 1991, summarizing *Hearing Women's Voices,* Diocese of Chicago.

5. See Mary Lou Randour, *Women's Psyche, Women's Spirit: The Reality of Relationships* (New York: Columbia University Press, 1987). Her exploration emphasizes "intra-psychic, imaginary, self-reflexive ideas about relationship" that are an essential dimension of the "interpersonal matrix" of women's daily lives (3).

6. Linda Clark, *Music in Churches Project Report*, no. 4 (Boston University, September 1991). A significant number of respondents in her research defined "worship experience at its best" as conveying a sense of immediacy, the corporate nature of the church, a sense of intimacy and personal relevance, and satisfaction from the integrated wholeness of all liturgical elements.

7. Dr. Frank Sugeno, retired, Seminary of the Southwest, Austin, Tex.,

letter to author, June 6, 1990. Similar questions were raised by professors at Harvard and Chicago divinity schools.

8. Personal communication, name withheld for anonymity, June 23, 1991.

9. Eighteenth-century Church of England evangelicals who became Methodists provided the first major revision of Anglo-Protestant worship behavior by hallowing religious emotion as *the* legitimate experience of worship. See, e.g., David Lyle Jeffrey, ed., *A Burning and a Shining Light: English Spirituality in the Age of Wesley* (Grand Rapids, Mich.: Eerdmans, 1987).

10. Nancy Van Scoyoc, *Women, Change, and the Church* (Nashville: Abingdon Press, 1979), was among the first to document women's concerns about issues that they "could" — or would not be welcome to — bring to their Protestant (Methodist) church, or expect to receive help on from their clergy.

11. See Maggie Ross, *The Fountain and the Furnace: The Way of Tears and Fire* (Mahwah, N.J.: Paulist Press, 1987), for a descriptive and devotional reclamation of early religious texts on the spiritual significance of tears (3).

12. "Primary groups" are a sociological term signifying the most intimate and profound emotional bond, often family or kinship groups. When congregations formally cultivate primary group structures, they are sometimes named "cell groups." Carl F. George, *Prepare Your Church for the Future* (Tarrytown, N.Y.: Fleming H. Revell, 1991).

13. Robert Wuthnow, introduction, *Faith and Philanthropy in America*, 11–12.

14. Mordechai Rimor and Gary A. Tobin, "Jewish Giving Patterns to Jewish and Non-Jewish Philanthropy," in Wuthnow et al., *Faith and Philanthropy in America*, 161.

15. See Darling, *New Wine*, and Mary S. Donovan, *A Different Call: Women's Ministries in the Episcopal Church, 1850–1920* (Wilton, Conn.: Morehouse-Barlow, 1986).

16. Mary S. Donovan, "Beyond the Parallel Church?" in *Episcopal Women: Gender, Spirituality, and Commitment in a Mainline Church,* ed. Catherine M. Prelinger (New York: Oxford University Press, 1992), 185–236.

17. One church bulletin announced the formation of "The Casserole Brigade"; unstated assumptions were that members thus are 'given permission' to visit each other with the gift of food, on a structured rather than spontaneous basis.

18. Mrs. Ruth Bacon Vickary, Oral History, EWHP File, Episcopal Archives, Austin, Texas.

19. Carman Hunter, personal conversation with author, Brooklyn, New York, 1990.

20. Donovan, *A Different Call*. Also, R. Pierce Beaver traces the ecumenical story in *All Loves Excelling: The Story of Protestant Missions in the Nineteenth and Early Twentieth Century* (1968; Grand Rapids, Mich.: Eerdmans, 1980).

21. Peter L. Berger, *The Sacred Canopy: Elements of a Sociological Theory of Religion* (New York: Doubleday, 1969).

22. Tilly, "Family History, Social History, and Social Change," 319–30. The phrase "communities of memory" is from Bellah et al., *Habits of the Heart*, 8.

23. Hopewell, *Congregations*, 7.

24. Riley, "Aging, Social Change and Ideas," 43.

25. Betty Friedan, *The Feminine Mystique* (New York: Norton, 1974).

26. She used the Hebrew word for the feminine face of God (Anderson, *The Feminine Face of God*, 2), a sophisticated choice for a self-educated layperson who has not studied at a seminary.

27. Wade Clark Roof called this self-determination within religious organizations "the new voluntarism" in "The Third Disestablishment and Beyond," paper, *Mainstream Protestantism in the Twentieth Century, Its Problems and Prospects* (Council on Theological Education, Presbyterian Church USA, 1986), 29.

28. See Warren Susman, *Culture as History* (New Brunswick, N.J.: Rutgers University Press, 1973), now published as *Culture and Commitment, 1927–45* (New York: G. Braziller, 1973).

Chapter 7. Unfinished Business

1. Mary Catherine Bateson, *Composing a Life* (New York: Atlantic Monthly Press, 1989), 171.

2. See, e.g., Rosemary Radford Ruether and Rosemary Skinner Keller, eds., *Women and Religions in America: A Documentary History*, 3 vols. (San Francisco: Harper and Row, 1981–84).

3. Nancy Hewitt, keynote address, Southern Association of Women Historians Conference, University of North Carolina, Chapel Hill, June 1991.

4. Supplement, "The Face of the Future," *Time* 142, no. 21 (Fall 1993).

5. John L. Kater Jr., "Whose Church Is It Anyway?" *Anglican Theological Review* 76, no. 1 (Winter 1994): 44–60.

6. Robert Coles, *A Witness to Idealism* (Boston: Houghton Mifflin, 1993). See also interview, *Christian Century* (December 1, 1993): 1208.

7. Elisabeth Schüssler Fiorenza, *But She Said: Feminist Practices of Biblical Interpretation* (Boston: Beacon Press, 1993).

8. A conference in November 1993 called "Re-Imagining God" has roused much journalistic and denominational ire. See, for example,

"A Controverted Conference" in the *Christian Century* (February 16, 1994); "Women's Conference and a 'Theological Crisis,'" *Christian Century* (March 23–20, 1994): 306; and three long essays, pp. 339–44, in *Christian Century* (April 6, 1994).

9. A 1993 list of Episcopal women's organizations or groups associated with the tenth-anniversary meeting of the umbrella-consortium known as the Council of Women's Ministries, named twenty-seven entities including women in religious orders, various administrative commissions, and racial or ethnic group representations.

10. Grace D. Cumming Long, *Passion and Reason: Womenviews of Decision Making* (Nashville: John Knox-Westminster, 1993), 13.

11. The concept is Judith Plaskow's, from "Facing the Ambiguity of God," *Tikkun* 6, no. 5 (September–October 1991): 70, quoted in Catherine Madsen, "A God of One's Own: Recent Work by and about Women in Religion," review essay, *Signs* 19, no. 21 (Winter 1994): 480–98. She names it a promising direction in feminist theological thought (493).

12. Adrienne Rich, *Of Woman Born: Motherhood as Experience and Institution* (New York: W. W. Norton, 1986).

13. Clarissa Atkinson, *The Oldest Vocation: Christian Motherhood in the Middle Ages* (Ithaca, N.Y.: Cornell University Press, 1991).

14. Elizabeth Carter and Joan K. Peters, *Married in America: Working It Out Against the Odds* (New York: Macmillan, forthcoming).

15. Thomas Moore, *Care of the Soul: A Guide for Cultivating Depth and Sacredness in Everyday Life* (New York: HarperCollins, 1992).

16. Sallie McFague, *Models of God* (Philadelphia: Fortress Press, 1987).

17. See Carol J. Adams, ed., *Ecofeminism and the Sacred* (New York, Continuum, 1993).

18. Long, *Passion and Reason.*

19. Sheila Briggs, "Women and Religion," 408–41, in *Analyzing Gender: A Handbook of Social Science Research.* ed. Beth Hess and Myra Marx Feree (Beverly Hills, Calif.: Sage Publications, 1987).

20. Margaret Miles, "Theory, Theology, and Episcopal Churchwomen," in *Episcopal Women*, ed. Prelinger, 330–44 (337). She prescribes a two-stage institutional revolution: women creating the strength of a genuine collective voice, then using it to speak out against injustice in the larger culture.

21. Darling, *New Wine.*

22. Bateson, *Composing a Life*, 171.

23. Jay Dolan, *Transforming Parish Ministry: The Changing Roles of Catholic Clergy, Laity, and Women Religious* (New York: Crossroad, 1990), 96–105, and 267–80 for "The Lay Ministry Explosion."

24. Janet Morley, *All Desires Known: Prayers Uniting Faith and Feminism* (Wilton, Conn.: Morehouse-Barlow, 1988), 4.

25. Bateson, *Composing a Life*, 73.

26. See Ann Swidler's review of Robert Wuthnow, *Sharing the Journey: Support Groups and America's New Quest for Community* (New York: Free Press, 1994), *New York Times Book Review* (March 20, 1994): 19.

27. Sandra Schneiders, *Beyond Patching* (New York: Paulist Press, 1991), 87ff.

28. See Jane Redmont, "Sex, Power, and the Sacred: It's Time to Talk," *Harvard Divinity School Bulletin* 20, no. 3 (1990–91): 5, for a similar summary of women's shifting views about what constitutes a godly life.

29. Briggs, "Women and Religion," 437.

INDEX